The World beyond the Windshield

THE WORLD BEYOND THE WINDSHIELD

**Roads and
Landscapes in
the United States
and Europe**

*Edited by Christof Mauch
and Thomas Zeller*

Foreword by David E. Nye

Ohio University Press
Athens

Franz Steiner Verlag
Stuttgart

Ohio University Press, Athens, Ohio 45701
www.ohioswallow.com
© 2008 by Ohio University Press

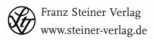

Franz Steiner Verlag
www.steiner-verlag.de

15 14 13 12 11 10 09 08   5 4 3 2 1

ISBN 978-3-515-09170-1 (Franz Steiner Verlag hardcover)

Library of Congress Cataloging-in-Publication Data
The world beyond the windshield : roads and landscapes in the United States
and Europe / edited by Christof Mauch and Thomas Zeller.
    p. cm.
Includes bibliographical references and index.
ISBN-13: 978-0-8214-1767-6 (hc : alk. paper)
ISBN-10: 0-8214-1767-3 (hc : alk. paper)
ISBN-13: 978-0-8214-1768-3 (pb : alk. paper)
ISBN-10: 0-8214-1768-1 (pb : alk. paper)
    1. Roadside improvement—United States. 2. Roadside improvement—Europe. 3. Scenic byways—United States. 4. Scenic byways—Europe. I. Mauch, Christof. II. Zeller, Thomas, 1966–
    TE177.W67 2008
    713.0973—dc22

                                                                    2008000738

. . . the road the human being travels,
That, on which blessing comes and goes, doth follow
The river's course, the valley's playful windings,
Curves round the cornfield and the hill of vines,
Honoring the holy bounds of property!
And thus secure, though late, leads to its end.

Friedrich Schiller, *The Piccolomini* (1799),
translated by Samuel Taylor Coleridge

Contents

Contents

Figures

Foreword

A century has passed since the motorcar raced into history, and during that time in the Western industrial nations the automobile and the high-speed road have passed from novelties for the rich to conveniences for the many to necessities for nearly everyone. In this process, the car has been naturalized. Children now think it normal to sit in a car while moving at 120 kilometers per hour, but the drivers of 1920 thought half that speed was daring. It requires an imaginative effort to recall the almost utopian promise of the early automobile and the uncertainty about how best to provide suitable pathways for this new vehicle. Historians have focused on the conversion of city streets and roads to the new traffic demands of cars and trucks, on the competition between mass transit and individual cars, and on the marketing battles between electric-, steam-, and gasoline-powered vehicles. Yet, curiously, until this present volume, the creation of fundamentally new kinds of roads has remained a somewhat neglected subject. Christof Mauch and Thomas Zeller have put together a tightly focused clutch of essays that share three concerns. First of all, they recover the moment of highway innovation from circa 1920–39, when planners in several nations worked out alternative solutions. Americans, inspired in part by Frederick Law Olmsted's carriageways in Boston, in New York's Central Park, and even in Yosemite, sought to build roads that would provide not merely transportation but recreation and enjoyment of nature. Indeed, the sinuous curves and occasional steep hills of these suggestively named "parkways" made them unsuitable for trucks. They were intended for automobiles only, and all horse-drawn traffic was banned. In contrast to these free public highways, Italians developed the first limited-access *autostrade* as toll roads, built and owned by private enterprise. The model they imitated during construction was the railroad. The engineers preferred long, straight highways, with no sharp curves or steep gradients. Somewhere between these two possibilities lay the German autobahn, constructed in great haste at a rate of a thousand kilometers per year, inspired by U.S. parkways but a largely separate development driven forward by Hitler, who built ahead of demand. This book recalls the debates between German engineers seeking the appropriate design for the original autobahn and later debates in postwar Germany, when engineers in East and West reappropriated these roads for new ideological purposes. The East Germans, for example, replaced modernist bridges destroyed in the war with stone bridges, asserting that this was more in keeping with socialism (as well as a necessity due to steel shortages). Meanwhile, the British lagged behind in limited-access road construction, beginning the M1 from London to the North only in the late 1950s. In short, this book is a wonderful case study of how each nation made its own sense of a new technology. The funding, appearance, and intended uses of the autobahn, the autostrade, the parkways, and the M1 were quite distinct. That theme alone would be quite enough to make this a welcome volume.

But there is much more. In a second strand of analysis, the contributors make clear that consumers of highways are by no means passive and that their intentions vary a good deal. Henry Adams, who in his autobiography contrasted and found irreconcilable the dynamo and the Virgin, might seem an unlikely automotive enthusiast. Yet as early as 1902 he declared in a letter, "My idea of paradise is a perfect automobile going thirty miles an hour on a smooth road to a twelfth-century cathedral." This was a high-speed escapade for a driver at the time and a somewhat fantastic idea, as there were few smooth roads and even fewer that were paved. The car was still an unexpected interloper on country roads and not a practical form of travel. Adams was not eccentric but rather a typical car owner of the era: a wealthy man making journeys for the pleasure of it, accepting poor roads and breakdowns as part of the game. The authors here are concerned not with this first generation of drivers but with the next, which demanded smoother roads that excluded horses and were safe at high speeds.

As more people began to own cars, it quickly became apparent that they did not all drive with the same intentions and values. If some drove only to reach a destination, others felt the journey was its own justification, whether cruising in the city or jaunting along on back roads to nowhere in particular. Some roads, indeed, were built more for pleasure than for practical transportation, including two analyzed here, both built in the Black Hills of South Dakota during the 1930s. They were intentionally designed to give drivers powerful and often disorienting experiences, such as the one provoked by the gigantic face of Mount Rushmore's George Washington suddenly emerging at the end of a tunnel. Likewise, the early invention of drag-racing, the subculture of the hot rod, and the enduring popularity of motorcycles are all reminders that roads provided many possible pleasures. Some, such as midnight racing on a new freeway not yet open to the public, were illegal; but this apparently increased the thrill for those involved. Today's advertisements suggest that driving retains some of the heady excitement felt by those first drivers. They depict not the traffic jams that limited-access roads were expected to eliminate but a new car streaking through wide-open countryside. This imagined landscape beyond the windshield and our possible interactions with it are the second theme.

Yet the present volume does not simply celebrate the romance of "life on the road" or "mobility for its own sake." Rather, a third strand of analysis in these essays treats the struggle to define and then to promote an aesthetic for these new limited-access, high-speed motorways. Rejecting the disdainful view that they are a "nonplace" somehow outside of architecture and culture, these essays present us with both the aesthetics of builders and those of drivers. Internationally, builders hardly agreed. German engineers of the 1930s wanted their roads to be embedded in the landscape, but more for nationalistic than for ecological reasons. Italian engineers, somewhat surprisingly, took little interest in the aesthetics of their new roads in the 1920s and began to be concerned only half a century later. However, if the Italians built roads with little regard for design and landscaping, and if Germans rushed to build their autobahn while still disagreeing about these matters, the British, who built almost no modern roads at all for thirty years, nevertheless set up committees concerned with the beautification of roadways and organized plantings around the few bypasses they did build. Progress in highway landscaping was erratic at best. If Americans began well by creating the parkway, by midcentury many U.S. engineers had rejected the parkway's graceful curves and genteel vistas, emphasizing instead functionality and speed in their new interstate highways. The contributors also remind us of the accompanying suburban sprawl, the automotive scrapheaps, the junkyards, and the billboard blight, which had become all too obvious by the early 1960s. As the ugliness spread, it spurred beautification campaigns, notably the one spearheaded by Lady Bird Johnson, at the urging of her husband, President Lyndon Johnson. Yet even her success was limited to surface appearances. Only in the 1970s did many road-builders begin to think at all environmentally. Just as important as the builders' intentions were the consumers' driving experiences. What did it mean when driving became widespread and therefore democratic? How did some drivers develop oppositional practices that gave new meanings to the road? Was the road not, in a very real sense, a medium of communication?

As we look back over the early decades of road-building, the first generation demonstrates how different cultures found different answers to these questions. One may have many purposes on a road or a journey. In that interwar generation, car cultures had only begun. For us, driving has become quotidian, a not-always-welcome part of experience so "natural" that it is nearly unconscious. It is easy to forget that highways are quite literally cultural constructions. This volume helps us to understand the choices that led to the present road systems and to realize that the road network was not a hegemonic inevitability. We cannot glimpse the end of our collective journey with the automobile, but this book maps out how it began and what it once meant.

David E. Nye

Acknowledgments

The editors would like to thank the staff of the German Historical Institute in Washington, D.C, particularly Christa Brown and Bärbel Thomas, for their help in organizing the conference "Landscapes and Roads in North America and Europe: Cultural History in Transatlantic Perspective." A number of the original conference presentations formed the basis of this volume. Two anonymous reviewers offered valuable suggestions that helped to improve the individual chapters and the introduction. We are grateful to David Lazar, senior editor at the GHI, for suggesting the title for this volume. Our very special thanks go to Mary Tonkinson at the GHI, who edited the manuscript with skill and grace. Thanks also go to Brian Madetzke at Custer State Park, who provided the book's cover images as well as several illustrations for chapter 4. At Ohio University Press, we are indebted to senior editor Gillian Berchowitz for adopting the manuscript and to Beth Pratt for shepherding it so professionally through production.

Introduction

Christof Mauch and Thomas Zeller

Seeing the world through the windshield is for most of us one of our earliest memories. Before car manufacturers started installing individual television screens for children in roomy suburban minivans, middle-class toddlers in car-owning households came to know much of the world around them by being driven around towns and cities and through the countryside. A 1953 General Motors advertising jingle, "See the USA in your Chevrolet," was the anthem for a widespread strategy of sightseeing and road trips. Guidebooks, tourist brochures, and movies told drivers and passengers what to look for—and what to avoid. The view through the car's windshield has redefined how we perceive the world around us. At the same time, what travelers have seen from their driver or passenger seats has changed over time as different types of roads—from meandering country roads to speedways—have been designed to serve a variety of purposes. The chapters in this volume, by looking at historical examples from the United States and Europe in the twentieth century, explore the relationship between the road and the landscape that it traverses, cuts through, defines, despoils, and enhances. This relationship is dynamic and never fixed, and precisely because its results—the view from the road toward the world beyond the windshield—are so ubiquitous, it has received only fleeting attention from historians. However, these roads, landscapes, and vistas are neither necessary nor accidental but the outcomes of historical negotiations. In some cases, as in that of the American parkway, the view from the road was the be-all and end-all of the highway; in others, as in the case of the Italian *autostrada,* the view of a fast, efficient transportation machine celebrating either Fascism or its absence was the goal. For twentieth-century roads, landscapes were intended or unintended, but always present. As such, they reverberate with past decisions while providing physical and cultural foils for our understanding of the environment. Road landscapes are located at the intersection of culture, the built environment, and what is usually called "nature." Thus, studying the relationships between roads and landscapes promises to yield insights into how different societies have tried to shape the environment before their eyes and in their minds.

Exploring such relations also allows scholars to demystify (or at least enrich our understanding of) one of the central aspects of the road trip. Especially in the United States, the experience of driving a car for long distances across the country has become more than an economical way of getting from one place to another; it is also a ritual charged with national resonances. Road literature celebrates individual highways (for example, Route 66, still famous after its demise); specific landscapes; and, most importantly, the act of self-discovery while spending time behind the wheel. Examples of this genre include Jack Kerouac's 1957 classic *On the Road;* Tom Wolfe's *Electric Kool-Aid Acid Test,* published in 1968; and the 1969 film *Easy Rider,* directed by Dennis Hopper. "The great American road," as one scholar aptly put it, "has become a magic screen for the fears and desires of travelers with means and a light skin—most who have written about it."[1] In much contemporary road lore, the landscape tends to be interchangeable: "Missouri looked precisely the same as Illinois, which had looked precisely the same as Iowa."[2] The papers in this volume go beyond such mythmaking and interrogate the road and its landscapes rather than the qualities of individual self-discovery associated with them. Additionally, they challenge the way white middle-class motorists have experienced landscapes by asking for whom such roads and landscapes were built, who benefitted from them, and whose visions were supplanted by technocratic imperatives.

While millions of miles of roads and highways have dramatically changed the face of our environment over the past century, there is still a widespread notion that roads—especially the more modern constructions—

are major interventions in rather than integral parts of our landscapes.³ One of the original meanings of *landscape* is, as John Brinckerhoff Jackson reminds us, "a picture of a view" or "the view itself."⁴ Landscape architecture and landscape painting have a common tradition; and the phrase *to landscape* means to beautify. What we have in mind when we think of a picture is therefore often "some pleasant prospect," "a piece of the countryside," or "the particular setting of some memorable place."⁵ Several influential scholars in landscape studies have claimed that the logic behind a landscape is the order of beauty. William Hoskins, for instance, in his groundbreaking works on the English landscape, puts forth his belief that the natural environment was much more pleasant in the Middle Ages than in recent times.⁶ His antimodern bias is typical of an earlier generation of landscape scholars. Leo Marx, in his seminal work *The Machine in the Garden*, emphasizes a sharp distinction between the pastoral and progressive ideals that characterized early-nineteenth-century American culture and that ultimately evolved into the basis for later debates about excessive road-building and twentieth-century technological developments.⁷ Furthermore, the very fact that we have coined such words as *roadscape, townscape*, and *cityscape* reflects our understanding that landscapes exist beyond the "traditional" ones, and that these are clearly distinct from one another.

The contributors to this volume do not think of landscapes and roads as opposites. For them, as for Jackson, "roads belong in the landscape."⁸ They are aware that the dichotomy between unspoiled nature and human intervention is a cultural construction. In reality, there is hardly a square inch on this planet that has not been physically altered by man's presence on earth. Pollution and climate change have had an impact on the highest mountain peaks in the Himalayas and on whatever life exists at the bottom of the deepest ocean. The ecology of landscapes is in constant flux even where no paths or roads run and where no man walks. Both natural and cultural developments leave their traces on the physiognomy of our landscapes.

The authors of these essays are particularly interested in the technological, social, and aesthetic changes that have evolved in connection with the construction of roads. Environmental historians, historians of technology, and cultural historians have paid only scant attention to this central aspect of modern, mobile life.⁹ Odology, the science or study of roads, may seem an exotic discipline, but it tells us much about the values that we hold: it appears that there is nothing inevitable about the relationship between roads and landscapes.[10] Human activities and belief systems, economic calculations and political regimes have been responsible for changes in the physical construction, the design, and the perception of roads. Why did the Romans build straight roads rather than curved ones? Why did Americans replace parkways with freeways? Why is it that the local system of roads has been connected with or replaced by highways over the past few decades? What is the relationship between highways and urban sprawl? What triggered the success of automobile-based tourism? It is important to realize that all these questions can be understood only from a historical perspective.

The way in which we imagine our environment today differs signficantly from earlier forms of remembering and understanding. Today we are trained to imagine landscapes in general or abstract terms. Our knowledge is technical and geographical. We think of roads not so much as particular places but as representations on maps, not as localities but as networks or systems. This is partly due to the high degree to which we are interconnected through empires of communication and movement—in space and cyberspace. Comprehending this kind of imagination requires historical reflection, which the chapters in this volume provide. Also, it is necessary to re-situate the road, to understand it as a shaped space.

The modern highway has been described as "a managed authoritarian system of steady, uninterrupted flow for economic benefits."[11] The idea behind it is a unified transportation system connecting the economies of different regions into a single market.[12] Beginning in the late eighteenth century, turnpikes, canals, and, later, railroads were established to ship people and goods across long distances. Before that time, roads served mainly local and regional goals. Streets and roads were public spaces, shared by pedestrians and horses, and no distinction was made between commercial and recreational traffic.[13] There is no need to romanticize the pre-motorcar road, but it is worth noting that roads did not always have the primary and universally enforced function of moving self-propelled traffic quickly. Today, of course, there are hundreds of thousands of miles of roads on which walking or any activity other than (fast) driving is prohibited by law. Some countries even require and enforce a minimum speed on their freeways. That roads can be spaces of social discrimination and exclusion was apparent to any traveler in the southern United States up to the latter half of the twentieth century, who would have witnessed segregated service facilities and other kinds of discrimination. Yet even more subtle forms of exclusion have found their way into road design. In his oft-cited article "Do Artifacts Have Politics?" Langdon A. Winner perpetuates the erroneous notion that Robert Moses's parkway bridges on Long Island were designed with low clearances in order to keep buses and the African Americans who rode them from traveling on these roads. While more recent scholarship has debunked this particular myth, the point remains that the exclusion of common-carrier traffic on parkways was socially as well as aesthetically motivated.[14]

The motivations for road construction have differed over the years. In early modern times and throughout most of the nineteenth century, roads became necessary when the establishment of a comprehensive postal system promoted regular coach service. In the three decades between 1804 and 1834, the number of postal routes in the United States increased more than eighty times. The postal service was very interested in punctuality—more so, in fact, than the early railroad administration.[15] Close connections and transportation across ever-increasing distances required a high degree of organization. The central instrument for time management was the schedule of coaches, which made travel more "manageable" and more predictable. One scholar described Europe's early-modern mail systems as "infrastructures of the Enlightenment."[16]

Centralized countries in Europe made early attempts to unify and standardize engineering knowledge about roads. In seventeenth- and eighteenth-century France vast networks of streets radiating from Paris were built to link the capital with the seaports and the agricultural regions. Such a design served the economic interests and military needs of the king and the ruling elite. Scholars have called the national networks of roads a "centrifugal" or a "palace" system, in contrast to the "vernacular" system formed for ordinary people.[17] In other European countries the upper classes often used corvée labor to construct roads. From 1555, for example, every common laborer in England and Wales had to perform four days of unpaid labor annually[18]—but this practice did not necessarily lead to a centrifugal system or a convergence of road designs. Economic interests were often at the core of road-building practices or specific designs of roads. In Great Britain, for instance, the concept of turnpikes—that is, publicly chartered and privately owned toll roads—emerged in the early eighteenth century. This concept became popular in the United States as well, where states like Virginia opted for turnpikes because of a political aversion to public investment in infrastructure projects. Different models of road-building emerged: in some countries and regions, especially in the Anglo-Saxon world, roads were built to supply a scarcity that blocked economic activity, while in continental Europe roads were sometimes built far ahead of demand in the hope that they would stimulate commerce through excess capacity. Cold War economists interested in development labeled the former model "development by scarcity," and the latter "development by excess."[19] The present volume presents case studies of both models.

Throughout most of the nineteenth century, rivers, canals, and railroads were more critical to transportation than roads. Roads and streets mattered inside cities, but ships and trains, not carriages and coaches, were the main carriers for industrialization in Europe and North America. It would be wrong to assume, however, that the volume of street traffic decreased during the railway age; rather, it expanded as passengers and freight needed roads to get to and from the railway stations.[20] The design and construction of roads was relatively inexpensive and technologically less ambitious than the construction of canals and railroads. Especially in Britain, the railroad right-of-way became synonymous, at least in the early years, with sizable engineering projects: excavations, dams, embankments, tunnels, and viaducts dotted the landscape of railway-based transportation. Hard, level, and smooth surfaces were preferred by railroad builders because the massive weight of trains and locomotives, along with the relative weakness of steam engines, made such topography especially desirable. Early engineers and surveyors in the United States, such as Robert B. Stanton, saw no contradiction between the "beautiful railroad" and "grandiose landscapes."[21] Although railway construction made physical intrusions into European and American land- and cityscapes, these intrusions allowed trains to run much faster than any other nineteenth-century traffic: early railroads were three times faster, for instance, than horse-drawn coaches. Railroad construction thus set a precedent for large-scale technological intervention, or the "conquering of geography"; it also set a rather high standard for speed in future transport and communication. The building of vast networks of highways and miles of straight roads for cars and trucks—with bridges and passes cutting through mountainous landscapes—seemed less radical after the completion of such gigantic projects as the transcontinental railway across the United States.

The acceleration of travel had a profound impact not only on concepts of space and time but also on habits of visual perception. What Wolfgang Schivelbusch in his studies on railway travel labels the "panoramatic gaze" became the characteristic view of motor journeys in the twentieth century: the faster cars moved through the landscape, the less important the foreground became. Travelers would increasingly focus on individual objects in the middle ground and, as these objects quickly disappeared from sight, would gaze at the landscape panorama in the far distance.[22] In the early twentieth century a new generation of motorists, mostly elite, affluent, urban car owners, celebrated the fact that automobiles allowed them not only to stop their cars whenever they chose but also to enjoy the scenery beyond the frame of the railway compartment's window. (The notoriously unreliable early cars broke down often enough, however, to afford their owners new vistas that they did not necessarily desire to see.) While railroad companies played a significant role in the establishment of America's national parks in the nineteenth century, it was the automobile that would become the vehicle of choice for the exploration of unique landscapes in the twentieth century.[23] Thousands of miles of scenic roads were built to take tourists to breathtaking sights. Dramatically designed roads that led to spectacular overlooks were created in scenic places, and campgrounds and motels were established to serve motor tourism. In the United States the construction of transcontinental roads, such as the Lincoln Highway, was promoted with the explicit goal of letting Americans discover the beauty of their country while authenticating the experience of the early pioneers who had traveled across the continent from east to west.[24] Often the beauty of such landscapes as the Pacific Coast both invited and justified roadbuilding. Such nationally charged roads, along with the more quotidian ones, soon became part of service-based transportation landscapes filled with gas stations, motels, and fast-food outlets for people on the move.[25] Only a few areas were, in principle, supposed to be left "wild" and without roads. Among these were several areas belonging to Native American tribes. According to the early (and now outdated) philosophy of the Bureau of Indian Affairs and foresters such as Robert Marshall, native peoples needed no more than what nature provided. Land without roads therefore seemed to be an adequate condition for reservations. But a pro-development attitude among Native Americans and at the Bureau of Indian Affairs contributed to the demise of roadless areas even on reservations.[26]

While access to spectacular landscapes played an important role in the construction of roads in remote areas around the globe, other factors, such as transportation, were even more decisive in the development of vast networks of roads and highways in Europe and North America. The United States, in particular, built up an empire of roads more quickly and efficiently than any other nation in the world. Political squabbles over state-versus-federal responsibility for these roads became a major obstacle to highway development in the first half of the twentieth century.[27] In the interwar period some states began to tax gasoline in order to raise funds for road construction and maintenance. The federal Bureau of Public Roads, under the guidance of the technocrat Thomas MacDonald and aided by money from Congress, supported the building or improvement of more than ninety thousand miles of federal-aid highways during the 1920s. The Bureau also sponsored and conducted road-building research, which not only defined standards for roads but also helped to ensure that university-trained engineers enjoyed professional authority over these projects. But the Depression and World War II slowed down these activities. In 1940 most of the roads and streets were still unpaved, and the automobile was used mainly for local driving. This changed dramatically after the war. "In 1940 there had been roughly 27 million registered passenger cars in the country; by 1950 that figure had almost doubled; a decade later, it had trebled. By 1970 there were more cars than there were households in the United States, and in Los Angeles in that year there were more cars than there were people."[28] By the 1990s the mileage of the paved roads alone in the United States was close to 2.4 million. These equaled the combined miles of all the paved roads in Canada, Germany, the United Kingdom, Japan, France, Poland, Brazil, Hungary, Mexico, Italy, and China.[29] In 2000 the highway system in the United States was 40 percent longer than that of the systems in twenty-five European states combined; today there are almost 4 million miles of paved and unpaved roads in the United States.[30] The major legislative force behind the paving of the nation, the Interstate Highway Act in 1956, first failed in Congress because of the enormous costs it imposed on the federal budget. Only when the Eisenhower administration reintroduced the bill as a major defense project during the Cold War did Congress give its approval. Ever since, the alleged military motivation for these roads has been the stuff of rumors and Internet lore. However, the primary motivation for starting what became the longest engineered structure ever built was not defense but the increased circulation of passengers and freight on a comprehensive American network. Beginning in the late 1950s, resistance to these projects grew locally, especially in urban areas; by the 1970s the environmentally detrimental effects of freeways had become obvious.[31] Today debates over whether and how many roads should be built in the last roadless areas of the American West are among the most important ones for environmentalists.[32]

Even though it is often difficult to tell from photos where a particular highway may be located, the meanings of landscapes and the designs of roads vary not only from era to era but also from country to country or from region to region. Even different ethnic traditions may account for variations in road design. Thus, in Texas, pre-automotive-era roads built by the Spanish population always radiated from major towns, whereas the roads built by Germans in the same region were constructed in ways designed to serve specific commercial and social purposes.[33] In some countries, such as Italy, a surge of highway construction in the 1920s eclipsed aesthetic considerations. The rapid modernization of the country was deemed more important than the beautification of the highway system.[34] In Germany, landscape architects characterized the straight roads of the Italians and Americans as inappropriate. They advanced a design doctrine for German highways that rejected everything foreign. Whether their proposals for curvilinear roads and the exclusive use of native plants were indeed realized, however, is still debated.[35] Several states claimed to have a truly national style in road-building, but these claims were sometimes inaccurate. In the German Democratic Republic, for instance, politicians and landscape architects promoted a unique alternative to the Western ideals of the Bauhaus and the national style, but they ended up building roads in much the same way as German engineers of the 1930s.

Donald Meinig argues that landscape concepts have been more progressive in America and more traditional in Europe. For him, Jackson's "eagerness for the future" (that is, the American focus on vernacular landscapes, such as parking lots and trailer courts) and William Hoskins's "obsession with the past" (as in the idealization of early modern landscapes) are "expressions of temperament as well as nationality."[36] In succinct terms, Stephen Spender, in his studies on transatlantic interaction, emphasizes that "Americans fear the European past" while "Europeans fear the American future."[37] In reality, Americans have been very antiurban (and certainly not progressive, to use Meinig's terms) in their preferences for green suburban communities; they live, as Sam Bass Warner has argued, "in one of the world's urbanized countries as if it were a wilderness."[38] Furthermore, while different nations and cultures have brought forth individual styles and designs in road-building, technological and cultural transfer have contributed greatly to a convergence of engineering and aesthetics in different parts of the world. In effect, the papers in this volume challenge the claims of many contemporary writers, politicians, and engineers that their respective nation-states developed and possessed "essentially" national technologies. The intersection of landscape and road instead shows that these ideas and realities were as international as they were parochial, and that the intense competition between countries and political blocs in the twentieth century fostered the national branding of technology at a time of increased exchange of professional knowledge about technology; confrontation and emulation could go hand in hand. Overcoming nationally centered narratives of automotive history is one of the goals of this volume.

According to American observers, their parkways were paragons of this technological genre in the first half of the twentieth century. Timothy Davis discusses American parkways as a landscape of national identity, explores why parkways became carriers of meaning at this particular point in American history, and analyzes how they seemed to reconcile the tensions between modernity and traditional values. Federally funded highway projects presented a highly selective version of American history and destiny yet became model roads for other parts of the world as well.

Rudy J. Koshar extends the debate on landscape and roads by tracing the intimate relationship that has developed over the past century between driving and citizenship. Koshar claims that everyday usage, not the intention of designers, makes roads what they are. His effort to bring the driver back into the picture is based on a larger understanding of citizenship in modern societies, which includes driving cars as a civic activity, not just as a technical skill. Challenging previous claims in the literature, he asserts that driving automobiles helped to spread democracy and egalitarian aspects of consumerism across the United States and Germany. Owning and driving a vehicle became tantamount to participating in a modern democracy. For Koshar, even Hitler's autobahn was a proving ground for democratic driving practices.

Anne Mitchell Whisnant examines the complex politics behind the land-scaping of the Blue Ridge Parkway, built and maintained by the National Park Service. Whisnant argues that the dominant narrative of the parkway is one of harmony between the road and its surrounding scenery. She shows, how-ever, that this notion obfuscates more than it reveals, since the Blue Ridge Parkway was by no means an uncontroversial project. Rather, the National Park Service decided to portray the Southeastern Appalachians as a backward, antimodern part of the United States and used the design and construction of the road to reinforce this notion in the minds and eyes of Parkway travelers. Whisnant's essay serves as a powerful reminder that political interests and cultural stereotypes more often than not influence the design of roads.

Suzanne Julin discusses how scenic roads were constructed and be-came tourist attractions themselves. According to her case study of South Dakota's Black Hills, the tourist industry encouraged road planners to pro-duce a stunning landscape that would prove to be unique and filled with unexpected features and vistas. The highway seemed to reveal itself to the adventure-seeking automobile tourists, while in reality it had been carefully designed to create a dramatic drive. The designers' control was omnipresent yet barely visible.

Carl A. Zimring studies the evolving interests of the scrap-metal indus-try and the outdoor-advertising industry. Their commercial motives pitted them against environmentalists and parts of the federal government, in particular Lady Bird Johnson, the nation's First Lady in the mid-1960s. Zimring asserts that, in the end, economic rather than environmental us-ages of space prevailed, but only after a long battle.

Three papers on European roads highlight the intimate marriage be-tween totalitarianism and extensive road-building. Massimo Moraglio de-scribes Italy's extraordinary program of road-building during the 1920s and the subsequent growth of the autostrade network. In sharp contrast to highway planners in the United States and Germany, managers of the Ital-ian highway system deemed it unnecessary to hire landscape architects to beautify or co-design the roads. Instead they relied on models of increased communication, circulation, and modernization in what they considered to be the most efficient form possible. Until the 1960s, they continued to portray roads as symbols of "progress."

Thomas Zeller examines the continuities and discontinuities in our un-derstanding of the autobahn as West German society transitioned from dictatorship to democracy. Knowledge of the landscape and of road-building technology, far from being fixed, was highly contested and remained fluid during these decades. Zeller interprets the professional debates between civil engineers and landscape architects as social struggles deriving from their respective roles in two contrasting political systems. Politics and technology were resources for each other, and civil engineers managed to harvest these resources more successfully than their counterparts.

In the case of East Germany, politicians and landscape architects were hoping to establish a visible alternative to National Socialism. As Axel Dossmann points out, GDR landscape architects pursued designs that would be distinct from the Bauhaus (whose Dessau birthplace ironically came to be located in East Germany) and from the International Style. In so doing, the planners ended up promoting a type of classical design (in bridge-building, for instance) that mirrored Nazi concepts and ideals. Both aesthetic and ecological considerations were secondary in the planning of GDR highways; and from the 1960s onward, its civil engineers drew much of their road-building knowledge and ideas from West German technical literature.

When Great Britain considered the building of motorways in the postwar period, debates arose over how to design roads that would reflect a national identity then in the process of redefinition. Peter Merriman examines in detail the dialogue that developed between British civil engineers and landscape architects. While the former insisted on "orderly" roads, the latter's ideas were based on horticultural knowledge and the country's long history of sculpted landscapes. Only in the late 1950s, according to Merriman's research, did landscape consultants enter the design process.

While most of the essays in this volume are concerned with extra-urban roads, Jeremy L. Korr analyzes the urban and surburban road that circles the U.S. capital. Korr points out that the Washington Beltway serves multiple constituencies within a framework of federal, state, county, and municipal authorities and demands. Korr's case study shows that many of the public's questions about safety, noise, and landscape were not addressed appropriately by transportation officials either at the time of the highway's construction or later. Even when public hearings were organized, residents who sought to discuss the planning process felt excluded; their concerns were not adequately acknowledged by politicians and engineers, who were reluctant to relinquish managerial control over the project.

Taken together, the essays in this collection tell us much about how roads are placed in landscapes. They are a reflection of automobility and its ever-increasing role over the past century. They teach us one way to read the world beyond the windshield, with historical awareness of the cultural preferences, power relations, and contingencies of the historical processes that have jointly helped to shape these roads and landscapes. Whether we abhor them or take delight in them, they have become part of the fabric of human existence.

ONE

Driving Cultures and

the Meaning of Roads

Some Comparative Examples

Rudy J. Koshar

I

In the conclusion to his *Roads: Driving America's Great Highways,* the Pulitzer Prize–winning novelist and screenwriter Larry McMurtry comments that "fiction seems mainly to be asking two questions: Where does the road go? And how is one to marry?"[1] McMurtry concedes perplexity on the latter question, but on the former he exhibits more certainty. "I wanted to drive the American roads at century's end, to look at the country again, from border to border and beach to beach."[2] His plan took him across the United States, not in one extended trip but in a series of short and medium treks from Dallas to Laredo on I-35; from Baltimore to Burlington, Colorado, on I-70; and from Detroit on I-75 to Michigan's Upper Peninsula, where McMurtry pays homage to the vivid portrayals of life in the northern woods by Ernest Hemingway and Janet Lewis. But McMurtry insists that his travel memoir takes the road itself as a destination as much as it values the people, stories, and landscapes encountered along the way. He likens America's interstates to the great rivers of the world, on which traveled intrepid explorers, such as the Americans Lewis and Clark, as well as bourgeois tourists like those nineteenth-century representatives of the British

Empire who plied the Ganges. Riverine travel came alive through the narratives these people told of their voyages and through the searching explorations of self and society to which those voyages gave rise. The meaning of such passageways, whether rivers or roads, finally came down to "the travelers themselves, characters so powerful, so twisted, so packed with sensibility that even the striking places they travel through frequently have trouble competing for our attention."[3] The travel writers told stories about the real world, about what was *out there*. But the shape and content of their stories always also led back inside, to the perception of existence and how that perception was projected outward onto the byways of human interaction.

McMurtry's point is relevant to the thesis I develop in this essay, which asserts that modern roads and highways derive their social resonance not from the actions of engineers or political authorities but rather from people who drive cars. Recent scholarship on the history of road-building in Europe and the United States elucidates a rich pattern of conflict and negotiation among economic interest groups, the state, engineers, construction companies, political and civic authorities, and the media. This research extends from accounts of the building of parkways, boulevards, and even legendary roadways in the United States, such as Mulholland Drive in Los Angeles, to analyses of the rapid construction of the German autobahn system, of such stunning mountain roads as Austria's Großglockner Alpine Highway, and of urban traffic systems in West and East Germany.[4] Scholars acknowledge that the "view through the windshield" has been a constitutive element in such projects, as engineers, builders, and politicians sought to mobilize or satisfy the car-driving publics that would use the new roadway systems.[5] Drivers' perspectives, or rather what authorities deemed those perspectives to be, were crucial in the process of proposing, designing, and building roads from which natural parks, cityscapes, and even industrial environments could be viewed. Even so, scholarly acknowledgment of the driver's role in modern roadway systems has rarely dealt adequately with the fact that the most socially resonant meanings of boulevards, parkways, and superhighways have evolved only after certain patterns of everyday usage were established. Regardless of how engineers or urban planners have envisioned the function and character of roads and arteries, it is quotidian use that has determined the shape of transportation systems. Who could have engineered the cultural meanings that became associated with Route 66 in the United States?[6] Usage patterns may sometimes have developed roughly along the lines anticipated by property developers and engineers; but often they did not, as the quantity of traffic either fell below or far exceeded predictions, or as certain streets and boulevards attracted "undesirables" who drag-raced or cruised their way through urban and rural neighborhoods. As a recent study avers, "automotive history should always also be a history of streets."[7] But the obverse is true as well: the history of modern roads must also be a history of cars and of the people who use them.[8]

Inattention to drivers as shapers of roads is one aspect of a larger scholarly indifference toward the social history of driving, as anthropologist Daniel Miller has pointed out.[9] The extensive historical literature on the automobile is replete with accounts of the major manufacturers and engineers, studies of labor relations and business practices, and analyses of design and aesthetics.[10] Recently, environmental perspectives have entered the picture, often with dire consequences for scholarly attitudes toward the car, which were already one-sidedly negative. Yet the most direct and palpable aspects of automotive history, the experiences individuals have of driving their cars; of entering and exiting flows of traffic; of negotiating, successfully or not, the multiplicity of roads and intersections that driving entails; of parking, touring, and promenading—all or most of these still escape the historian's attention. Even recent discussions of American "road-trip literature" miss the mark here, largely because they are fixated on artistic representation rather than quotidian social practice.[11] Sociologist John Urry points out that modern civil societies not only presupposed but also required mobility in a multitude of forms to foster participation.[12] The car achieved domination in the United States quite early compared to Europe, where stronger initial resistance and more intense competition from other modes of transportation slowed public embrace of the automobile. The contingency of this development, its unexpected and discontinuous qualities, will be examined below. Nonetheless, "automobilized" civil societies did become a key benchmark of modernity, if not always a full social reality in much of the industrialized world,[13] just as new hybridized relations between humans and machines, between drivers and their cars, came to shape social and cultural perspectives even when many did not drive cars or drove them only irregularly. To ignore or underestimate the citizen-drivers of modern societies, that is to say, to overlook the fact that very often citizens *are* drivers, in imagination as well as in actual practice, is also to ignore how those societies have been constituted on the ground, or in our case, on the road.[14]

To illuminate the general process whereby roads acquire meaning through social usage, I will here sketch out three distinct, though related, driving practices—the "pioneering," the "democratic," and the "oppositional"—each of which has assumed a particular appropriation (or creation) of roads and streets over the past century. By *practice* I mean making "use of a semiotic code to do something in the world."[15] As William Sewell argues, putting something into practice entails the ability not only to deploy a cultural code in stereotyped situations but also to elaborate and modify it and to adapt it to unexpected conditions. When drivers drive, they use a code, the "rules of the road" as they are understood in particular cultures. But different drivers adapt that code to the kind of car they are driving; to their needs and dispositions; to the assumptions they make about their ethnic, national, class, or gender status; to the types of roads and landscapes through which they drive; and to the determinate political and economic relations that have produced the roads in the first place. Their practice is not only a formulaic or mechanical behavior designed to meet specific functional needs but also a semiotic act, an effort at negotiating meaning through use of a shared code.

My analysis will focus mainly on the United States and Germany. It is not meant to offer a comprehensive catalogue of driving modes but rather to tease out some distinctive relations between driving patterns and the cultural appropriations of roads since the early part of the twentieth century. In so doing, it will necessarily underemphasize topics such as landscape technologies, the history of roadway construction, and the development of signage and roadway semiotics (advertising, roadside architecture), to say nothing of the themes of automobile design, safety regulations and the history of accidents,[16] the evolution of drivers' education and licensing, and the history of car makes and models. Some of these themes will be touched on below, but for the most part they must await elaboration in future research projects. Above all, this essay is meant to be transnational and synthetic rather than explicitly comparative across national borders or distinct time periods.

II

The road-making practices of driving find a most literal expression in my first example, which I refer to as the pioneering mode. It should be noted that I use this term not to suggest a Whiggish or teleological narrative of the rise of the car. Rather, my terminology is intended to underscore the radical contingency of automotive transport at the end of the nineteenth century. Not only was the car an untried medium of individual mobility, but automotive technologies based on gas, electric, and steam alternatives competed with one another for dominance. Moreover, the quality of roads varied widely; they were often no more than paths in the United States, where organizations such as the League of American Wheelmen (a bicycling group) and the Good Roads Association would make great efforts to develop existing roads and create new transport networks, especially in rural areas, where road improvement promised to boost agricultural economies and prevent depopulation.[17] The sheer novelty of the car also reinforces the point that the automobilized civil societies of the twentieth century had uncertain beginnings, as mobile individuals at the end of the nineteenth century were more likely to be transported by rail or carriage or on horseback than by car. Competition between public and private transportation shapes a large part of the story of individual automotive experience.[18] Mobility, a sine qua non of modernity, meant something quite different at the dawn of the twentieth century from what it would mean just twenty years later in the United States, or a half century later in Europe. For all these reasons, the idea of pioneering driving practices here refers to the discontinuous and experimental qualities of early car use rather than to some celebratory narrative of the automobile. Even so, we should not fail to mention that the terminology does indeed reflect a kind of heroic story, since at no previous point in history had a form of individualized transport enabled people to move about with a rapidity and ease only imagined in the past. Scholarship on early childhood development repeatedly emphasizes the revolutionary change in perspective brought about by a child's ability to take its first steps entirely unaided. The concept of a pioneering driving practice is meant to convey the same kind of first step, a truly radical break with what had gone before.

In the pioneering mode, drivers often literally had to create their own roads, or rather paths, through landscapes that in some cases had never been traversed by an automobile. I am referring specifically to the first transcontinental trips in the United States between 1899, when the first attempt was made to cross the country by motorcar, and 1908, when the first family drove across the United States by car.[19] Automotive historians on both sides of the Atlantic have focused generally on speed as the definitive characteristic that drew an initially elite audience to the automobile in the United States, France, England, Italy, and Germany. Races, reliability competitions, and even amateur "sports" driving of the kind associated in Germany with often-reckless *Herrenfahrer* from the aristocracy or wealthy bourgeoisie were indeed important constituents in the building of early automotive cultures in Europe and North America.[20] Yet although historians have put more emphasis on these spectacular driving practices, it was the early transcontinental trips that may have done more to create an auto-buying public, at least in the United States. Whereas racing and speed were central to the technological development of internal combustion engines, transmissions and drivetrains, suspension systems, brakes, and other important mechanical features of the car, the qualities of reliability and durability as evidenced in the early long-distance pioneering trips convinced a wider public that the automobile was there to stay.[21]

Let us concentrate here only on the first trip, which was planned as a spectacular excursion from New York City to San Francisco in 1899 by John D. Davis and his wife, Louise Hitchcock Davis. The couple ended their trip in Chicago after experiencing numerous mechanical breakdowns and other complications, prompting one newspaper to call it "the bust of the century."[22] Yet the trip began with broad publicity and significant popular interest, and it had an impact well beyond the three months it took Davis and his wife to traverse the nearly twelve hundred miles along the way. Sponsored by a Connecticut automaker and two newspapers, the couple drove a two-cylinder Duryea. For Davis, whom a doctor had ordered to seek healthy western air, as well as for his wife, the trip meant both adventure and pleasure. *Scientific American* highlighted the touristic appeal of the trip when, early in the Davises' excursion, it wrote: "[T]here is no more delightful way of seeing the country than to view it from the comfortably cushioned seats of an automobile vehicle."[23] But the element of leisure was only one of many motivations for the trip and certainly not the primary one, as it would be in driving practices that evolved later in the history of auto use. Trip sponsors were thinking internationally, as they hoped that the Duryea's exploits would prove the competence of American automobiles, still regarded as inferior to French competitors. Moreover, the Davises not only intended to make a detailed report on the quality of roads; they also planned to determine whether navigable roadways for autos existed at all,

1.1. John and Louise Hitchcock Davis as they made the first attempt to drive coast to coast in 1899. Palmyra Photographs collection, album 3:20, negative 03:834, reproduced courtesy of the Department of Rare Books and Special Collections at the Rush Rhees Library, University of Rochester, Rochester, New York.

especially west of Ogallala, Nebraska, about which press reports disagreed, and between Denver and San Francisco, auto routes for which little official information was available (fig. 1.1).[24]

As he prepared for the trip, Davis studied a map issued by the League of American Wheelmen, one of the main supporters, beside car clubs and rural groups, of the Good Roads Association. This reflected a general attribute of early automotive routes in that the car traveled on roads designed either for other means of transportation or to be shared with other vehicles and pedestrians. In decades to come, auto-only roads would be considered both desirable and feasible; and later in the twentieth century, planners would begin to establish separate routes for pedestrians, bicyclists, streetcars, buses, and autos. But Davis's map-reading revealed important elements of the pioneering driving mode that were shared with other driving practices as well.

First, the maps (and the routes finally employed) suggested not merely possible functional paths but a national-cultural itinerary. Since at least the eighteenth century, Americans had believed that engagement with "wilderness" and the "frontier" was a constitutive experience of national identity. Some two decades later, environmentalists would decry the notion that a meaningful frontier experience could be derived from automobile touring; as Aldo Leopold wrote, "[I]f we think we are going to learn by cruising around the mountains in a Ford, we are largely deceiving ourselves."[25] But this is precisely what the Davises' encounter entailed and what their route-planning implied, namely, the finding of an East-West itinerary through which the country's roads and frontiers, and thereby the nation itself, as well as its characteristic natural vistas and stunning natural monuments, could be viewed and mapped. The creative and inventive aspects of the landscape experience in the pioneering mode come through most clearly in this instance, as did its contribution to later road-building projects. For if there was a national culture of auto road-building in the United States, then a chief part of it was the attempt to construct a grand "linking" thoroughfare from East to West, a kind of "main street across America," as the famous Lincoln Highway was called, that brought the Atlantic and Pacific oceans, the two great natural wonders bounding the country, together across the rugged body of the nation.[26] Indeed, the Lincoln Highway and analogous projects suggested that not even natural wonders sufficed to express national identity in the United States. The mode of transportation itself— whether a Conestoga wagon, a steam locomotive, or a car—was the decisive symbol of Americans' need for ceaseless travel across the continent.[27]

Second, road-mapping and attempting to traverse the nation were by no means mere exercises in "imagining" community, as present orthodoxy would have it.[28] Through planning and driving, the individual actively mediated a relation between the car and the road and, in so doing, entered the national community in a specific and palpable sense. We can speak here, using Heidegger, of a "referential totality"[29] in which human agents formulated the task of driving and encountered the mechanical equipment (the car and the road) needed to fulfill the task in a constantly reciprocal and self-perpetuating dynamic. The balance of energies between the car, the driver, and the road varied in different driving modes, as did the manner in which this balance connoted national belonging.[30] In the pioneering mode the rigorous physical demands of driving could hardly be ignored. The Duryea broke down almost daily, and the trip fell behind schedule from the moment the two-cylinder vehicle left New York City. Bad roads and the fragility of the automobile combined to create a highly uncertain trip that finally had to be discontinued. Yet it would be wrong to assume that this was only a frustrating or negative experience for the Davises. Writing from Buffalo, Louise Hitchcock Davis observed: "[I]t would be monotonous to go speeding across the continent without accident or mishap of any kind. One might as well fall back in the cushioned chair of a Pullman car. But the joy of being thrown into a ditch, of having cylinders break while the motor is running at top speed, of having a wheel come off, letting you gently down to earth, and of all sorts and conditions of mishaps, is something too exhilarating for words."[31]

Early automobilists' apparent pride in their ability not just to weather such mishaps but also to quickly recover from them, either on their own or (as was often the case for the Davises) with assistance from capable blacksmiths along the way, appears to have been a transnational and cross-class phenomenon, as suggested by aristocratic gentleman-drivers' accounts of their early automotive adventures in Europe. No less a personage than the brother of Kaiser Wilhelm II, Prince Heinrich, was seen repairing his Benz automobile on German roads in 1911, thereby earning the deep admiration of the car-owning public.[32] In all such cases the physicality of the car experience was linked to efforts to participate in a direct way in the community, which, in the case of the transcontinental automobilists, was defined by the American frontier experience.

The first attempted transcontinental car trip in the United States heralded the coming decade of automotive pioneering.[33] The Davises' trip was followed in 1901 by another unsuccessful attempt, by Alexander Winton. Two years later, however, Dr. H. Nelson Jackson and Sewall K. Crocker crossed the United States from San Francisco to New York City in a 1903 Winton touring car nicknamed "Vermont" (fig. 1:2).[34] Several additional crossings followed, each accompanied by more fanfare, more advertising investment, and more impressive speeds and times. In 1908, the businessman and sports enthusiast Jacob Murdock, his wife, his three children, and two mechanics traveled from Pasadena, California, to New York City in thirty-two days. This accomplishment merits analysis, for it marked the first time an entire family had made the crossing. But I mention it here only to suggest its relevance for things to come.

Exaggerating the resolve with which he had planned the adventure, Murdock would later write that he meant the trip to demonstrate that an or-

I.2. Horatio Nelson Jackson and Sewall K. Crocker in their Winton touring car named "Vermont," in the early days of their transcontinental drive from San Francisco to New York City in 1903, the first successful cross-country trip by automobile. Photograph reproduced courtesy of the Department of Special Collections at the Bailey/Howe Library, University of Vermont.

dinary family, children included, could withstand the rigors of transcontinental motoring.[35] In making this claim, he envisioned a different sort of driving practice, one oriented less specifically to exploration and adventure, although these experiences would continue to be among the goals of even the most comfortable automotive touring of the late twentieth century. Murdock's trip opened a window on a mode of driving in which people learned to "motor democratically," in the words of the English automotive journalist Owen John.[36] In this instance, roads were not primarily exploratory itineraries of national being but pathways constituting a democratic public sphere, places where individuals and families performed a cultural code based on tolerance, reciprocity, and freedom as they drove or rode in cars (and later station wagons or minivans) designed to travel safely yet efficiently, in much the same way that commerce and manufacturing were intended to function in a smoothly flowing capitalist society. Cars and their drivers were analogous to freely circulating capital in this interpretation, and drivers on the road operated according to the principle of "one man, one vote."

The democratic mode presupposed that a certain "culture of control" had already been put in place through which the requisite technical, political, and cultural requirements of working transportation systems were met.[37] The bicycle played an important role here, as its proponents advocated new paving techniques, safety measures, and other improvements that would redound to the benefit of the automobile. In both America and Europe, roads had to be adapted to car use, which meant that sharply cambered streets had to be fixed, the incline of steep slopes reduced, and markers and signals created or improved. Among the main proponents of such changes were the automobile associations, which have come in for substantial scholarly criticism for their resistance to many government regulations and their aggressive intent in rewriting the rules of the road to suit selfish needs.[38] Accurate though such criticisms may be, the fact is that the roads did become less dusty and dangerous for drivers as well as pedestrians and animals over time. Additionally, it is important to note that such cultures of control were subject to immense national and regional variation, and that the meaning of democratic driving practices evolved in relation to historically specific conditions in different countries.

Just as roads acquired new meanings in the evolution of this tradition, so the referential totality of car, driver, and road changed. The transformation of motoring clothing signaled a deep structural shift. Owen John associated nondemocratic driving with the masks, goggles, and full-length dusters worn by early automobilists as they careened over the roads.[39] Not only did these costumes scare the devil out of farm and domestic animals, they also alarmed local people and enhanced the sense of anonymity and class distance surrounding the first motorists. But drivers were soon able to shed such accoutrements, making the people behind the wheel more visible and identifiable to pedestrians as well as to other drivers. A new transparency characterized roadway interactions. In addition, as cars became less labor-intensive and more reliable, drivers honed their motoring skills, and roads improved. This led to an emphasis on technique, safety, and comfort rather than physical stamina and a "warrior mentality."[40] Contemporaries often bemoaned such changes, as Herrenfahrer criticized the "feminization" of cars and the ease with which driving could be learned. "Today, the automobilist is for the most part an automaton," wrote one chagrined driver in 1913.[41] Women had been active participants in automotive history from the beginning, as the example of the first transcontinental attempt in the United States demonstrates. But they became even more prevalent in the democratic mode, most often as passengers but increasingly as drivers.[42]

In the democratic mode, perhaps because of a degree of direct and indirect feminization, the car's "domestic" features predominated, as the automobile developed analogously to the bourgeois home, becoming a site for "dwelling within the car" rather than "dwelling on the road."[43] Electric starters, closed bodies, glass windows, better sound insulation, cloth seats, more informative dashboard instrumentation, and later the introduction of radios in car interiors—all such technical, safety, and design increments added up to a cumulative change that was nothing short of revolutionary when considered in terms of its social consequences. What had been gained by the shedding of elaborate automotive clothing seemed to have been lost by closing off the car from its surroundings. Critics might suggest that the domestication of the car—its transformation into a more secure, semi-isolated unit relatively insulated from the sights and sounds of road traffic—paralleled the privatization of culture in the twentieth century. In this shift, it may be argued, roads lost their function as conduits for a participatory civil society and instead became sites of passive, consumerist pleasure. The evolution of roadside architecture, shaped not only by scenic rest stops but also by the auto camp, the motel, the garish horde of advertising signs, and later the strip mall—all signaled the powerful commercial dynamic that informed the driving experience.[44] The landscape experience shifted from "wilderness" in the pioneering mode to a commercially mediated chain of natural and urban vistas. Scholars have analyzed more sinister trends, as they argue that the automobile and suburbia aided whites' persistent efforts (already widespread before the age of cars) to isolate themselves from blacks, immigrants, and blue-collar workers.[45] In such instances highways and roads served not only to link driving with the intense commodification of daily life but also with social and racial segregation. But I find the argument of the car's isolating effects only partially convincing, or at least in need of strong qualification, as will be noted below.

Democratic motoring emerged most decisively in the United States before World War I, partly as a result of the rise of middle-class car ownership but also partly due to American farmers' embrace of the car in general and the Model T in particular by the late 1920s.[46] Auto ownership in Europe grew more slowly, although by the 1920s and 1930s both England and France had seen the automobile become an important symbol of middle-class family life, and even a small minority of workers had gained access to the previously circumscribed circle of auto ownership.[47] But these patterns should not obscure countervailing tendencies such as the "motor-phobia" documented by Uwe Fraunholz for Germany or by Ronald Kline for the United States.[48] From farmers who opposed the dust and noise raised by speeding automobiles in rural America to stone-throwing adolescents who bombarded wealthy automobilists' cars as they passed through German villages before World War I, individuals reacted critically and on occasion even violently to the spread of automobiles. Nonetheless, Fraunholz's data could be adduced for the opposite purpose, namely to document how scattered and quantitatively insignificant protests against the car were.[49] Moreover, given the extraordinary rapidity with which cars became ubiquitous in the United States, one can only conclude that popular acceptance of the car dramatically outweighed the envious, critical, or hesitant voices. In the United States the period during which automobile ownership was limited to the elite passed quickly, although it lasted much longer in Europe. But there, too, the demographics of car ownership were influenced much more by the larger structural and historical characteristics of income patterns and consumer markets than by any organized resistance to the automobile.

Germany was also part of the story of democratic driving practices even when auto ownership there fell far below what it was in France or England, the two European leaders in car use until the late 1950s. During a 1930s visit to the United States, the German engineer Ferdinand Porsche commented on the "courtly" behavior Americans demonstrated as they drove.[50] He had in mind the rather slow, orderly, and relatively polite motoring practiced by Americans in a variety of venues, from national parks to tree-lined urban boulevards. He no doubt overlooked the yahoos screaming down American rural roads in their Ford V-8s, and New Yorkers might have scoffed at such a comment as they bristled their way through daily traffic jams. But Porsche's observations were meant only partly as straightforward observation. He had journeyed to the United States in order to learn more about American automotive manufacturing, labor relations, and designs as he took on the task of building a "people's car" for Germany.[51] He also knew that many Germans, including some who were trying to articulate a new driving culture adequate to the nascent autobahn system, opposed speeding and other kinds of reckless behavior on Hitler's superhighways. Thus, his positive assessment of Americans' driving practices could serve as a spur to developments back home.

That German drivers were still uncertain about how to negotiate their nation's roads cannot be doubted. Indeed, the country's driving culture existed in a liminal state, suspended between the devil-may-care traditions of the Herrenfahrer and practices more attuned to the age of mass automobility and to navigating roads dedicated exclusively to car traffic. The German autobahn system, a decidedly precocious phenomenon in a country where auto ownership was still limited, presented both an important challenge and a significant opportunity in this regard. My argument is that it was an important context for the learning of democratic driving practices, even in Hitler's Germany, where the state's ultimate goal was totalitarian mobilization in preparation for a war of racial conquest.

It was not Porsche only but many others who looked to America for inspiration. The automotive journalist Heinrich Hauser was one of the most articulate advocates of *Motorwandern,* or "motor wandering," which featured moderate driving in scenic landscapes, knowledge of which enhanced both individual pleasure and pride in the nation. It entailed a cooperative attitude and a slow pace, which drivers observed not only on the superhighways but also on country roads. Like Americans, Germans were to let the elements and their own personal spontaneity be their guide rather than adhering slavishly to preordained routes or itineraries. Hauser argued that the autobahn system was ideal for such driving experiences, and he counseled Germans to learn to use these new arteries as quickly and efficiently as possible.[52] Developed at a time when there was a scarcity of cars in Germany, Hauser's vision was just as precocious as the autobahn system that formed its backdrop. Even so, because it took its cue from an American image of the individual driver with access to leisure pursuits of his or her own choice, it was part of what Raymond Williams would have termed an "emergent" culture of democratic driving practices in Germany.[53] Yet Hauser's position was always deeply ambivalent, for he would criticize consumer society and the "Americanization" of Europe after World War II.[54]

At first glance, other advocates of autobahn driving appeared to emphasize individual experiences less than Hauser did. Hauser praised Hitler, as so many commentators did, for his grand road-building scheme, but he always came back to the individual driver. By contrast, C. Volkhardt, an engineer and contributor to a popular car magazine of the time, *Motor-Kritik*, urged Germans to learn the new rules of the road because Hitler had intended for them to be used in a particular way, that is, as auto-only routes supporting speeds of up to a hundred kilometers per hour. "The incorrect or even dangerous use of the autobahn contradicts directly the Führer's intentions, and it is therefore to be punished even more severely than faulty driving on normal streets," he wrote.[55] Volkhardt followed this declaration with a catalogue of "Autobahn sins." He chastised the estimated 25 percent of all drivers who didn't keep to the right unless passing, and he noted that truckers were especially egregious offenders. People who weaved in and out of their lanes, lovebirds who dawdled along without paying attention to surrounding traffic, drivers who continued to sit in the passing lane even after they overtook slower-moving cars, and those who failed to consult their rearview mirrors—all deserved criticism, argued Volkhardt, if not harsher penalties, such as fines, imprisonment, and impounding of the offenders' cars—a system similar to the one allegedly used in the United States. Paradoxically, even Hitler lent a hand in this project, as he strongly condemned reckless or inappropriate driving on the autobahn.[56] Of course, Hitler had his sights set on war, so his admonition to the autobahn sinners was not meant primarily to promote new civic values on the roadways but rather to conserve manpower and raw materials.

All such discussions of wanderers and "sinners" on the autobahn oscillated between an emphasis on roads as "vistas of delight," to use a phrase from interwar Britain,[57] and an emphasis on the public responsibilities of road users. But both facets were always present, regardless of whether commentators pinpointed elements of consumer fantasy, pleasure, and individual choice or of civic obligation and official control. Between these two poles, democratic driving practices developed, shaped by specific national (and regional) driving cultures, but always with an eye toward harmonizing individual choice with civic and political purpose, private interest with public engagement.

Road-builders also tried to balance such interests and priorities. As Mumford argued, the international language of transportation planning conceived of the road not as a social locus but as a major structure whose function was to enable speedy circulation of auto traffic. A linear notion of progress shaped this functionality, just as similarly linear notions influenced liberal political practice.[58] The autobahn system appropriated the evolving American parkway ideal, initially shaped by Frederick Law Olmsted and extended by midcentury planners such as Robert Moses. This ideal was based on linking urban civilization with nature and intercalating the private automobile as a symbol of public life in a modern consumer society. In the case of the autobahn, nature took on a particularly important role, as the new superhighways were built through forest, heath, and mountain, offering stunning natural landscapes that German as well as foreign observers found delightful and exhilarating.[59] German road-planners claimed that such landscapes wedded nature and technology in a revolutionary new synthesis. But it is more likely that the autobahn's natural vistas promoted what John Brinckerhoff Jackson has called an "abstract, preternatural landscape of wind and sun and motion."[60] In the "abstract world of the hot-rodder," which is really the world of the ordinary (male) tourist and his family, according to Jackson, people see not traditional, picturesque landscapes of forest and village. Instead, theirs is a world of motion in which natural and man-made settings constitute abstract patterns best appreciated through the windshield of a car or perhaps from the window of a plane. They do not get back to nature as much as they appropriate a glimpse of nature as they drive, ski, or paddleboat through it. "The new landscape," wrote Jackson, "is composed of rushing air, shifting lights, clouds, waves, a constantly moving, changing horizon, a constantly changing surface beneath the ski, the wheel, the rudder, the wing."[61]

German adaptations of the American model of extraurban parkways and the abstract world of the hot-rodder reflected the political culture in which they occurred. A major feature of the German case is that Hitler thought in distinctly "postliberal" terms as he excluded a whole category of people from participation in the new autobahn system. Nazi Germany was not a liberal community but a "racial meritocracy" in which, theoretically, everyone who was "racially correct" had access to societal resources;[62] racial comrades were in turn invited to use the roadways as paths to territorial expansion, especially in the East, where the superhighways would lead first soldiers, then settlers, administrators, and tourists, into a German imperium. But those deemed racially unfit were initially harassed, then excluded or murdered. In all such cases the autobahn's landscapes were to reflect German social values, not liberal Western ideas of commercial progress and linearity. This search for authenticity resulted in truly tortuous efforts to create unmistakably "German" bridges, roadside plantings, and even gas stations consonant with each *Heimat* (homeland, or regional) style.[63] If drivers of the interwar democratic mode were experiencing a consumerist, abstract world, then in the autobahn system this world would be shaped by the political determinants of a system based on racial hierarchy and imperial conquest.

A most striking feature of the German-Jewish philologist Viktor Klemperer's best-selling memoirs of his life in Nazi Germany is his detailed account, scattered throughout the first volume, of how deeply his exclusion from German driving culture hurt him. It was not only a matter of losing his mobility, a right to which citizens throughout the Western world laid greater claim as the twentieth century wore on. Rather, the initially irritating, then more serious and debilitating prohibitions against Jews' owning or operating cars also removed a pleasurable and challenging element of Klemperer's life. Klemperer was no natural driver; his recollections are filled with painful moments in which he took driving lessons, learned how to maneuver his used Opel in and out of his garage, and got into fender-bender accidents, which would create moments of truly high anxiety for him and his wife. Yet he found the autobahn "magnificent," and his passion for driving was unlimited: "Car, car over all, it has taken a terrible hold of us," he wrote in 1936.[64] In his love of driving and his determination to be a safe driver, Klemperer practiced democratic driving—until 1939, when his use of the car was transformed into a subversive activity, indeed, into a crime against the racial state.

Klemperer became an unintentional subversive, but many other drivers quite willingly adopted this stance. My third example touches on oppositional driving practices such as those developed by hot-rodders and "joy-riders" in Europe and America. In this mode, cars and highways became sites of dissidence, if not resistance. Antielite and antibourgeois, sometimes based on illegally "borrowing" cars (as in joyriding in interwar England and Germany) but often also including the populist cultural practice of customizing automobiles (as in the American hot-rod scene starting in the 1930s, or in the "tuning cultures" of Japan and the American West Coast over the past quarter century), such resistant driving exploited the temporal and spatial gaps of roadway systems, transforming what might be a sedate urban boulevard by day into a racetrack in the early morning hours.[65] Youth and working-class tinkerers have often been drawn to such driving cultures. Unlike drivers in the pioneering and democratic traditions, these individuals practiced what Michel de Certeau calls the "subtle art of 'renters,'" which is to say they did not enact a comprehensive vision of roads and society but selectively adapted elements of the dominant system to their own needs and interests.[66] In this they also differed from the gentleman-drivers, whose perspective was not only more "strategic" but also aristocratic or elitist rather than populist.

Let us move to the post–World War II hot-rodding scene in the United States for a brief glimpse of this phenomenon. The history of American hot-rodding goes back to before World War I, when, for example, Los Angeles police arrested 115 juveniles for "joy-riding" in 1913.[67] In the 1920s, people began racing automobiles on desert lakebeds in Southern California or on Los Angeles streets, where the speeding of "wild-eyed kids in hopped-up jalopies" was decried as a public nuisance in 1941.[68] After 1945, the term *hot rod* had at least two overlapping but different meanings. It referred to "a highly visible, relatively affluent, teenage lifestyle which seemed to turn on drive-ins, noise, jalopies held together with chewing gum and dangerous driving on public highways," as analyzed by H. F. Moorhouse.[69] But it also referred to a specialized, more self-regulated, and technologically demanding form of sport racing undertaken by older men, many of them ex-GIs, on the broad, flat desert stretches of California landscape. This second variant became institutionalized through characteristic publications, such as *Hot Rod* magazine, and organizations, such as the National Hot Rod Association.

Of the two variants, it is the former that interests us here, in part because its oppositional features are more clearly outlined. Hot-rodding contrasted with the sedate driving practiced by the average American, but its focus was not without an important international dimension. Hot-rodders considered street and drag racing to be typically American activities, less refined and more spontaneous than the driving of sportscar enthusiasts, who favored European automobiles, and less regulated than European-inspired Grand Prix racing.[70] The drag strip or urban boulevard on which hot-rodding took place was contrasted with the "typical" European road. The former was unerringly straight, intentionally or unintentionally designed for the optimal display of power and speed; whereas the latter's curves and variations in no way required high horsepower but rather deftness of touch and a degree of nuance. If the symbol of American hot-rodding quickly became the "rebel without a cause," it should nonetheless be noted that its "all-American" and nativist tendencies were very strong and explicitly articulated. The street-racing rebel was unwilling to leave home, and his "cause" was often patriotic and even nationalistic.

In the oppositional mode, moreover, the relationship between car and driver was more direct and intense, much as it had been in the pioneering mode or in the practices of the Herrenfahrer. Likewise, the oppositional mode was usually accompanied by more explicit reference to masculine identities: racing and street-rodding were often extensions of dating rituals, and women appeared as pinups in car magazines or as audiences for, rather than full participants in, street-racing cultures. Shaped by masculine preconceptions, street-rodding presupposed a mastery over automotive technology and the ability not just to excel in the driving of a car but actively to shape it, modify it, and maximize both its performance and its "machinic" visual cues.[71] The alleged passivity of the democratic driving mode was the explicit counterpoint to the technoactivism of oppositional driving practices. But to stop at the masculinist elements of such activism would be incomplete. Hot-rodders' engaged approach to automotive technology was not only an assertion of male values but also an important mark of civic participation. Even when they assumed the rebel's posture, they followed the precepts of an automobilized civil society, which demanded rapid circulation through the "scapes" and "flows" of modernity. In this process the acquisition of technical skills became an important measure not just of hot-rodders' collective and individual identity but also of societal competency as such. Contemporary scholarship on the meanings of citizenship has done relatively little to factor technical practices into the equation, much less to consider hot-rodders as "citizens" at all.[72]

If democratic driving practices lent themselves to living within the car, the oppositional mode returned the driver to living in the road. The road was valued not for the way in which it eased the individual's orderly traversal through urban or rural landscapes but for its ability to communicate to the driver. Its texture and relationship to surroundings were to be experienced directly, not subdued or rendered as elements in a commodified set piece accessible through the windshield of a domesticated interior. In the oppositional mode, the road spoke to the driver, who interpreted its language through feedback gained from the engine, steering wheel, suspension system, and sound of the tires. Had Jack Kerouac's *On the Road* not been suffused with the dissoluteness of "beat" culture, it would have been the perfect anthem for proponents of oppositional driving, who valued the "romance" of roads and the traffic they enabled. Even slow "cruising," a kind of urban promenading undertaken mainly by youthful drivers everywhere, fits the argument of the road as a source of direct communication.[73] Cruising ostensibly nullified some of the effects of dissident driving because it was based on that courtly progression that fit the democratic motoring tradition. Yet cruising derived much of its allure from rolled-down windows, revving engines, and open sexualized display—rather a contrast to the domesticated and relatively inward-looking vehicle of democratic driving.

The landscape experience mirrored this new type of engagement with the road. In the oppositional mode, it was neither natural nor commodified vistas that demanded attention but the environment of the machine. This is not to say that oppositional driving practices departed from the tradition of visuality that had characterized the pioneering and democratic modes. Instead, oppositional driving foregrounded the gleaming surfaces of automotive bodies, the sheen of asphalt roads on hot afternoons, and the hard glare of plate-glass windows in the summer sun. It was as if oppositional drivers had turned road-planners' intentions inside out as they raced or promenaded through urban streets; not natural scenes or grand urban monuments, not "the environment" or history, but the immediate sights and sounds of the traffic itself excited the driver. Their perspective was not that of a sublime "windshield wilderness" but that of the fleeting image glimpsed in the rearview mirror, as Reyner Banham once wrote of driving in Los Angeles. Banham might just as easily have been writing about the oppositional mode when he argued that the driving experience was one of "heightened awareness that some locals find mystical."[74] For the landscape experience of the dissident drivers was oriented not so much to the physical surroundings, whether appropriated tangibly or abstractly, as to the expressionistic impulses satisfied by racing, weaving in and out of lanes, and testing the car's mechanical limits. Landscape surfaces were reduced to emotionally laden catchments apprehended in the act of fast, often dangerous driving. It is worth asking if the dissident mode, or at least significant parts of it, did not take on a normative rather than transgressive character in the late twentieth century as the Los Angeles landscape experience analyzed by Banham came to characterize more and more driving practices, at least in the United States.

III

My goal in this essay has been to direct attention to the cultural work that makes modern motor roads what they are: not only arteries for rapid transportation but also complex systems of societal communications in which the interactions of drivers and cars connote larger systems of civic belonging. This approach leaves little room for current theories of the road as a "non-place," which Marc Augé defines as a space without relational or historical features. The non-place has no anthropology, in this view, because it is not "concerned with identity."[75] Augé argues that "supermodernity" is defined by the production of non-places, including not only roads and railways but airplanes, transit points such as airports and waiting rooms, cable and wireless communications networks, and motor vehicles.

Conversely, in my approach, driving always entails a dynamic, meaningful relation among individuals, the car, and the road. Different driving traditions or practices have evolved (and continue to evolve) over time, each of them linked with particular modes of interaction between the car and its operator. In each practice, moreover, we find that driving lends itself to characteristic understandings of the self as a participant in society, which is to say that driving enacts citizenship, just as citizenship implies certain kinds of driving practices. Above all, driving practices may emphasize close interaction with the road, as in the pioneering and oppositional traditions, or interpolate the car as a semi-isolated and domesticated unit protected from the road, as in the democratic mode. But none of them can do without the road as a site of social engagement. After all, a person who travels on a high-speed freeway as he or she listens to music, talks on a cell phone, and eats a snack is "concerned with identity" even if the roadway has been designed exclusively for traffic circulation rather than the social, economic, or recreational functions roads once performed. Finally, my discussion presupposes that no single or definitive meaning may be attached to roads and highways, regardless of what builders and their sponsors in state and society intended. Only when the multiplicity of driving practices and everyday usage of roads are taken into account will we be able to write a complete social and cultural history of roads and landscapes.

TWO

The Rise and Decline

of the American Parkway

Timothy Davis

The American motor parkway rose to prominence in the 1920s and '30s as an international model for the harmonious integration of engineering and landscape architecture. Parkways were celebrated by the popular and professional press, embraced by the driving public, and widely emulated not just in the United States but abroad. The main reason for this acclaim was that parkways reconciled complex and often competing cultural concerns. At the height of their popularity, parkways were championed by engineers, landscape architects, city and regional planners, patriotic societies, scenic beautificationists, leaders of the tourism industries, public officials, popular journalists, and elite architectural critics. Parkways began to recede from prominence after 1940, when changing social practices, accelerating technological developments, and shifting cultural concerns made it increasingly difficult to accommodate such diverse interests in single, multipurpose environments. This essay recounts the parkway's rise to prominence and summarizes its subsequent marginalization, tracing this trajectory in relation not just to aesthetic and technological concerns but to cultural and ideological issues as well.

From a technical perspective, parkways were clearly the most advanced motorways in the world from the mid-1910s to the mid-1930s. They were safer, faster, and more efficient than conventional roads. Aesthetically, parkways afforded a cure for the much-decried problem of roadside blight while updating established principles of landscape design in order to address the needs and speeds of contemporary motorists. As public amenities, they provided access to far-flung parks and beaches while serving as multipurpose recreational areas in their own right. From a broader planning perspective, they played a crucial role in revitalizing rural regions and reshaping the form and function of the modern metropolis. Parkways made good business sense as well. They proved to be powerful economic engines, gentrifying their immediate surroundings, boosting suburban real-estate values across the board, and nurturing the nascent heritage-tourism industry. With their attractive naturalistic scenery and comforting rustic allusions, parkways were cast as quintessential American landscapes and active agents in the drive to define and promote idealized American values. This was particularly true of federal projects such as the Mount Vernon, Colonial, and Blue Ridge parkways, which were explicitly intended to inculcate a highly selective vision of American history and destiny. While parkways reified traditional values and conventional aesthetics, they also captured the imaginations of modernist critics and artists, who praised their sinuous streamlined curves and hailed them as embodiments of modern conceptions of space, time, and motion.[1]

Along with their overt practical value and symbolic appeal, parkways performed a critical cultural function with far-reaching implications, both in the United States and abroad. By serving simultaneously as icons of modernity and touchstones of tradition, parkways helped to mediate the tension between progress and nostalgia, which numerous historians have identified as a dominant cultural concern of the period between the two world wars.[2] Most Americans embraced the material rewards of modernization, but few sought a radical break with the past. Popular interest in history—especially colonial and early American history—remained strong as the country looked for a "usable past" to provide continuity, stability, and a sense of direction in a rapidly changing world. By uniting traditional landscape aesthetics and allusions to America's pioneer past with state-of-the-art highway engineering, parkways grounded the present in the past, reconciling modern desires for material and social progress with the paradoxical longing to recapture the simple virtues and clarity of purpose commonly ascribed to the premodern era. By combining nature, celebratory public history, and technological progress in harmonious compositions that could be experienced through the medium of recreational driving, parkways designers united America's most rapidly growing popular pastime with prominent themes of American national identity. While the parkway's practical benefits are readily documented, a more intangible reason for their widespread appeal was that by being both emphatically modern and resolutely traditional, they helped Americans to negotiate the disjunctive experience of modernization during the tumultuous period between the two world wars.

Parkways were not twentieth-century inventions, of course. Frederick Law Olmsted and his partner Calvert Vaux introduced the term "park-way" to describe the attractive approaches they designed for Brooklyn's Prospect Park in 1868. The idea of connecting suburban parks with urban centers and elite residential districts by means of landscaped parkways soon became a key element of American city planning. Parkways were seen as a way to spread the benefits of parks throughout urban areas and as powerful economic stimulants that enhanced property values, encouraged upscale residential development, and bolstered a city's reputation as a place for business, residence, and tourism. As the connective tissue of metropolitan park systems, moreover, parkways played an important role in enlarging the scope of American city planning from isolated projects to comprehensive improvements.[3]

Stylistically, the first parkways resembled European boulevards. Brooklyn's Eastern Parkway consisted of a central drive bordered by broad, tree-lined margins, which were flanked by smaller roads for commercial vehicles and access to abutting properties. The series of drives and bordering parkland that Olmsted planned for Boston's Muddy River in the 1880s, now known collectively as the "Emerald Necklace," redefined the parkway as a picturesque lane winding through an elongated park embellished in the naturalistic style favored by Anglo-American landscape designers. The Boston project also represented a middle stage in the evolution from traditional boulevard to modern parkway with respect to circulation. The riverside location limited access on one side of the main roadway, but traffic entering from adjacent streets remained a source of danger and disruption. Despite these improvements, the advent of the automobile rendered horse-and-buggy-era parkways obsolete on both practical and aesthetic grounds. Not only were the tight turns and frequent intersections

unsuitable for automobile traffic, but the intricate picturesque compositions favored by nineteenth-century landscape architects became increasingly difficult to apprehend as speeds rose from a leisurely horse-drawn
pace to a heart-pounding thirty-to-forty miles per hour.[4]

The primary impetus for the parkway's rising popularity had less to do
with refined aesthetic arguments than with pragmatic concerns for safety
and efficiency, augmented by a broadly shared contempt for the excesses
of commercial roadside development. Conventional highway departments
had made significant progress in alleviating the "dust menace" and "getting the farmer out of the mud" through the adoption of modern paving
methods. By the 1920s, however, it was apparent that simply paving over
old roadways was not an adequate solution to America's highway crisis.
The chief problem with conventional roadways, most critics agreed, was
the combination of poorly designed intersections, hazardous road alignments, and rampant and uncontrolled commercial development. Exacer-
bating the dangers posed by at-grade intersections and unregulated side
streets was the long-standing legal precedent that guaranteed landowners
access to roadways passing by or through their property. With the growing popularity of the automobile, the frontage-right rules were turning
America's roadways into congested, unsightly, and dangerous linear slums.
Merchants lined the highways with brightly colored billboards and constructed a chaotic array of roadside establishments to capitalize on the
burgeoning market of motoring Americans. The entrances to these establishments disrupted the flow of through-traffic, while the eye-catching signs
and garish architecture distracted motorists and disappointed sightseers
in search of rural scenery. The general consensus was that outmoded
and unregulated highway development was ruining the appearance of the
countryside, stifling urban and suburban growth, and preventing Americans from enjoying the full potential of the automobile age.

What was needed, in the eyes of contemporary planners and popular
critics, was a new type of roadway geared to the social and technological
requirements of modern, automobile-dominated life. Professional journals were filled with prescriptions for highway modernization, scenic-
improvement groups excoriated the billboard and roadside-merchandising
industries, and middlebrow magazines published polemics about the dangers and disappointments of the American roadside. *Fortune* magazine
quoted academic experts on the perils of modern highway travel, *Life*

complained that the American roadside had become "the supreme honky-tonk of all time," and the *Saturday Evening Post* called for "a new and happier era of highway construction," in which engineers and landscape architects joined forces to "make motor travel as stimulating to the eye as it is to the speedometer." Benton MacKaye and Lewis Mumford issued a call in the pages of *Harper's* and the *New Republic* for a new approach to highway development based on "motor-age principles."[5]

By the mid-1920s it had become apparent that the most significant progress in answering this widely felt need was being made in the rapidly expanding network of parkways spreading from New York City into Westchester County and Long Island. By combining established parkway design techniques with new technologies and adapting them to higher speeds and longer distances, designers such as Jay Downer, Gilmore Clarke, and Hermann Merkel invented a new type of roadway that accommodated modern automobile traffic without sacrificing the parkway's characteristic recreational and environmental functions. The new parkways along the Bronx, Sawmill, and Hutchinson rivers were flanked by wide tree-lined borders that greatly reduced the number of accident-prone exits and entrances while screening out unsightly billboards and other roadside commerce. The safety and efficiency of these "limited-access" parkways was enhanced by grade separations that eliminated cross traffic at busy intersections. Parkway alignments followed graceful S-curves, rising and falling in gentle harmony with the surrounding terrain. This made driving more enjoyable while minimizing unsightly excavations, reducing hazardous curves, and eliminating blind spots. Careful attention to the three-dimensional quality of road design resulted in improved sight lines and eliminated the dangerous and unpleasant roller-coaster effect of climbing up and down hills in rapid succession. Following existing contours also reduced the need for cuts and fills that scarred the sides of conventional roadways. While the use of median strips preserved attractive terrain in select locations, the expense of constructing separate roadways kept this safety feature from being employed on a wide scale during the first decade of parkway development. The modern concrete bridges and grade separations that were essential to the parkway's safety and efficiency were given rustic surface treatments and integrated into the surrounding terrain with the help of picturesque plantings. Together with the rustic guardrails and lampposts and the carefully composed landscaping, these attributes tempered

Fenimore Road Bridge, Bronx River Parkway
Scarsdale, N. Y.

2.1. Classic Bronx River Parkway scene showing curvilinear alignment, grade-separated interchange with masonry-faced concrete bridge, rustic guardrails, and naturalistic landscaping, ca. 1925. Vintage postcard from the author's collection.

the modernity of the parkway's sophisticated circulation features with re-assuring allusions to vernacular traditions and classic landscape aesthetics (fig 2.1).[6]

The Bronx River Parkway was the first of these new roads to be com-pleted, opening with considerable fanfare in November 1925. It proved to be tremendously successful, both as a scenic pleasure drive and as a com-muter thoroughfare. With the new parkway providing convenient access to New York City, formerly remote areas of Westchester County experienced a tremendous real-estate boom. This parkway-driven prosperity stimulated realtors and civic boosters to join park promoters in advocating the con-struction of landscaped, limited-access parkways throughout the region. Soon Westchester County and southern Long Island were in the midst of a parkway-building frenzy. Westchester County alone constructed another seventy miles of parkway over the next twenty years. These additions in-cluded the Saw Mill River Parkway, the Hutchinson River Parkway, and the Cross County Parkway. New York park czar Robert Moses, meanwhile, pressed for construction of a series of parkways running between New York City and the beaches and parks he was developing on Long Island. The Southern and Northern State parkways employed many of the design features that characterized their Westchester County counterparts.

While these parkways were widely heralded as the safest and most efficient motor roads in America, they were developed by park commissions and intended to function as mixed-use recreational environments. Conceived and constructed as integral components of ambitious local and regional park systems, these gleaming modern motorways were often flanked by bridle paths and walking trails. At select locations the parkway corridors broadened to include community parks, golf courses, lakes, and athletic fields. Many led to state parks and beaches that were heavily used by both urban and suburban residents. Another key element of traditional park and parkway design—the prohibition of buses, trucks, and commercial vehicles—ensured a more relaxed and attractive driving environment and allowed designers to work with narrower roadways and more sinuous curvature.[7] Most of these parkways were designed by teams of landscape architects and engineers working in close collaboration, with landscape architects generally playing the lead role in matters of road layout and landscape design.

Despite the success of the Bronx River, Westchester County, and Long Island parkways, the highway-engineering community did not rush to embrace parkway design principles. Downer, an engineer, and Clarke, a landscape architect, appealed repeatedly to the highway-building fraternity, presenting Westchester County parkways as examples of the fruitful collaboration of landscape architects and engineers. In speeches and professional journal articles they insisted that the parkways' aesthetic attributes presented significant practical advantages. Winding alignments were safer than the long straightaways linked by short-radius curves that were favored by highway engineers. Gently sloped and rounded banks resisted erosion better than the steep raw cuts left by standard construction methods. Saving topsoil and replanting roadsides with native vegetation reduced costs and produced a more stable, maintenance-free environment.

Senior officials of the U.S. Bureau of Public Roads quickly recognized that the new parkways were not just more attractive than ordinary roadways but safer and more efficient as well. The problem, however, was to convince skeptical state-highway engineers, budget-strapped planners, tightfisted politicians, and the American public that parkway design principles could be translated to large-scale highway development. Most engineers and highway officials viewed landscape architects as extravagant artistes intent on driving up the costs of roadway construction with gratuitous ornamentation.

Parkways might be appropriate for limited recreational uses in well-heeled suburbs, they believed, but indulging the landscape architects' desire for serpentine curves and broad, landscaped rights-of-way was as alien to the engineers' culture of mathematical precision and economic calculation as was acceding to the whims of woman-dominated scenic beautification groups, with whom landscape architects were often linked in the professional mindset.[8] Both constituencies were marginalized as dilettantes and "prettifiers" who had no business meddling with the serious masculine enterprise of large-scale highway development.

The long-awaited construction of a memorial roadway from Washington to Mount Vernon provided BPR officials with an ideal forum for convincing rank-and-file engineers that parkway techniques could be efficiently and economically applied to arterial-highway construction. When the BPR was put in charge of the project in 1928, the agency went to great lengths to present Mount Vernon Memorial Highway as a "model modern motorway," casting it as a national—and even international—paradigm of contemporary motorway design. Even the name "Mount Vernon Memorial Highway" was calculated to further the goal of persuading mainstream engineers to adopt parkway design principals. As a tourist-oriented roadway restricted to private vehicles and surrounded by a wide band of multipurpose parkland, the project clearly fit the conventional definition of a parkway.

The BPR prepared articles on the parkway's design, conducted tours for visiting officials, and produced impressive booklets and detailed technical pamphlets outlining the project's design features. Grading plans, cross-sections, and circulation diagrams emphasized the practical value of free-flowing traffic provisions and underscored the harmonious integration of landscape architecture and highway engineering. Compelling photographs, taken before, during, and after the construction process, documented the transition from tangled woodland or cluttered roadside to attractive, efficient parkway landscape. The most elaborate of these publications was the 1934 USDA bulletin *Roadside Improvement*. The Nazi highway engineer Fritz Todt found this document so impressive that he reprinted it in German to help guide development of the *Reichsautobahnen*. The memorial highway garnered worldwide attention when the BPR hosted an international road conference in Washington in October 1930, using the project to showcase American achievement in motorway development. The BPR conducted tours of the construction site and published a detailed brochure loaded with compelling graphics. Excerpts from this publication and related reports appeared in such international journals as the Italian highway-construction magazine *Strade*.[9] The German road-building journal *Die Strasse* published numerous accounts of American parkway development during this period. Nazi engineers even traveled to Westchester County to inspect the American parkways. Gilmore Clarke hosted the visitors and later maintained that the Germans "took our ideas" as the basis for the *Reichsautobahn*. Clarke contended that the Nazi designers paid little attention to the more subtle details and broad-based goals of parkway development, however, producing a more efficient but aesthetically inferior product.[10]

Clarke's dismissal of the German *Reichsautobahnen* was undoubtedly motivated by a mixture of nationalism and personal pride, but his comments reflected important aesthetic, technological, and cultural differences between American parkways and the Nazi superhighways. Despite a shared appreciation for native plants and natural scenery, German and American landscape architects embraced different philosophies of landscape design. While German landscape architects carried their racial theories into the realm of roadside landscaping, American parkway designers were concerned more with appearances, economics, and a highly malleable sense of contextuality than with scientific concepts of ecology or politically laden ideologies espousing the supposed superiority of indigenous species.[11] American parkway designers favored native species, but Anglo-American "naturalistic" landscapes were unabashedly contrived compositions, wherein the landscape designer "improved" existing topography and plant growth to produce the visual effects codified by aesthetic theories developed in painting, poetry, and earlier park design. The American approach emphasized native plants but in subtly manipulated proportions designed to increase the prominence of attractive species and to minimize or eliminate naturally occurring but less aesthetically appealing vegetation. The result resembled a traditional landscape painting, simplified for viewing at higher speeds, rather than an unadulterated "natural" forest pierced by the rigid geometry of a stark modern pavement. From the parkway designer's perspective, the German approach produced "a horrid clash of nature and technics."[12]

Technical factors also figured in the visual disparities between parkways and autobahns. German designers may have intended their roads to harmonize with their surroundings, but given their commitment to significantly higher travel speeds, there was simply no way they could replicate the picturesque intimacy of parkway landscapes. The high design speeds of the *Reichsautobahnen* required wider pavements, gentler grades, broader curves, and more extensive excavations. The autobahn's high speed also mandated greater consistency in engineering and design standards, giving rise to criticism that the German roadways were as monotonous as railroad beds. American landscape architects were willing to countenance lower design speeds, sharper curves, and greater variation in order to integrate parkways into the existing terrain and provide a broader array of scenic diversity. On a cultural level, the parkway's subtle manipulations and carefully contrived borders created an ideal middle landscape, a pastoral interlude that historians such as Leo Marx have identified as holding an enduring appeal for Americans seeking a balance between the opposing poles of nature and culture. Parkways served to reconcile the machine and the garden, mediating between the biological banality of "raw" nature and the harsh technological efficiencies of modern highways or, parkway advocates contended, the German autobahns.[13]

The *Reichsautobahnen* were not the only foreign roadways to be unfavorably compared with American parkways. Demonstrating a keen awareness of the ideological implications of road design and terminology, Mount Vernon Memorial Highway landscape architect Wilbur Simonson rebuked reporters for referring to the BPR's project as a "boulevard" rather than as a parkway or highway. Asserting that the term *boulevard* implied an ostentatious formal avenue developed "for 'show,' in the French style," he maintained that the BPR's model motorway embodied American ideals, both aesthetically and symbolically. While boulevards and avenues served as intimidating expressions of authoritarian power and elite rule, the BPR's informally landscaped parkway was a quintessential American public road—"simple," "unostentatious," and "democratic." Boulevards were explicitly artificial constructions, moreover, while the memorial highway's informal landscape reflected American reverence for unadulterated—or at least seemingly unadulterated—nature. Warning that the continued use of inappropriate terminology threatened to subvert the project's pragmatic goals and symbolic intentions, Simonson assailed the press for employing "the ill-chosen French 'boulevard' in reference to this splendid and truly American memorial highway" (fig. 2.2).[14]

As part of the BPR's efforts to celebrate its achievements and promote parkway design principles, the agency produced a thirty-minute film singing

2.2. Collingwood area of the Mount Vernon Memorial Highway with fully developed landscaping, 1946. From the U.S. Bureau of Public Roads Collection, National Archives and Records Administration.

the parkway's praises and portraying the development process in meticulous detail.[15] Toward the end of the film, the parkway's broad appeal was underscored in a dynamic sequence depicting late-model automobiles speeding along the shores of the Potomac. The technical aspects of the film were clearly geared toward a professional audience, but these scenes of speeding automobiles sweeping along intersection-free concrete roadways with long, sinuous curves winding through attractive woodlands undoubtedly appealed to the legions of motorists who embraced the harmonious integration of modern roads, modern cars, and naturalistic scenery as the ultimate manifestation of America's ability to combine reverence for nature and traditional values with social and material progress.

While the BPR promoted the memorial highway as "America's Most Modern Motorway," the agency went to great lengths to call attention to the project's historical associations and ideological implications. Not only did the memorial highway link sites of surpassing national significance, but the route itself was designed to encompass landmarks related to George Washington and other founding fathers. Design details such as broken-pediment Colonial Revival–style signboards underscored the parkway's symbolic function, as did the Colonial Revival concession stand at the Mount Vernon terminus. The drive from Washington to Mount Vernon was presented as a patriotic undertaking with wide-ranging cultural significance. In addition to appreciating the technical superiority of American highway engineering and enjoying the parkway's scenic beauty and opportunities for healthful outdoor recreation, motorists were expected, in the words of one supporter, to experience "a thrill of Americanism" while zipping along the shores of the Potomac at the exhilarating rate of thirty-five miles per hour (fig. 2.3).[16]

The engineering achievement of constructing the memorial highway was presented as a patriotic accomplishment in its own right. Simonson and others repeatedly described the project as a fitting memorial to George Washington, asserting that the founding father's surveying background would have predisposed him to appreciate the parkway's technical excellence. Taking advantage of the project to emphasize the national significance of road-building, the American Association of Highway Officials timed its annual meeting to coincide with the highway's opening celebration. *American Highways* magazine commemorated this event with a striking cover photo of stalwart engineers assembled on Mount Vernon's iconic portico. The back cover further underscored the patriotic associations of highway engineering with a woodcut of George Washington in surveyor's garb, ostensibly enacting the role of America's first highway builder. The BPR's film portrayed the parkway not just as a memorial to George Washington but as an illustration of "the progress made in highway engineering" since the birth of the republic. Elaborate models of the Mount Vernon terminus and cloverleaf interchange were displayed in the U.S. Capitol Rotunda, surrounded by paintings of momentous events in American history.[17]

The popular and professional press acclaimed the project as an exemplary union of modern motorway development, landscape design, and patriotic sentiment. Articles on the memorial highway's design, construction, and cultural significance appeared in newspapers, popular magazines, and virtually every major planning, engineering, and park-development publication. Leading engineering periodicals echoed the BPR's pronouncements about the practical value of parkway design, providing detailed technical information and invoking the BPR's characterization of the project as "America's Most Modern Motorway."[18] Landscape architects were equally enthusiastic, applauding the highway for demonstrating the value of cooperation between engineers and landscape architects. Popular publications focused on the parkway's recreational potential, scenic beauty, historic associations,

2.3. Cover of the March 1932 issue of *American Motorist* magazine. From the Library of Congress Collection of Prints and Photographs.

and commemorative significance.[19] *Literary Digest* praised the project as "a yardstick among highways," proclaiming that the new roadway would be "as pleasing to the eye as it is to the rumble seat."[20] Invoking the themes of nature, patriotism, and technological prowess, *American Motorist* applauded the BPR for having "perpetuated Washington's memory by a boulevard of which he would be proud from a practical, patriotic, and picturesque point of view." Reiterating these sentiments in a formulation that emphasized the cultural resonance of road-building, the magazine enthused: "At last there is a highway built for beauty with history for its roadbed and the American ideal for its goal."[21]

While the National Park Service (NPS) was not directly involved in the development of Mount Vernon Memorial Highway, the agency embraced the notion that parkways could serve as linear lessons in American history and values. Colonial Parkway, begun in 1930 and largely completed within a decade, catered even more explicitly to the period's veneration of early American history. Modern concrete bridges were clad in red-brick veneer, the sinuous modern pavement was subtly textured to mimic the rough surfaces of Colonial-era roads, and the route connected three of Virginia's most venerated historic sites: Jamestown, Yorktown, and Williamsburg. The parkway served as the primary circulation for Colonial National Historical Park, one of the Park Service's first large-scale ventures into historic-site management and heritage tourism. As with most public-history enterprises of this era, the Park Service's initial historic sites and interpretive activities enshrined heroic sagas of "great men and events," preserving presidential homes, battlefields, and sites and buildings associated with momentous developments, such as the first permanent Anglo-Saxon outpost in the New World and the surrender of British forces that sealed the success of the American Revolution.

The Blue Ridge and Natchez Trace parkways were meant to tell a more populist story, extolling America's agrarian roots and preserving relics of the nation's hardy pioneer past. Along with providing recreational opportunities and presenting spectacular views that reaffirmed the long-standing belief that America was "Nature's Nation," these long-distance rural parkways were explicitly intended, in the words of NPS landscape architect Stanley Abbott, to "provide the look of homespun in an east that is mostly silk and rayon" (fig. 2.4).[22] Stretching for hundreds of miles through the backcountry of Virginia, North Carolina, Mississippi, Alabama, and

2.4. Rocky Knob area of the Blue Ridge Parkway, ca. 1940. This image exemplifies key design and cultural aspects of the National Park Service's long-distance parkway. Vintage postcard from the author's collection.

Tennessee, the Blue Ridge and Natchez Trace parkways were linear odes to America's agrarian past. With miles and miles of sleepy pastures, split-rail fences, and quaint log cabins, they afforded motorists a soothing respite from the pressures of modern urban life.

These pastoral idylls were as contrived as any English landscape park or romantic painting. While BPR engineers attended to the technical aspects of parkway-building, NPS landscape architects composed carefully calculated scenes of rural bliss. Abbott and his colleagues referred to this enterprise as improving the "roadside picture" and evinced little concern for the literalistic notions of historical accuracy that would come to dominate later public-landscape debates. Buildings that failed to conform to pioneer stereotypes were torn down, charismatic structures were moved to more accessible locations, and new construction emulated regional vernaculars. Traditional agricultural practices were promoted through leases and scenic easements. While parkways ostensibly celebrated traditional folk values, the folk themselves were not accorded the most respectful treatment. Parkway development displaced significant numbers of rural residents, though some elderly individuals were granted lifetime tenures to enliven the NPS's drive-through dramatization of America's arcadian landscape. NPS officials appeared untroubled by the social cost of parkway development to the local populations, many of whom had lived on the land for generations. The displacement of a few "backward mountaineers" was seen as a small price to pay for the greater good of enabling millions of Americans to experience a sense of cultural regeneration by driving along a roadway designed to memorialize the nation's mythic roots.[23]

This combination of recreational motoring and aggressively nationalistic heritage tourism was by no means unique to the American parkway. Nazi autobahn designers and political leaders similarly believed that encouraging interregional travel and showcasing highly selective natural and cultural landscapes would promote a shared national culture based on idealized folk values and the redemptive power of nature and rural life. Nor were the Germans and Americans alone in this enterprise, though few other countries could devote comparable resources to the development of state-sponsored tourist infrastructures. As numerous historians of the late-nineteenth and early-twentieth centuries have demonstrated, cultural leaders and ordinary people throughout the developed world were engaged in a process of defining, redefining, inventing, and manipulating various aspects of their real or imagined heritage, both to counter the social dislocations and uncertainties wrought by modernity and to strengthen the power and identity of the nation-state. These activities ranged from renewed interest in folktales, ballads, and "traditional" crafts to the staging of pageants and festivals to the creation of "living" museums, the veneration of vernacular architecture, and the alignment of local, regional, and national political agendas with purportedly indigenous cultural ideals. This "romantic nationalism," as it has been called, was particularly prevalent in the United States, Britain, and northern Europe, where it strongly influenced popular culture and "high art" and appealed both to outright conservatives threatened by the changing social and racial dynamics of modern life and to putative progressives who sought to combine traditional values with advances in various social and technological spheres.[24]

Parkways embodied both strains of romantic nationalism. The allusions to Anglo-American history and folk values soothed contemporary anxieties about the impacts of immigration and urbanization on American life, while the gleaming concrete roadways winding through natural scenery and traditional agrarian landscapes epitomized the reconciliation of modern and anti-modern impulses. By reinterpreting the winding country road and the iconographic American landscape through the quintessentially modern medium of the streamlined motorway, parkway designers provided a populist counterpoint to the work of avant-garde artists such as Aaron Copland and Martha Graham, who also sought to evoke traditional idioms and values through modern modes of expression.

The rapidly growing network of suburban commuter parkways was even more dramatically modern and was celebrated as such by a wide variety of contemporary commentators. As metropolitan New York continued its parkway-building binge, an article in the British art magazine *The Studio* proclaimed that Moses's Long Island parkways offered a preview of the "New York of Tomorrow," which promised "a new way of living and working" based on "a fusing of the arts and technical skills in close collaboration with nature." Thanks to Moses, the magazine declared, "the highway has become munificent and a thing of beauty."[25] *Fortune* magazine asserted that parkways had joined New York's fabled skyscrapers as icons of progress that visitors to the world's most modern metropolis "simply *must* see."[26] Parkways were widely marketed through the popular medium of postcards. Vibrant colorized photographs of streamlined cars sweeping along serpentine curves extolled their scenic beauty and emphasized their engaging modernity. While it is difficult to recapture popular perspectives on parkway development, sentiments expressed on postcards provide some sense of the vivid impressions these new motorways made on their users. A California visitor to Westchester County scrawled, "Everything is Parkways back in New York" on the front of a Bronx River Parkway postcard that portrayed the gleaming roadway nestled between rugged timber guardrails and soothing greenery. On the back he observed, "I thought L.A. and vicinity had a lot of paved roads & highways, but I never saw anything like N.Y. & vicinity." Underscoring the parkway's naturalistic landscaping and rustic features, the anonymous writer praised the scene's "quaint" appearance as well.[27]

The preeminent articulator of the essential modernity of the American parkway was the architectural critic Sigfried Giedion, who saw parkways as exemplifying the "space-time continuum" that he cast as the core of modernist perception. Praising "the great sweep of the highway, the beauty of its alignment, the graceful sequence of its curves," Giedion enthused: "The space-time feeling of our period can seldom be felt so keenly as when driving, the wheel under one's hand, up and down hills, beneath overpasses, up ramps, and over giant bridges."[28] For less esoterically inclined commentators the most common rhetorical device for emphasizing parkways' modernity was to align them with streamlined automobiles and other emblems of modern industrial design. Applauding the virtues of Mount Vernon Memorial Highway, BPR landscape architect Simonson declared: "[T]his broad paved highway will simulate in its flowing lines, the spiral curves, the horizontal and vertical transitions, and the banked turns of a fast transport aircraft in flight."[29] Not only was "streamlining" one of the dominant popular symbols of modernity, but the association had legitimate technical underpinnings as well. Traffic experts had developed elaborate theories ascribing automobile accidents to the "friction" produced by poorly designed roadways, hazards that parkway designers literally "streamlined" away.[30] Simonson insisted that "'streamlining' the flow of high-speed modern motor traffic" with teardrop safety islands, spiral curves, beveled curbs, gently rounded side-slopes, and outwardly flared guardrails expressed the designer's determination to ensure that "the practical needs of traffic circulation and aesthetic attractiveness are harmonized."[31]

Even as the classic 1930s motor parkways were being lauded for their masterful integration of naturalistic landscape aesthetics, technological progress, and traditional American values, these competing concerns were beginning to pull apart the disparate elements of the parkway movement. Changing cultural and technological factors made it difficult, if not impossible, for a single environment to accommodate the conflicting demands for higher speeds and larger traffic volumes, extensive reaches of undeveloped scenery, and increasingly elaborate public-history presentations. Not only did efficiency-minded highway engineers realize that they could appropriate the parkway's innovative circulation features without wasting money on scenic improvement and associated recreational developments, but landscape architects and environmentalists were coming to the conclusion that motor-road development was incompatible with evolving park and preservation ideals. The multipurpose parkways epitomized by Mount Vernon Memorial Highway gradually gave way to more specialized environments: urban expressways, high-speed toll roads, remote scenic parkways, and an ever-broadening array of recreational areas, wilderness preserves, and historical parks.

By the mid-1930s, the parkway movement was clearly diverging in two directions: the relatively low-speed scenic and recreational parkways promoted by the National Park Service, and the commuter parkways proliferating around major American cities. Connecticut's Merritt Parkway was the

scenic vs commuter

2.5. New England's Merritt Parkway, ca. 1948. This image shows the design emphasis changing from aesthetics and recreation to transportation efficiency. Vintage postcard from the author's collection.

most widely acclaimed of this new generation of commuter parkways (fig. 2.5). It was heralded as a marvel of modern motorway development and an engaging example of landscape design. Despite its tree-lined borders and prolific plantings, the Merritt was decried by parkway purists on the grounds that its relentless straightaways and lack of associated recreational features made it more of a glorified traffic artery than a comprehensively designed and context-sensitive multipurpose recreational development. Los Angeles's first true modern motorway illustrated the parkway's changing fortunes. The Arroyo Seco Parkway was conceived as a classic recreational amenity, but by the time it was completed in the early 1940s, it had become a stripped-down traffic artery. Its new name, the Pasadena Freeway, proclaimed the changing form and function of urban motorways. Freeways—the term was coined in 1930 by planning authority Edward Bassett to denote freedom of movement, not the absence of tolls—would reshape the American landscape in the postwar era, with a distinctly different balance between the competing concerns of efficiency and landscape aesthetics.[32] Higher speeds and larger traffic volumes demanded wider, straighter roads that were difficult to reconcile with traditional landscape values. The growing preference for efficiency over aesthetics provoked great concern in the landscape-architecture community but caused little consternation to highway engineers, who were clearly regaining their hold over the American road-building establishment.

Two seminal events occurred in 1939 that prepared the way for this reorientation, one popular and the other largely bureaucratic and technocratic. The General Motors Pavilion at the 1939 World's Fair introduced the world to "Futurama": a thrilling vision of the highway system of the future. Conceived by the noted industrial designer Norman Bel Geddes, this sprawling diorama of high-speed streamlined motorways spreading across the American continent captured the public's imagination and made a profound impact on the politicians that controlled highway-building purse strings.[33] That same year the newly retitled Public Roads Administration released the results of a detailed study that was intended to set the blueprint for federally sponsored highway construction. *Toll Roads and Free Roads* lacked the public appeal of Bel Geddes's futuristic extravaganza—in fact, few outside the road-building and legislative communities were even aware of its existence—but this dry government report had a profound impact on the subsequent development of the American landscape. Concerned primarily with bureaucratic and technical matters, *Toll Roads and Free Roads* devoted a mere three paragraphs to aesthetic and recreational issues. The few illustrations that accompanied the report echoed Bel Geddes's vision of stripped-down high-speed motorways arcing across the countryside with no concern for local topography or landscape development. *Toll Roads and Free Roads* affirmed the parkway's limited-access circulation concept as the basic framework for modern highway design and contained a brief reference to the practical benefits of gentle side-sloping; but the report conspicuously failed to endorse the more subtle and diverse aspects of parkway development that had temporarily found favor in the upper reaches of the federal highway-building establishment. Landscape architects were placed in a distinctly subordinate position in this new order, no longer equal partners in the design process. Their contribution was reduced to the cosmetic adornment of intersections and embankments constructed according to strictly utilitarian engineering principles. Adding insult to injury, the federal highway establishment reinterpreted *parkway* in a manner that reflected complete contempt for the comprehensive design principles formerly associated with that term. In the PRA's new lexicon, *parkway* referred simply to the sodded strips lying alongside the stretches of concrete that formed the central focus of the engineers' endeavors.[34]

The first major American roadway to embody this new approach was the Pennsylvania Turnpike, opened with great fanfare in 1940 and immediately touted as "America's Dream Highway." This 160-mile thoroughfare allowed motorists to speed at seventy or more miles per hour along a fully divided and grade-separated four-lane concrete motorway with gentle grades and minimal curves. Highway engineers and the motoring public loved it. Along with dramatically improving regional transportation, the Pennsylvania Turnpike became an attraction in and of itself as motorists flocked to the new roadway to enjoy the thrill of driving at high speeds without interruptions or distractions in a distinctively modern environment. Landscape architects assailed the turnpike's numbing straightaways and strip-mine-like excavations, casting it as a giant step backward in motorway design. An entire issue of the journal *Landscape Architecture* was devoted to critiquing the turnpike's faults and bemoaning the profession's marginalization from meaningful participation in motorway development—a refrain that would be repeated at frequent intervals, particularly after federal authorization of the interstate highway system funneled billions of dollars into road construction.[35]

Parkways would continue to be built in the postwar era, but they would never again capture the public imagination and professional attention they had commanded during the golden age of parkway development in the 1920s and '30s. The National Park Service pressed on with construction of the long-distance recreational parkways it had begun before World War II. As scenic, recreational, and historical landscapes, the Blue Ridge and Natchez Trace parkways remained immensely popular, but no one would claim that their narrow, winding drives reflected state-of-the-art engineering principles. The pioneering prewar commuter parkways were increasingly condemned as inadequate and unsafe. Freeways, expressways, and interstate highways won favor with engineers, planners, business interests, and politicians, as they clearly surpassed parkways in their ability to accommodate large volumes of traffic safely and efficiently. The public also appeared to be enamored of high-speed motorways. Magazines, postcards, games, movies, songs, and other expressions of popular culture celebrated their dynamic aesthetics, form-follows-function pragmatism, and promise of seemingly limitless thrills and opportunities (fig. 2.6). Times would change, of course, but in the 1950s much of America was embracing modernity's throw-out-the-old-and-bring-in-the-new ethos. The picturesque sensibilities

2.6. Aerial view of the Los Angeles Freeway Interchange, ca. 1965. Vintage postcard from the author's collection.

and antimodernist overtones of traditional parkways must have appeared distinctly out of synch with contemporary concerns. Many of the most prominent parkways were, in fact, updated during the 1950s and '60s, their serpentine curves straightened, pavements widened, and picturesque landscapes either pared away or dramatically degraded by mismanagement and neglect. Rustic guardrails and lampposts gave way to steel beams and metal light standards that were easier to maintain and less vulnerable to lawsuits by litigious parties intent on blaming outdated designs for accidents caused by inattentive drivers and inappropriate speeds.

Traditional parkways continued to have their place, of course, but as specialized landscapes to be enjoyed on rare and carefully bracketed occasions, like a trip to the museum or a hike in the backcountry. With recreational practices tending toward more active physical exertion and environmental sensitivities growing by leaps and bounds in the 1950s and '60s, motoring was no longer seen as the ideal way to experience America's scenic splendors. A number of proposed parkway developments were stopped in their tracks by environmentalist opposition. Others, notably the Natchez Trace, languished for lack of funds, no longer able to garner the popular attention and political support they had enjoyed during the parkway movement's heyday. While they were overshadowed by mainstream highways, the last generation of regionally oriented parkways demonstrated that it was possible to adapt classic parkway design techniques to higher speeds and traffic volumes. Completed during the 1950s and 1960s, the Taconic, Garden State, Palisades, and Baltimore-Washington parkways might not have been as fast and efficient as conventional expressways and interstates, but they managed to combine reasonably high speeds and enhanced safety with varied and attractive landscape design.

Over the past decade or so, the parkway's cultural resonance has begun to experience a resurgence. Several parkways have spawned historic-preservation initiatives aimed at preventing further alterations and remediating inappropriate modifications. The Historic American Engineering Record has documented parkways across the country, and scholars are chronicling their development and ruminating on their cultural significance.[36] Several parkways have been named to the National Register of Historic Places, and efforts are underway to designate the Blue Ridge Parkway a national historic landmark. Both the Blue Ridge and Natchez Trace parkways have already been placed on the Federal Highway Administration's list of All-American Roads. The term *parkway* has regained popularity both as an honorific designation and as a means of elevating the status of speculative residential developments and mundane industrial parks. Public entities are also resurrecting the term to cloak controversial road-building projects in a more comforting guise or to enhance the cachet of modestly landscaped suburban boulevards.

By the 1970s mainstream highway-builders were even beginning to acknowledge the advantages of paying greater attention to aesthetic and environmental concerns. The legacy of classic mid-twentieth-century parkway design can be seen in the sinuous curves and landscape sensibility of some of the later interstates built in particularly scenic regions such as Vermont, New Hampshire, and Colorado. While the super-wide pavements and minimal curvature mandated by modern interstate-highway standards prevent a complete return to the intimate, picturesque qualities of classic parkway design, these recent trends suggest that it is still possible to harmonize concerns for safety and efficiency with attractive and context-sensitive landscape design. Given the resurgence of early-twentieth-century urban design techniques under the guise of the New Urbanism, a return to parkway-based urban and regional development would be a logical extension of contemporary planning ideologies. While the New Urbanism promotes many beneficial social, aesthetic, and environmental goals, the popularity of neotraditional planning may also portend a revival of the romantic and essentially conservative visions of an idealized American heritage that played an underlying role in the parkway's rise to prominence during an era of cultural anxiety and socioeconomic uncertainty. Perhaps parkways will once more gain favor as appealing middle landscapes capable of reconciling the perennial tensions between progress and nostalgia, nature and technology, recreation and transportation. If parkways are to be regarded as progressive rather than reactionary environments, however, the earlier emphasis on Anglo-American traditions must give way to more inclusive visions of national character that better reflect the multicultural composition of contemporary society.

THREE

The Scenic Is Political

Creating Natural and Cultural Landscapes
along America's Blue Ridge Parkway

Anne Mitchell Whisnant

America's Blue Ridge Parkway—a 469-mile limited-access scenic highway through the mountains of North Carolina and Virginia that is the most visited site in the country's national park system—is often profiled in popular and travel magazines along the lines of a 1985 *Southern Living* cover story commemorating the fiftieth anniversary of "The Good Road of the Blue Ridge." The road, it noted, "celebrates every mile of the country through which it travels . . . without altering the countryside." Roadside exhibits, it observed, "both honored and celebrated" the "unromantic life" of "mountain highlanders": "stripped of clutter and pretense . . . full of independence . . . [and] fueled by ingenuity and self-sufficiency." The piece concluded soothingly that "the parkway never seems an intruder among these mountains"; instead, it has become "evidence of how well, how honestly, and how intelligently we can treat the earth if we but try."[1]

Most Parkway travelers probably agree. More than twenty million of them—people like Bob and Frances Allen, who have been coming to the Parkway since their honeymoon in 1955—drive leisurely along the road connecting the Great Smoky Mountains and the Shenandoah national parks each year. "It's like being in another world," Bob Allen told the Asheville (NC) *Citizen-Times* in a 2002 interview for the paper's feature story about "what makes this scenic highway so special." Paul Ingrassia of Waynesville, North Carolina, was more specific: "People like to travel the parkway because they get glimpses of God. . . . They get glimpses of something outside of the realm of the world they are living in day to day. It's their little escape from the box of society."[2]

Obscured by the road's seamless integration into the surrounding mountains, however, is the fact that the landscape of "America's favorite road" is highly constructed (as opposed to natural), its shape as much a product of more than fifty years of very worldly political decisions as it is of the natural topography and scenery it showcases.[3] Built beginning in 1935 through the cooperative efforts of state highway departments in North Carolina and Virginia and federal agencies of President Franklin D. Roosevelt's New Deal, and completed in 1987, the Parkway has been as politically controversial as any other large public-works development. Creating the Parkway scene required more than the talents of landscape designers and engineers working in a stunning physical setting. Instead, "the Scenic" was also political: its construction required the arbitration of disputes over substantive issues across boundaries of power.

Travelers on the Parkway rarely see evidence of these parts of its history, however; and those tourists seeking a glimpse of God might have been surprised to have encountered instead S. A. Miller of Ashe County, North Carolina, who owned land along the Parkway route and complained to President Franklin D. Roosevelt in 1937 that "the Park to Park highway isn't any benefit to us according to what they tell us. We aren't allowed to put any buildings near it and not even cross it to our land on the other side."[4] Or L. F. Caudill of Sparta, North Carolina, who repeatedly ripped down the barricade on a now-illegal access road that connected his property to the Parkway. Or Fred Bauer of the Eastern Band of Cherokee Indians, who opposed the Parkway's intrusion into Cherokee lands and argued in 1939 that "a system of public roads, with freedom to stop at any farmhouse, and visit or trade as desired, would be enjoyed more than a restricted parkway with everything planned just so."[5] Rather than being captivated by thoughts of mountain scenery, drivers in the Cherokee area—who had anticipated construction of a regular state highway from the Cherokee reservation eastward to the nearest metropolitan area of Asheville—were dismayed to learn of plans to build a land-gobbling, limited-access scenic parkway over the same route instead.[6]

In truth, then, drivers' views of the Blue Ridge Parkway during its seventy-year history have varied considerably depending on their cultural frames of reference, their class position, their geographic location, and their particular needs. Yet the intense conflicts the Parkway has generated are nearly invisible to most present-day travelers, as the Parkway landscape itself almost mysteriously conceals its history and the complicated, contentious, and significant issues involved in its development.

Perhaps partly for this reason, the history of the Parkway has generated little scholarly interest since Harley E. Jolley's slender volume on the topic came out in 1969. Nearly every account of the Parkway's development has repeated a set of ideas, advanced in Jolley's book, that has come to constitute conventional wisdom about the road: the Parkway originated primarily to provide jobs for an undifferentiated population of suffering mountaineers; it was thus essentially a benign and broadly beneficial "road of peace" and a "godsend for the needy"; local citizens, who shared a common interest in building up the tourist industry, unanimously welcomed it; the several controversies that did erupt in the early years were relatively small speed bumps along the road to Parkway progress; and, finally, these controversies neither reflected significant costs associated with building the road nor revealed substantial social divisions. "From the beginning," intoned Jolley, "the Parkway . . . benefitted from the helping hands of countless people, each making a contribution toward the common goal of establishing a unique recreational highway." It was "a road for pleasure . . . [which] emphasized the work of nature while de-emphasizing the work of man."[7]

As the *Southern Living* article and countless others like it suggest, this version of the Parkway's origins and meaning has been widely popular largely because it seems to fit so well with what Parkway travelers do see: dramatic mountain views, split-rail fences, and solitary log cabins and grist mills, all in a tranquil and apparently undisturbed natural landscape. Because of strict Park Service regulations, electric power lines, billboards, speeding traffic, and the bustle of commerce barely intrude. Crowds at any one spot on the long road are rare; it is not uncommon for travelers to experience almost total silence. Such scenes have proven perennially attractive to a public that craves escape from the stresses of modern life and prefers to view the past as simple and straightforward.

Yet an uncritically nostalgic vision of both the Parkway itself and the region through which it winds only obscures the real story of what was in fact a hotly contested project with lasting consequences for the residents of western North Carolina and southwestern Virginia. As the most visited site in the American national park system, the Blue Ridge Parkway is a cornerstone of the southern Appalachian tourism industry, and Parkway development was part of the promotion of that industry. Any account of either the Parkway or the mountain tourism industry that uncouples the two misses major parts of the stories of both and hinders productive discussion of how various forms of tourist development affected all sectors of the mountain population.[8]

To rethink the history of the Parkway and to understand why such rethinking has been so long deferred, we must look at the Parkway landscape with a more discerning eye, interrogating the politics both inherent in and generated by scenic-parkway design and examining the ways in which the artificially constructed Appalachian pioneer scenes along the Parkway have rendered the politics of Parkway development all but invisible.

Political Conflicts and the Shaping of the Parkway Landscape

In the first place, we must look at how conflicts that were essentially political shaped the Parkway landscape. Rather than arising organically from the geography of the region itself and harmonizing with it (as the *Southern Living* perspective implies), the Parkway's physical form in fact inscribed on the landscape several critical political decisions made during its history. Those decisions reflected power differentials among the stakeholders and, in turn, determined the distribution of the road's costs and benefits. Thus the Parkway is as much the product of political processes as of the "natural" features of the surrounding mountain landscapes. Rather than "deemphasizing the work of man," the Parkway quietly embodies the very human story of the politics of tourism development in the southern Appalachian mountains.

AMERICAN PARKWAYS

Creating this scene was an explicit goal of Parkway planners; indeed, the road's status as a "parkway" prescribed a set of design standards and concepts that achieved their highest popularity in the pre–World War II years, well before the Interstate highway system and expressway models became ascendant. When they began to think about the Blue Ridge Parkway, planners drew on more than twenty years of parkway-building experiences in other parts of the United States. The nation's first real motor parkway was the Bronx River Parkway, started in 1913 and completed in 1925. Like most of the parkways that were to follow, this one was an urban road, but it did include many of the features that came to distinguish a parkway from an ordinary roadway: it was flanked by parklands, with intersecting roads carried over it on bridges; it was carefully landscaped to eliminate unsightly roadside dumps and billboards; and, in keeping with its design as a leisurely recreational drive, it limited speeds, banned commercial vehicles, and offered easy access to recreational facilities.[9]

Through the 1920s, New York led the nation in parkway-building, as Westchester County embarked on construction of a large network of parks and parkways. Long Island State Park Commission Chair Robert Moses adopted the idea, directing development of another parkway system, which included the Southern State Parkway, the Wantagh State Parkway, the Meadowbrook State Parkway, the Northern State Parkway, and several others. In the 1930s, Moses built other parkways in hopes of relieving New York City's growing traffic problems. These latter roads were, however, designed mostly to provide swift, uninterrupted traffic flow, not recreation, leisure, and scenery, which, according to one observer, meant that they "were not, for the most part, parkways at all" but early efforts at freeways.[10]

Other cities—Milwaukee, Cleveland, the District of Columbia—also built or planned parkways in the 1930s and, following the practice in New York, usually constructed them alongside rivers, often with labor supplied by the Civilian Conservation Corps. Designers of these parkways, in keeping with the original parkway concept, aimed to preserve greenery and provide spaces for recreation.[11]

Most of the parkways that preceded the Blue Ridge attempted to combine a visually attractive roadside landscape with engineering that enabled easier and faster commuting. One parkway that succeeded in doing both was Connecticut's Merritt Parkway. Construction of this four-lane, 37.5-mile parkway—another in Robert Moses's parkway system—was begun in the early 1930s and completed in 1940. It sought to ease the congested commute from New York City to the Connecticut suburbs. Protected by a three-hundred-foot-wide right-of-way along its length, the Merritt Parkway was a controlled-access, limited-use highway (buses and trucks were prohibited) characterized by extensive, thoughtful landscaping and creative, artistic bridges. Lacking the stoplights that slowed traffic on the old road to New York, the Merritt did reduce commuting time to the city; but as traffic increased, so did regulation of recreational uses such as roadside picknicking, which had become dangerous. With time, the people who, according to parkway historian Bruce Radde, "took too literally the *park* in *parkway*" were pushed out as the Merritt's objective of providing a faster commute overwhelmed the highway's recreational purposes. Nevertheless, when compared with later expressways, some of whose features the Merritt employed, this parkway "was rooted in the picturesque, romantic landscape tradition of Frederick Law Olmsted. True to its name, it was designed as a way through a park."[12]

For a time it seemed as if parkways might be the transportation wave of the future. Federal agencies embraced this parkway-building trend with gusto as the need for public-works projects coincided with the New Deal's focus on conservation and recreation. Along with the Blue Ridge Parkway, the National Park Service built two similar parkways in the 1930s: the Colonial National Parkway, connecting historic sites in the Williamsburg, Virginia, area; and the Natchez Trace Parkway, following the old trading and Indian trail through Tennessee, Alabama, and Mississippi.[13]

Flushed with their initial success, New Deal road- and park-builders waxed eloquent about the possibilities of parkway development. One Saturday afternoon in April of 1935, Bureau of Public Roads Chief Thomas H. MacDonald—architect of much of America's early federal highway system—and National Park Service Assistant Director A. E. Demaray went on nationwide radio to tout the "Parkways of the Future."[14] With the Marine Band simulating the clatter of wagon wheels in the background, a narrator recounted the steady progress of America's transportation revolution: from covered wagons to railroads ("telling the Indian that the White Man had come to stay!") to autos to airplanes and, now that "the past is gone but the future remains," to "parkways of the future." After musing for a few moments on the gradual rise in pleasure travel and park visitation, MacDonald and Demaray asserted: "We have found that the instinct of people to seek the open country or the gypsy trail is very strong"; but people not living near state or national parks, Demaray elaborated, "often have missed the enjoyment of natural scenic beauty along the highways because of roadside nuisances, such as unsightly billboards, and also because of hot-dog stands and gas stations." MacDonald added that parkways would help to fulfill people's need for "natural scenic beauty," giving them the "impression of being out in the great open spaces, far from industrial or other commercial developments." If the parkways then under construction—Blue Ridge, Colonial National, and Natchez Trace—proved as popular as expected, the two continued, then "construction [would] be expanded. If the use justifies, it may be that eventually a great parkway will lead from New England, from Maine or the Green Mountains, on south to connect with the Shenandoah–Great Smokies parkway, and on farther south, into Georgia and perhaps to the Florida Everglades." His excitement building, Demaray linked the idea to a grand vision of American progress:

> I can, in imagination, see still other parkways stretching westward
> . . . offering a maximum of comfort and enjoyment through scenery
> such as our pioneer forefathers first saw as they walked or rode
> horseback or drove their covered wagons, paving the way for that
> extension of our country which made possible the first national
> parks, those of the West. The pioneers opened that country for us
> . . . [,] and we, in turn[,] may open it up in an entirely different way
> to those who come after us.[15]

Demaray's ambitious scheme for a network of parkways crisscrossing the nation never materialized, however. Paradoxically, the vision was washed away in the next wave of automobile-inspired progress, the expressway, whose design emphasized direct travel along standardized roadways where drivers would interact but little with surrounding landscapes. Indeed, according to one student of American tourism, the federal parkways are in no way typical of national approaches to road-building but rather "stand in contrast to the nation's other highways built with federal funds."[16]

Nevertheless, these New Deal parkways, including the Blue Ridge, emphasized recreation and scenery and were only secondarily concerned with speeding travelers to their destination. As the Interior Department's 1935 building regulations noted, these parkways aimed "to make accessible the best scenery in the country [they] traverse[d]. Therefore, the shortest or most direct route [was] not necessarily a primary consideration."[17] In many ways, then, these parkways, especially the Blue Ridge and its sister the Natchez Trace, were unlike any that had been built before: they were rural; their purpose was completely recreational; and they were far longer than any of their precursors. As a result, they required substantial new thinking about regulations and design.

BLUE RIDGE PARKWAY ROUTING, DESIGN, AND CONFLICT

Implementing the design features characteristic of a scenic parkway generated intense conflict around issues of routing, basic engineering, land acquisition, and access and use regulations. Arbitration of these disputes was as central as the design vision in determining what the road would look like and whom it would benefit (or harm). The route of this unique parkway—which local tourism boosters throughout the southern mountains recognized as a potential boon to the industry—was, from its inception in 1933 through completion of the final link in 1987, a topic of ongoing conflict. Beginning with a nearly year-long debate in 1934 over whether the road would pass through North Carolina and Virginia only or would venture into Tennessee as well, and continuing with many smaller routing controversies, the question of where the special scenic road would go spawned numerous battles.

In 1934 the project's proponents initially proposed two routes: one that would have traversed parts of Virginia, North Carolina, and Tennessee (favored by citizens in Knoxville); and one that lay entirely within Virginia and North Carolina and offered easy access to the latter state's mountain tourist center in Asheville. In all three states the paramount concern was the projected boost the highway would bring to regional (especially urban-area) tourism.

A federally appointed committee, with the support of the new landscape architect hired by the National Park Service, initially recommended the route endorsed by Tennessee partisans. After months of intense behind-the-scenes lobbying by North Carolina's Parkway supporters—who enlisted the aid of Ambassador Josephus Daniels, former editor of the state's major newspaper and longtime friend of Interior Secretary Harold Ickes and President Roosevelt—Ickes overruled the committee and chose the Virginia–North Carolina route.[18]

This turn of events reflected the influence wielded by Asheville's business community, which not only ensured that the highway would benefit the town's long-established but Depression-battered tourism industry but also determined which landowners would be affected. Because the topography of the two routes differed substantially, route selection dictated the type of parkway that would be built—one that would run for much of its length along the ridgetops rather than through a more undulating terrain of mountains and valleys. In turn, this placement of the road further limited its usefulness as a means of transportation or engine of informal tourism development for local residents.

The outcomes of several smaller-scale routing battles in subsequent years also reflected the adjudication of political contests over who would retain use of specific lands and how tourism profits would be distributed. In the late 1930s the Eastern Band of Cherokees, whose Qualla boundary lands sat at the southern end of the Parkway, mobilized their tribal government and took advantage of innovative New Deal policies toward Native Americans to fend off an effort by the state of North Carolina to route the Parkway through their most fertile valley farmlands. By far the best-organized grassroots opponents of the Parkway, the Eastern Band eventually forced its rerouting along a neighboring ridge.[19]

At Grandfather Mountain, North Carolina, powerful businessman Hugh Morton delayed Parkway construction for nearly two decades in the 1950s and '60s through the clever strategy of enlisting powerful allies in state government and effectively combining arguments for the environment and against communism. Ultimately he compelled adoption of a route that skirted the middle of the stunning mountain, left ownership of the area in his hands, and yet provided ready access to numerous tourist attractions (including the "mile-high swinging bridge") that he soon developed into a lucrative business. Clearly, in both the Cherokee and Grandfather Mountain cases, final Parkway routing reflected political power relationships rather than impartial decisions made on the basis of objective criteria.

In addition to fundamental questions of routing, design, and appropriate land use, regulations governing the creation of a rural scenic parkway (as opposed to a regular highway) have often generated controversy. Since the early 1930s, the interests of tourists have consistently trumped those of local residents and commercial haulers. Except for a short period during World War II, commercial vehicles have always been prohibited. Speed limits are set at an intentionally leisurely forty-five miles per hour. Roadside development has been severely curtailed in hopes of preventing the tacky, congested, and "unsightly" buildup that by the late 1920s had already marred many American highways. In these respects the Blue Ridge Parkway—whose major design features were established in the 1930s—

borrowed many elements from American parkways built after 1925, when the Bronx River Parkway was completed; but in planting such a road in a rural setting and doing away almost completely with the idea of providing a faster, more pleasurable means of commuting around cities, Blue Ridge Parkway planners developed something with little precedent.[20]

To preserve the "scenic" part of the "scenic parkway," the National Park Service required the state highway commissions, which were responsible for land acquisition, to appropriate (through their power of eminent domain) an exceptionally wide right-of-way. North Carolina's state highway officials, who had lobbied hard to get the Parkway built, adhered enthusiastically to the NPS's recommendations. There the Parkway strip averaged close to a thousand feet wide, while it was somewhat narrower in Virginia, whose officials were less cooperative with the project. Nowhere, however, was the right-of-way less than two hundred feet wide. The Parkway (technically "an elongated park . . . to contain the roadway") thus consumed much more land than the sixty or so feet that an average highway of the time required—and more than even many previous parkways had taken.[21] This policy kept nearby landowners and residents at a much greater distance from the Parkway than they had had in relation to other roadways, and thus magnified its impact on landowners whose property the road bisected. Parkway land acquisition, mostly complete by the late 1940s, was thus an area of sharp conflict as landowners coped with the shock of having to relinquish so much land.

Since controlled access was considered critical to maintaining both Parkway safety and scenery, federal regulations also prohibited most landowners from connecting private roads or driveways directly to it. Access from other highways was tightly controlled via widely spaced entrances and exits. Leniently enforced at first, particularly on the Virginia sections of the Parkway, these regulations were much more strictly observed from the late 1930s onward.[22]

The combination of land acquisition, design features, and access and use restrictions proved frustrating to neighboring residents, who pushed against them in a number of ways. Those who did so met with widely differing responses. What kind of response was forthcoming depended on a particular property holder's access to the levers of political power.

North Carolinian S. A. Miller was one of the few small landowners who complained directly to federal officials, but the sentiments he expressed in a 1937 letter to President Roosevelt were likely widespread: "It goes through the middle of my farm. . . . Maybe some people would say, that the land on the Blue Ridge isn't any good. Well we people have made our support on it and it is some good to us and the Park to Park highway isn't any benefit to us according to what they tell us. We aren't allowed to put any buildings near it and not even cross it to our land on the other side."[23]

Other landowners protested with the "weapons of the weak," such as trespassing, carving illegal access roads, venturing onto the noncommercial road with trucks, and cutting timber on what was to become the right-of-way. Connie Johnson of Glade Valley in Allegheny County, North Carolina, confounded the Park Service for nearly three years by repeatedly trespassing on Parkway lands to make use of an illegal access road. But such tactics proved unavailing; a federal-court injunction finally threatened Johnson with imprisonment should the trespassing continue. Miller, Johnson, and others like them were generally unable to bring about the changes in routing, land-acquisition plans, or engineering that more powerful constituencies were able to effect.[24]

At the same time, however, the Park Service tiptoed around Mrs. Bertha Cone, widow of textile magnate Moses Cone, who owned an extensive summer estate, known as Flat Top Manor, near Blowing Rock. Mrs. Cone was alarmed to learn that the planned route of the Parkway bisected her lands, cut across the entrance to her property, and spelled doom for a beautiful hemlock hedge that she and her husband had nurtured for fifty years. In hopes of getting the planners to adjust the route to go around instead of through her property, she wrote letters to everyone she could think of, including Secretary Ickes and eventually Roosevelt himself.[25]

Throughout the 1930s, the Park Service and North Carolina state officials treated the elderly woman gently, considered various possible routing alternatives, and finally informally agreed that land acquisition in the Flat Top area could be postponed until after Mrs. Cone's death.[26] In the end, their strategy paid off: North Carolina inherited the Cone estate in the late 1940s and deeded it to the Park Service, which opened a craft shop in the manor house and developed the land into the Moses Cone Memorial Park.[27] Meanwhile, by contrast, in the process of acquiring land in the Bluffs recreation area, the Park Service refused the simple request of one small landowner to retrieve the windows from his modest but newly built house.[28]

Not surprisingly, in view of these biases, North Carolina officials—pulled between a genuine desire to see the mountain scenery through the Parkway corridor preserved and a hope of encouraging what they termed "desirable" tourist development—openly favored large-scale tourism operators, who repeatedly demonstrated that they had the power to challenge the regulations and exploit the differences between state and federal officials over the Parkway's purpose.[29] The most glaring example was the set of concessions granted to the Switzerland Company, which, beginning in 1909, had built an exclusive summer colony through which the Parkway was set to pass. At Little Switzerland, "noncommercial" gave way to hard bargaining, creative propaganda, and timely legal action by a well-connected and wealthy developer who was also a North Carolina Supreme Court justice. The result was that the state supreme court gave the Switzerland Company a dramatically narrowed right-of-way, a generous cash settlement, and several access roads leading directly to the Switzerland Inn.[30]

Similar patterns emerged with regard to entrepreneurship and how the Parkway would—and would not—foster tourism. When the Park Service began to develop concessions facilities along the road in the 1940s, Parkway neighbors who had hoped to open small businesses catering to Parkway traffic ran head on into more frustrating restrictions. A Park Service official explained to one local businessman that, although service and supply stations would be established to serve travelers, "[p]ersons owning land adjoining the parkway land should not plan to begin any business venture as it will be impossible to build any access drives to the parkway."[31] The somewhat vague stipulation that concessions operators along the highway be "well-financed individuals" further undercut local entrepreneurs.[32] Initial contracts in 1942 went to National Park Concessions, Inc., a "non-profit distributing corporation" that already ran concessions at Kentucky's Mammoth Cave National Park and that was controlled by two National Park Service staff members and three "private citizens" who were "old hands in the operation of national park facilities."[33] With this decision, the Park Service signaled unambiguously that it would bar most small-scale local entrepreneurs from participating in commercial enterprises along the Parkway.[34]

The thorny politics always at play when large public works are planned clearly influenced the development of the Blue Ridge Parkway—configured in precise ways for this particular project in this specific place. But creating a scenic Parkway required planners to devise a pleasing aesthetic experience for travelers to enjoy on their way from one place to another. As its staff developed the Parkway scene, the Park Service deliberately concealed evidence of the political machinations that had so profoundly shaped the project. In addition to analyzing the imbalances of power and their concrete results, then, one must ask why the landscape that emerged from such a tangle of political controversies would come to be understood in a way that effaced the considerable debate and conflict in the project's history.

Great Picture Windows on Appalachian Life: History (Re)Presented on the Parkway

The Parkway's serene appearance—molded by the landscape architects on the Park Service staff and federal and state engineers—is partly explained by its infusion with a romanticized version of Appalachian regional history presented in roadside exhibits. The historical interpretation program has obscured the very currents within Appalachian, southern, and indeed American history that produced the highway. Consequently, a tourist attraction that, according to an early Parkway superintendent, was designed to open "great picture windows to expose a way of life hitherto heavily veiled from the eyes of the American tourist" in fact presents a highly idealized picture of that life, into which the Parkway itself and the forces that shaped it have not been, and in many respects could not be, incorporated.[35]

In the early 1940s, as the state-directed land-acquisition phase wound down and the parameters for construction and use had largely been set, the staff at Parkway headquarters turned their attention to detailed landscape design and cultural interpretation. The system of historical presentation and interpretation they developed worked in tandem with routing and landscape design to conceal the politicized process that had produced the Parkway. The Park Service's first interpretive plans repeated time-worn stereotypes that portrayed mountain people as wholly rural, isolated, and out of touch with the transforming currents of modernity. Since the latter half of the nineteenth century, when writers in search of "local color" and timber, coal, and railroad entrepreneurs in pursuit of abundant natural resources simultaneously "discovered" the southern Appalachians, various myths had flourished about the people who lived there. Rumored to be a culturally unique Anglo-Saxon remnant untouched by modernity, Appalachian people were alternately depicted as backward (moonshiners or feudists) or quaint and noble (craftspeople and ballad singers). Such images proliferated in fiction and nonfiction writings for genteel popular audiences and in popular films and cartoons. From the 1850s onward, a steady stream of articles in the popular press, religious journals, and other publications supplied the stock phrases for a developing discourse about southern mountaineers: "a strange land and peculiar people" (1873), "our contemporary ancestors" (1899), "our kindred of the Boone and Lincoln type" (1900), "Anglo-Saxons" (1901), "simple, homeloving folk . . . heedless of the march of events" (1907), and the ubiquitous "hillbillies" (1915).[36] Such characterizations could even be found in published compilations of English ballads collected in the southern mountains and in widely read nonfiction studies of mountain life, such as Samuel Tyndale Wilson's *The Southern Mountaineers* (which went through five editions between 1906 and 1915) or Horace Kephart's *Our Southern Highlanders* (1916). At the very moment of the Parkway routing battle, *National Geographic* promised that travelers through the new eastern national parks would encounter mountaineers in log cabins, "the friendly descendants of that sturdy stock which produced such men as Abraham Lincoln, Daniel Boone, Andrew Jackson, and Admiral Farragut." The *New York Times* informed a national audience that they would find along the new Blue Ridge Parkway "primitive mountain folk" whose speech was often laced with "a phrase or two of Anglo-Saxon origin almost without meaning to the modern grammarian."[37]

Such writings encouraged an influx of mountain workers who either hoped to "uplift" the downtrodden mountaineers or to "preserve" or "revive" their putatively disappearing but valuable culture. Thus, as booming coal, timber, and textile companies bought and transformed mountain land, drawing former farmers into wage work and bringing convulsive economic and social dislocation, church-affiliated missionaries and other social and "culture workers" came to the aid of mountain residents. While some of them established health clinics and literacy and agricultural programs, most were partial to crafts and cultural study. From the 1890s onward, numerous settlement schools and folk-craft programs that shared those broad goals were opened, and western North Carolina was a center of such efforts. Prominent handicrafts projects in the area included the Log Cabin Settlement, Allanstand Cottage Industries, Biltmore Industries in the Asheville area, and the John C. Campbell Folk School (1925) near Murphy. By the 1930s the Southern Highland Handicraft Guild, based in western North Carolina, had become a principal arbiter of "mountain crafts."[38]

Like others before them, National Park Service personnel working in the southern mountains foregrounded the scattered remnants of pioneer culture they expected to find in Appalachia in the choices they made about which cultural features to highlight along the Parkway. For example, an early inspection team passed over one section of the Parkway in North Carolina when the park ranger assigned to the area informed them that "there was nothing of particular interest for our purpose."[39] Although this section contained the estate of textile magnate Moses Cone and fashionable resorts at Linville and Little Switzerland, the story of the development of mountain tourist retreats for the wealthy (a story that stretched back to the early nineteenth century) was not a tale the Park Service was interested in telling.

What they promised to present was "some insight into the problems of the pioneers with their 'long rifles' who first penetrated the area, as well as the problems and life of their descendants"; but in fact the descendants were mostly dropped out of the equation.[40] The first master interpretive plan for the entire Parkway, drafted in 1942, asserted that the roadway could be the "narrator of the whole story of the mountains," which should include representations of the "lived-in mountains" along with both managed and wild natural scenes.[41] The plan acknowledged that the story to be told included elements of modernization and change. But actual recommendations focused on the Parkway's role in preserving the "pioneer cabins . . . , the grist mills, and the traces of old fence" associated with a way of life that was "swiftly passing and, but for the Parkway, . . . passed in many parts."[42]

Implementing the Park Service's view of regional history meant that even along a rather heavily populated and farmed section of the Parkway, where "only three log cabins were encountered," the pioneer story would be top priority as Park Service personnel set to work interpreting Appalachian life.[43] Logically but lamentably, then, the Park Service removed numerous modern homes from the right-of-way and focused early preservation efforts on the three log cabins and on Ed and Lizzie Mabry's Floyd County, Virginia, grist mill (fig. 3.1).[44]

One of the inspectors was disappointed to find that the "old Mabry Mill" was "not very old, dating perhaps between 1900–1920." He pointed out, however, that from a distance "the building is well weathered and

3.1. Mabry Mill is located in Floyd County, Virginia, at milepost 176.2 of the Blue Ridge Parkway. From the Library of Congress Collection of Prints and Photographs.

appears much older than it is," and thus might be used in an exhibit.[45] To create such displays, the NPS removed or camouflaged inconvenient evidence that modernity had indeed touched mountain people's lives. At the mill, the owner's 1914 clapboard frame house (quite typical of mountain farmsteads by that time) was torn down and replaced in the 1950s with a log cabin trucked in from another county. The Park Service erected displays on blacksmithing and whiskey-making while neglecting to mention the timber industry that up to the very eve of Parkway construction had been so dominant in and so devastating to the region.[46]

Elsewhere one of the early inspectors found other cabins, which, he suggested, could be restored and staffed with an "inhabitant of pure mountain stock" who would agree to "treat his field as he would ordinarily" and to make only "genuine" craft articles for display and sale.[47] Exhibits of "typical mountain farms" emphasized isolation and primitiveness and ignored both the diversity of mountain life and farmers' well-established community networks and routine participation in regional and national market economies.[48]

As the years passed, pioneer themes remained central to the Parkway's interpretation of mountain life, to the exclusion of most other elements of the region's complex history. A 1950 master plan reiterated the Parkway's mission to "make accessible . . . representative sections of the Appalachians, assuring the visitor the opportunity to appreciate scenes of great natural beauty and traces of the homespun culture of the mountain people" (fig. 3.2). Such people, the plan observed, would be "living exhibits" of a region "touched only by the backwash of history."[49] Ironically, however, while Park Service staff expressed such enthusiasm for the material remnants of mountain people's lives, they also worked to keep most actual mountain residents off "the Scenic." In fact they worried that, left in the hands of mountain people themselves, lands adjacent to the Parkway would present "a scene of poverty rather than one of rural pioneer life." Hence they hired an agronomist to coordinate a program of leasing Parkway lands back to mountain farmers, who were instructed in more picturesque farming methods.[50]

3.2. Puckett Cabin, located on Virginia's Groundhog Mountain at milepost 189 of the Blue Ridge Parkway, was built around 1875 by John Puckett, and it remained the home of his wife, Orleana Hawks Puckett, until a few weeks before her death in 1939 at the age of 102. From the Library of Congress Collection of Prints and Photographs.

The Park Service's difficulty in dealing with the multidimensional history of the southern Appalachians emerged in its handling of the Cone estate, an extensive property with a lavish residence built in 1900 near the long-established resort community of Blowing Rock, North Carolina, by textile baron Moses Cone. Acquired by the Park Service in 1949, the estate did not fit easily into the pioneer paradigm. Indeed, the Service initially tore down many of the outbuildings on the property and considered razing the manor house itself, which it deemed historically and architecturally insignificant. In the 1950s, however, the house was converted into a museum of pioneer life and a handicrafts sales center. In the 1960s and '70s, the Park Service contemplated constructing an "early Americana" village to display farm life, crafts, and the "centuries-old culture" of mountain people, which had supposedly persisted into the twentieth century (despite the pervasive influence of railroads, mining, textiles, timbering, and tourism). Paradoxically, the Park Service has never really considered allowing the Cone estate's own history to dictate interpretive efforts at the site.[51]

Debates over how to handle the Cone estate illustrate how the Park Service's commitment to making the Parkway "an elongated museum of folklore" foreclosed other voices and other meanings as development of the roadway proceeded in the post–World War II period.[52] By the late 1960s, however, the determination to present an idyllic picture of pioneer life began to clash with the inconvenient realities of the history of western North Carolina and southwest Virginia, which became better known as a wave of revisionist scholarship reinterpreted the Appalachian region.[53] At Virginia's Peaks of Otter park, one of the large "recreation areas" established alongside the Parkway (where food, lodging, camping, hiking, and other visitor facilities were located on a "bulge" of property bought for the purpose), the Park Service faced the dilemma of how to interpret the "Johnson Farm" house and surrounding buildings, acquired in the late 1930s. The bowl-shaped Peaks area, set among three prominent mountains and along a major overmountain turnpike, had drawn tourists since the mid-nineteenth century to a series of modest boardinghouses and hotels. By the time the Park Service obtained the lands, the small community that had flourished in the area had begun to decline; but there remained the comfortable and popular Hotel Mons and the large nearby farm of Callie Bryant, a descendant of the original Johnson family, which had settled there in the 1850s. Separated only by a short walk, the hotel and farm existed in a symbiotic economic relationship in which the farm provided food, flowers, and employees for the hotel; the hotel provided income for the farm; and hotel guests regularly visited the Bryant family home.[54]

Shortly after acquiring the property, the Park Service demolished the hotel and its numerous outbuildings, leaving only an empty field where summer crowds attracted to the cool air and the "Mons habit" of coming each year to the Peaks had once played lawn games. The clapboard farmhouse was left intact, although it was allowed to deteriorate until the mid-1950s, when the Park Service at long last began to develop interpretive plans for the site. In 1964 a Park Service report recommended revamping the site to appear as they surmised it might have around the turn of the twentieth century. Pursuant to that recommendation, workers in 1968 removed the tin roof, pried off the clapboard siding, tore off the porch, and exposed the smaller log cabin that was indeed underneath. For four years the lonely cabin stood in a now-isolated field. Certainly the Bryant family would not have recognized their former home.[55]

A new Park Service interpretive team that arrived in 1972 quickly realized that a lack of sufficient documentary evidence precluded presenting the farm as it had been in the late 1890s. They recommended instead that the farm be returned to its 1930s appearance (for which adequate documentation, including photographs, was available) and that interpretive efforts thereafter focus on the farm's role in the larger Peaks of Otter–area community. Once again construction teams swarmed around the house, rebuilding the porch and replacing the white siding.[56]

Despite these efforts, however, even into the 1990s the Park Service seemed unable to relinquish its commitment to the comfortable old myths. Later recommendations that the rest of the site be upgraded to reflect how *uni*solated the farmstead really was—by better marking of the Hotel Mons site and clearer indication of the road that had provided access to the farm— were never carried out.[57] As late as 2002, signs at the site still directed visitors up a long and circuitous (literally *mis*leading) path to reach the farm, rather than pointing out the quicker route that crosses the former Mons site. The serial interpretive process through which the farm passed reflects all too clearly the challenges the Park Service confronted in maintaining its picturesque fictions in the face of expanding new scholarship on the Appalachian region.

This new scholarship notwithstanding, the romantic *Southern Living* version of the Parkway's origins sketched above has proved remarkably durable, despite abundant evidence that early decisions about routing, design, access, and use inscribed on the landscape a much more complex version of regional history—one that is visible to those who know where to look. That more complicated history created a parkway that traversed North Carolina and passed near Asheville rather than a three-state parkway that ended near Knoxville, Tennessee; that kept most neighboring landowners at a distance; that could be entered directly from the exclusive Little Switzerland resort but not from most ordinary landowners' homes; that brought wealth to Grandfather Mountain's Hugh Morton but prevented smaller tourist operations from gaining a foothold; and that preserved the Cone mansion, many cabins, and the Mabry Mill but eliminated the frame and brick homes in which so many displaced landowners had lived.

So if the symbiosis between the Parkway's design and the Park Service's historic-interpretation program is so problematic and pertinent new scholarship is available, why not simply move to present a more accurate picture of Appalachian history—perhaps by allowing the Parkway itself to tell the political story so thoroughly yet so invisibly inscribed upon it?[58] The first impediment to such reconsideration and reformulation is the enormous political and economic investment that the Parkway now constitutes. For a Park Service perennially strapped for funds, modifying a large and widely dispersed array of buildings and sites that express an accepted if inaccurate historical narrative would be prohibitively expensive. Furthermore, from the standpoint of the large-scale corporate tourism industry, the Parkway has been a resounding success. Why alter elements that bring twenty million visitors to the region each year? Even some historic preservationists now view the Parkway (in its entirety) as a unique and historic "designed landscape" deserving of preservation as it is—stereotypes, confusions, and all. Finally, to tamper with the pervasive and persistent public affection for the "good road of the Blue Ridge" in a period characterized by pervasive antigovernment sentiment would be a political move fraught with peril.

Whether or not roadside exhibits ever change, however, it is clear that the Blue Ridge Parkway did not develop apart from the history of the region it traverses. Rather it is the product of a complex, multidimensional society that exists both within and beyond the mountains. Equally important, it has been an agent of profound social and cultural conflict and change *within* the region it both meanders through and seeks to explain to a traveling public charmed by a stunning landscape and a beguiling story.

FOUR

"A Feeling Almost beyond Description"

Scenic Roads in South Dakota's
Custer State Park, 1919–32

Suzanne Julin

In the late 1920s, writer and automobile tourist P. D. Peterson described his trip over the Needles Highway in Custer State Park, located in South Dakota's Black Hills. The mountain road twisted through eerie granite towers; led through narrow, roughly cut tunnels; and ascended and descended steep grades. Peterson declared that for motorists "the sense of conquering all these, affords a feeling almost beyond description to the soul of the driver."[1] The Needles Highway was part of a landscape planned, constructed, and promoted during the interwar years to bring automobile tourism to the region. This landscape, which included Mount Rushmore National Memorial and the park's Iron Mountain Road, brought tourists into a designed space that combined vistas of sublime natural beauty with modern automobile technology and accompanying feelings of freedom, accomplishment, and adventure.

The development of automobile tourism in the United States exerted a profound impact on the landscape, on the built environment, and on American society. Although people began touring by auto shortly before the beginning of the twentieth century, this travel was restricted in general to wealthy citizens with the money to buy and operate cars and the leisure to take long trips. After World War I, affordable cars and improved road systems opened up automobile touring to the wage-earning classes. Hundreds of thousands of Americans took to the road, many of them lured westward by the national parks, the promise of wide-open spaces and rugged landscapes, and the mystique of the Old West. Communities, states, and regions worked to gain the attention of these travelers, hoping to detain them long enough to boost the local economy and local pride.[2]

The developers of Custer State Park capitalized on automobile tourism. An early destination for tourism in the Black Hills region, the park was the cornerstone of its success. The development within its boundaries of the Needles Highway and the Iron Mountain Road bracketed the creation of Mount Rushmore National Monument, located at the edge of the park's game-sanctuary extension. The first of these two roads served as an inspiration for the memorial, and the designers of the second used the monument as a foil to the natural environment and as a focal point for the road itself. The landscape thus created offers an outstanding example of the effects of automobile tourism in the years between the world wars.

The expansion in automobile tourism following World War I occurred within the context of a wider social transformation in the United States. Corporations began to dominate business, and new employment opportunities drew immigrants and countrydwellers to cities, leading to an increasingly urban and complex nation. Increased production and consumption created pressure to acquire capital and material possessions. Progressive reformers turned to the organization of bureaucratic structures, efficiency, professional specialization, and regulation in their attempts to stabilize a rapidly changing social and cultural milieu. Americans were constrained by new hierarchies, new rules, and new economic demands.[3]

At the same time, this was a society of new freedoms. The middle and working classes enjoyed higher wages, a rising standard of living, and more time away from the workplace. The reduction of actual work hours led to acceptance of the value of leisure and a demand for greater recreational opportunities, while the pressures of modern life prompted people to look for escape.[4] They found that escape most fully in the mass-produced automobile. By enabling large numbers of Americans to travel cheaply and independently, the car created a broad category of potential tourists and offered access to areas and attractions formerly out of their reach.

Recreational driving and automobile tourism supplied Americans with an activity that combined technology, consumerism, appreciation of nature, the quest for adventure, and the illusion of personal freedom. Purveyors of tourism, both public and private, tapped into Americans' driving fever to develop attractions that would lure travelers to specific localities. In the first decades of the twentieth century, many of these sites were located on public lands, particularly in the American West. U.S. Forest Service lands and national monuments established under the Antiquities Act of 1906 provided some of these attractions.[5] The consolidation of the national parks under the National Park Service a decade later launched the development of an important public-tourism infrastructure.[6] Stephen Mather, director of the National Park Service from 1917 until 1928, encouraged expansion of the system and automobile travel to and within the parks.[7] Under Mather, the national parks became identified with the slogan originally coined by Salt Lake City promoter Fisher Harris, "See America First." Connecting this directive with the national park system gave a particularly patriotic and nationalistic cast to vacation travel, especially during World War I, when Americans had to forgo trips to Europe.[8] Travel within the United States became not only an adventure but also a demonstration of patriotism, further encouraging automobile tourism across the nation.

Once the war was over, a small group of state politicians and influential citizens collaborated to draw automobile tourists to the Black Hills, a small mountain range on the western edge of South Dakota. Bypassed by transcontinental railroad lines and far from any urban centers, this isolated region in the sparsely populated northern Great Plains seemed an unlikely site for a significant tourism industry. During the interwar years, however, the results of publicly funded tourism development created attractions that appealed to tourists traveling west and spurred growth of private tourism in the Black Hills.

Like many such parks, Custer State Park was established to protect natural resources, preserve areas of special scenic value, and provide opportunities for relaxation and recreation in pleasant outdoor settings. There was, however, another motivation behind the creation of this particular state park, one of the largest in the nation: the desire to appeal to automobile tourists.[9] Peter Norbeck, South Dakota governor from 1917 to 1921 and U.S. senator from 1921 to 1936 (fig. 4.1), led this effort. A Progressive Republican vitally interested in conservation issues, he was also an art enthusiast with a special interest in what he called "scenic design." Norbeck used his popularity, his political skills, and his policymaking power to promote the construction

4.1. Peter Norbeck, governor of South Dakota from 1917 to 1921 and senator from 1921 until his death in 1936, provided both the artistic vision and the political leadership for South Dakota's spectacular scenic highways in the Black Hills region. Photograph courtesy of the South Dakota State Historical Society—State Archives.

of roads in Custer State Park that would tempt motoring travelers. As an elected official and a member of the Custer State Park Board, he influenced the creation and design of these roads and set the stage for the area's most important tourist attraction, Mount Rushmore National Memorial. These features helped to make the Black Hills the first mountain landscape that thousands of western-bound tourists saw.[10]

In leading the development of Custer State Park, Norbeck demonstrated his Progressive conviction that government ought to use public resources to benefit the people. In this case the resources were scenic, and Norbeck maintained that citizens should have access to them. "A wilderness may be a thing of beauty," he wrote in 1927. "It must be preserved, but it must also be accessible to the public." In his view, accessibility called for the development of mountain highways, hotels, restaurants, tourist camps, golf courses, and mail and telephone service that would encourage visitors to come to the area, and that would make their visits convenient and pleasant.[11] His goals went beyond simply conserving public property and providing unobtrusive recreational opportunities in a natural setting. "We are looking mainly for tourists now," he told the park board's secretary in 1921.[12]

A generous appropriation from the state legislature and administrative and fiscal ties with other departments in the state government, including the state Highway Commission, allowed Norbeck and his colleagues to pursue such development. The park's road system, built in part with convict labor, was an important element in attracting automobile tourists. Although park roads were officially constructed by the Highway Commission, an agreement between the commission and the Custer State Park Board gave the board extensive control over their planning and construction; in essence, these roads constituted a separate highway system within the state.[13]

The design of this system owed a good deal to Norbeck's faith in his own judgment and to his lack of regard for what he viewed as bureaucratic and professional barriers. In road-building matters in particular, he disdained a rigid adherence to rules and on at least one occasion contemplated rejecting federal funds if accepting them meant conforming to standard engineering practices.[14] He quickly became frustrated with those who did not appreciate the need to build park roads differently from ordinary thoroughfares. When addressing the complaints of an engineer who objected to trees left near a road and insisted on a guardrail that would block the view, for example, Norbeck could not resist sarcasm: "I do not think it is necessary to make the guard rail so high that people can't jump off the bridge if they really want to. They might jump off the rim of the canyon, or they might climb up those tall trees (that we forgot to cut down), and commit suicide in that way."[15] In another case he took exception to the customary galvanized wire or cable guardrails because they were "out of harmony with the surroundings," and he declared that they should be replaced by logs or large rocks "laid on the edge of the road and in fact cemented fast."[16] Despite professional highway builders' disagreements with Norbeck's plans, his political power usually guaranteed him the freedom to shape the design according to his own goals. For Norbeck and those loyal to him, the appeal of the roads and the emotional impacts they exerted on motorists took precedence over modern standards of highway construction and sophisticated use of technology.

These emotional impacts resulted not only from the roads' environment but also from the very experience of driving them. Automobile tourists during the first decades of the twentieth century considered motoring an active pursuit, not a passive diversion. The car offered a physical challenge, one that many Americans were seeking. In 1899, when Theodore Roosevelt called on American men to be strong and vigorous, he used the phrase "the strenuous life." Roosevelt's words created an antidote for what many people saw as the draining tension of modern existence.[17] In motoring, the quest for a "strenuous life" and the need to escape from structured society combined with the fascination for new technology and the burgeoning consumer culture to establish a satisfying and popular mode of travel. Early automobile travel was strenuous indeed. These tourists wrestled with the machinery; coped with breakdowns, bad roads, and inclement weather; and improvised dining and sleeping arrangements. They sought out difficult landscapes to traverse, satisfying their tastes for adventure.[18] After their vacations ended, motoring tourists remembered hardship, adventure, and novelty rather than luxury and relaxation. Their new freedom demanded strength and stamina and produced a sense of hard-won accomplishment.[19]

Peter Norbeck was himself an avid motorist. In 1905 he and two companions were the first people to drive overland across western South Dakota to the Black Hills.[20] His appreciation for the automotive adventure extended to his belief that park highways should be designed to entertain and delight tourists and need not—indeed, should not—conform to conventional road-building standards. He once told an engineer concerned about exceeding a 7 percent grade that sections of the Needles Highway were at 11, 16, and even 22 percent grade. "Remember," the senator reminded the engineer, "this is inside the Park, not outside the Park, where the 7 per cent rule is important in commercial work."[21] He analyzed the attractions of a much-photographed road in the Black Hills: it was narrow, crowded by trees, and "crooked enough so one can see the roadway through the trees, which is not possible on a straight road," pointedly emphasizing features objected to by engineers interested in speed, efficiency, and safety.[22] Norbeck's conception of a park road system included not only access to scenery but also design that contributed to the driving experience.

Two of the scenic roads Norbeck helped to create during the interwar years incorporated these elements and became tourist attractions in their own right. The first was a fourteen-mile-long road through granite formations known as the Needles. Eroded over time into narrow spires, these remarkable formations are located in the highest and most rugged section of the Black Hills (fig. 4.2). Norbeck, often in the company of Scovel Johnson, a civil engineer employed jointly by the park and the state Highway Commission, and Cecil C. Gideon, the park gamekeeper, explored the area on

4.2. A roadside view of the "Cathedral Spires," which are among the most dramatic of the granite formations for which the Needles Highway is named. Photograph by Brian Madetzke.

foot and on horseback in order to determine a route. Gideon and Johnson took responsibility for on-site design and construction; Norbeck followed the process closely, even after being elected to the U.S. Senate and moving to Washington early in 1921. In letters from the nation's capital, he continued to offer detailed suggestions about the scenic elements of the road and the engineering process.[23]

The most difficult part of the construction, which was also the most dramatic part of the finished road, was a one-and-one-quarter-mile section in the midst of the Needles. This segment's sharp turns, switchbacks, and tunnels cut through solid granite cost almost five times more per mile to build than the rest of the road. Most of the boulders had to be dynamited out, and in several places the roadbed was blasted through granite ledges. As many as 165 men in eight separate camps worked on the road under Johnson's supervision.[24] Johnson shared Norbeck's conviction that they were building an extraordinary road under extraordinary conditions. In September of 1921 the engineer reported good progress despite constant problems and concluded, "[W]e'll get a road built in spite of the Devil, also snowstorms, rain and other Acts of the Creator."[25] Six weeks later Norbeck congratulated Johnson on the completion of the bulk of the road construction within a year's time. "I would like to see the Highway Department turn you loose with half a million dollars to complete and surface the highway system in the park," Norbeck told him.

Although work continued into 1922, a few adventurous motorists were able to drive the Needles Highway by early November of 1921.[26] The road promised to reveal scenery that had "been behind a closed door to tourists," according to a local newspaper report.[27] Highway Commissioner M. L. Shade, who had been closely connected with the construction, confirmed that notion after walking a portion of the highway in the spring of 1921. "[I] really had thought that I had seen most of the beauties of the park but I was amazed at what I saw on this trip," Shade noted.[28]

The road's design and the reactions of drivers who experienced it reveal its success as an attraction for motoring tourists. The road did not just provide tourists with a view of the Needles or a way to reach them; it took them *into* the Needles, wound around the formations, and passed through tunnels painstakingly blasted out and finished by Johnson and his crews. The proximity to the towering granite outcroppings contrasted dramatically with the distant vistas. The tunnels, the twisting road, the numerous switchbacks, and the sharp drop-offs provided drivers with an exhilarating experience, as P. D. Petersen noted in his description of the drive. John Stanley, the Custer State Park Board's secretary, chauffeured a landscape architect from Minneapolis over the road and reported to Norbeck that the man was "speechless in his appreciation."[29] While admiring the landscape and the road's design, the two men noted the incongruity of automobile traffic in such a remote place; they encountered at least ten other autos even though few people knew the road was open. "It seemed strange to meet cars way up there in those needles almost on top of the Black Hills," Stanley wrote.[30]

As these responses to the Needles Highway attest, Norbeck and his colleagues had created a new and exciting landscape for motoring travelers, one in which the road itself quickly became a dominant feature. Photographs and postcards depicting the Needles during the 1920s and 1930s almost invariably included a view of a portion of the Needles Highway, usually with a car navigating a turn, emerging from a tunnel, or parked in front of one of the formations. A 1927 article about the Black Hills in *National Geographic* included a full-page photograph of a portion of the road and one of the tunnels with a caption reading "Custer State Park's Greatest Scenic Asset." The rest of the caption explains that the road through "this jagged wonderland" exposes the park's "most striking scenery."[31]

Access to the Needles indirectly inspired the development of one of America's best-known cultural landscapes, Mount Rushmore National Memorial. Doane Robinson, poet, author, secretary of the State Historical Society, and tireless South Dakota booster, conceived the idea of carving the granite spires into massive statuary as another way to draw automobile tourist traffic to the state. He introduced his proposal at a meeting of the Black and Yellow Highway Association early in 1924, sharing his vision of a parade of western figures such as Lewis and Clark, Jedediah Smith, and Buffalo Bill Cody silhouetted against the sky.[32] Robinson saw no contradiction in using a work of monumental art to encourage tourism or in altering the natural environment to achieve that goal. "Tourists soon get fed up on scenery," he said, concluding that the proposed sculpture would add the "special interest" necessary to attract them to the area.[33]

Robinson quickly enlisted Norbeck. The senator, involved in a political campaign and at odds with the governor in office, kept a low profile during the early promotion of the idea to the public. However, he was crucial to its eventual success by pursuing political and financial support. He also served as an intermediary between the monument's mercurial sculptor, Gutzon Borglum, and various agencies that oversaw the work.[34] Borglum determined the location of the monument by rejecting the Needles in favor of a nearby granite mountainside, and he chose the monument's theme by insisting that the art should be national rather than regional in focus. He warned Robinson that the work must be taken seriously by critics if it was going to succeed in diverting tourist traffic to the Black Hills.[35]

By depicting the faces of four presidents, Borglum succeeded in designing a monument that appealed to patriotic sentiments and attracted wider interest than a project focused on Old West heroes would have generated. However, many South Dakotans objected to desecration of the natural environment in the interest of creating a pull for tourists. A magazine serving as the voice of promotion and development forces in the state glumly predicted that even if Borglum should create an ass on top of the mountain, tourists would ignore the beautiful scenery already present in favor of the novel sculpture.[36] One Black Hills newspaperwoman compared the undertaking to college students' attempts to place their class emblems in unlikely places. "We look tolerantly on their scrambling," she said, "knowing that they will learn in time to differentiate between physical altitude and real accomplishments. But we do not emulate them."[37] The Black Hills chapter of the General Federation of Women's Clubs officially opposed the carving.[38]

Robinson and Norbeck were neither amused nor deterred by the opposition. True Progressives, they continued to see the proposed monument as at once an important work of public art, a tool to increase the tourist trade, and an example of humans' ability to improve on nature. To a disapproving newspaper editor, Robinson wrote: "of course God made the Needles as he made every thing [sic] else that man has taken to himself and imporved [sic] and beautified. That is what God made men and things for. . . ."[39] Through a combination of determination and political maneuvering, Norbeck, Robinson, and other supporters of the sculpture brought the project to fruition. Norbeck and his allies persuaded President Calvin Coolidge to spend the summer of 1927 in the Black Hills and to speak at the ceremony marking the start of the carving. His presence conferred presidential approval on the Mount Rushmore Memorial, encouraging Norbeck in his ultimately successful quest for federal funds to finance the project.[40]

Mount Rushmore was born of automobile tourism. No railroads approached the monument area, but it became accessible to cars by road shortly after the carving got underway. The monument immediately began to draw tourists who, before the advent of automobiles, could not have reached the remote site. By 1931, officials estimated that in this state with fewer than a half million residents, 100,000 people visited the memorial annually.[41] Mount Rushmore, a work in progress from 1927 through 1941, became the focal point of Black Hills tourism and helped to make the area a gateway to the West for travelers from the midwestern and eastern parts of the country.

The creation of Mount Rushmore led to the formulation of Norbeck's final major road project and played a crucial role in its design. Early in May of 1930, Senator Norbeck wrote from the Black Hills to his secretary in Washington, "The Park looks glorious. . . . Tomorrow we go on Iron Mountain to settle on a very scenic route where the great point of Attraction is Rushmore."[42] The Iron Mountain Road linked Custer State Park's eastern gate to Borglum's studio near the sculpture, a distance of just over sixteen miles, and included components even more dramatic than those the Needles Highway featured. By the end of 1930, two thousand feet of the road had been roughed out; the most complex section was built over the following two years.[43]

Cecil C. Gideon and Owen Mann, by now the Custer State Park highway engineer, supervised the on-site planning and construction.[44] Norbeck had great faith in Gideon's design instincts and also appreciated Mann's ability to see park roads as distinct from commercial highways: "I do not have to quarrel with him all the time as I would with another man, who thinks he knows it all and carries his pre-conceived notions of road work into the Park."[45]

Norbeck oversaw the work from Washington and during his trips to the park, approving plans and contributing several elements that made the Iron Mountain Road unique. He patterned one of these features on a section of another road in the park where trees crowded the edges. His wife referred to this area as "the aisle of pines." Anxious to give drivers the experience of traveling in an isolated forest setting, Norbeck convinced Forest Service officials, who shared jurisdiction over part of the area, to allow the road to divide at particular points, taking motorists down one-way single lanes bordered by trees, thus creating the effect of paths winding through the woods.[46]

So-called pigtail turns and bridges became important components of the Iron Mountain Road. Norbeck's fondness for switchbacks influenced the design of the convoluted pigtails, which turned under themselves and allowed drivers and their passengers to look down and see where they were going, or up to see where they had been (fig. 4.3). At one location on the road, Norbeck originally proposed a triple spiral bridge between two tunnels but gave up the idea in deference to trusted advisors on site who considered the design impractical. In place of the triple spiral, Cecil Gideon worked out a nearly circular bridge on a trestle. The bridges were constructed with log supports and guardrails that provided the rustic effect Norbeck had hoped to achieve. This design conformed to a style of architecture known as Park Rustic, a uniquely American style institutionalized by the National Park Service after its establishment in 1916. Park Rustic used local materials and presented a rugged, handcrafted appearance.[47]

The road's most dramatic features proved to be its views of Mount Rushmore, some of them framed through rock tunnels on a line with the

4.3. One of the pigtail bridges on the Iron Mountain Road in South Dakota's Black Hills National Forest. Photograph by Brian Madetzke.

monument. Norbeck monitored the design of the tunnels carefully.[48] In March of 1931 the park superintendent wrote Norbeck that preliminary work on one of the tunnels was finished, revealing "George Washington's image in an unexcelled frame though a fringe of pines. Some of these will have to be trimmed or removed but I am leaving that for your suggestion."[49] Paul Bellamy, a Norbeck confidante who observed the tunnels as they were being completed, informed the senator, "[T]he views through each of the tunnels are magnificent. They are centered wonderfully well." One of the tunnels featured a curve at the entrance which obscured the view of Rushmore until the driver had nearly entered,[50] adding to the suspense of the drive. As work on the road progressed, Norbeck sought to avoid publicizing the fact that it offered stunning views of Rushmore, where only the carving of Washington was complete at that time.[51] This secretiveness was an extension of his desire to amaze drivers with unexpected features in scenic roads. Just as the Needles Highway not only revealed a landscape but also created one, the Iron Mountain Road brought nature, highway, and sculpture together in a contrived series of visual encounters.

By late June 1932 drivers could navigate the road and began to discover its surprises. From locations along the way, travelers could see the

4.4. View of the Mount Rushmore Memorial from the Iron Mountain Road in the Black Hills National Forest. Photograph by Brian Madetzke.

Needles and, on clear days, the White River Badlands to the east of the Black Hills.[52] Motorists were impressed by these views, but they were more intrigued by the complexity of the drive, with Mount Rushmore as the orientation point—although disorientation seemed to be a stronger theme (fig. 4.4). The tunnels, switchbacks, and pigtail turns created dizzying changes in direction. After driving the road, Paul Bellamy declared a motorist on it might think that he was drunk or that someone was moving the monument, "because first he sees it in front of him, and then behind him, and then on the left, and then on the right; sometimes he is above it and sometimes he is below it, sometimes he is approaching it and other times he's going away."[53] Another observer called the road "quite mad," appropriate for Alice in Wonderland. His description of the drive could have served as an advertisement for an amusement park ride. In part, it read:

> Under a log bridge, the sweep of a curve, and you're over it. The bridge curves of a pattern with the road, and mountains tumbled beneath are blue that merges into purple. . . . A tunnel is carved in solid rock and when you're inside, you know that it's also a hill, with an elevator-like drop. . . . You climb sharply into

immensity and another bridge . . . ends at solid granite. . . .
Through the granite is a gap which is another tunnel—long—and
sharply outlined against the end is light and the cameo-face of
Washington.[54]

On the Iron Mountain Road, adventurous driving experiences, mountain
scenery, and man-made sculpture combined to create a complex tourists' landscape.

Peter Norbeck and those who worked with him did not apply aesthetic
or philosophical labels to their accomplishments. However, the Needles
Highway and the Iron Mountain Road, along with Mount Rushmore, resulted in a landscape best described as sublime, a category emanating
from sixteenth-century European changes in how wilderness was viewed,
and buttressed by the Romantic movement of the eighteenth and early-
nineteenth centuries. In its extreme manifestations sublimity carried overtones of soul-rattling reactions to natural splendor, awe that inspired fear
or even terror, and a spiritual component that linked the mysteries of nature with the mystery of a creator.[55] The Needles Highway emphasized the
granite pinnacles, often described as grotesque, that dwarfed automobiles
and their drivers; the road itself seemed otherworldly. P. D. Peterson concluded that the highway must have been built with "divine guidance," the
only explanation he could imagine for humans' ability to construct it.[56]
Doane Robinson also pondered the road's spiritual qualities, with travelers
on it "looking out through windows of Heaven, down upon the mountain
peaks, so far below that the homes of men are as sparrows' havens . . .
and still above is the great maze of the Cathedral Spires."[57]

The natural environment of the Iron Mountain Road was more picturesque and less dramatic; this landscape's sublimity resulted from the in-
corporation of Mount Rushmore in its design. Iron Mountain Road awed
and astonished motorists with its sudden, fleeting views of a massive
sculpture in the midst of wilderness, glimpsed during turns, ascents and
descents, and through tunnels. The magnitude and the mystery of the
sculpture and its intense patriotic appeal carried spiritual overtones, a
sense acknowledged by Calvin Coolidge, who declared when dedicating
Mount Rushmore that its cornerstone had been "laid by the hand of the
Almighty."[58] The roads created by Peter Norbeck and his colleagues, combined with the emerging sculpture, created a truly sublime landscape.

Norbeck once told a friend that he would rather be remembered as an artist than as a senator.[59] As an artist, he was most nearly an architect. He conceived, created, and manipulated features and landscapes to establish mood and effect, and he inspired engineers, designers, and political supporters to collaborate in his visions. As a result, tourists experienced the thrills of driving challenging mountain roads in scenic surroundings. They might believe that the one-way lanes through the forest were expedient detours around an obstacle or that the rustic pigtail bridges were built of necessity from materials on site. They might believe that the steep grades, sharp turns, and meandering routes were unavoidable, rather than evidence of Norbeck's ability to supersede standard engineering practices within the park. They might even believe that the views of Mount Rushmore from Iron Mountain Road were coincidental. In reality, these elements were carefully planned to surprise and delight adventurous drivers.[60]

Other roads, scenic in their own way but more utilitarian in purpose, were built in Custer State Park during these years. Although other communities throughout the Black Hills constructed scenic highways through the mountain canyons and along the ridges, Needles Highway and Iron Mountain Road remained unrivaled. The "madness" of Iron Mountain Road and the eerie environment of the Needles Highway catered to motoring tourists' tastes for adventure and excitement, and gave them access to stunning landscapes that they could experience without leaving their cars. The designs of these two roads helped to influence the nature of tourism in the Black Hills and to integrate the area into America's western vacation lands during the post–World War I boom in automobile tourism.

FIVE

"Neon, Junk, and Ruined Landscape"

Competing Visions of America's Roadsides and
the Highway Beautification Act of 1965

Carl A. Zimring

While offering drivers expansive views of the nation's diverse terrain, America's highways have also supported a vast array of economic activities, including interstate commerce and such roadside industries as specialized lodging, restaurants, gas stations, billboard advertising, and scrapyards. Commercial development of the roadside is not uniquely American, yet since the end of World War II, the number and the nature of businesses alongside roads in the United States have aroused concern among environmentalists and politicians.[1] These concerns emerged in debates provoked by the Highway Beautification Act of 1965, which exposed growing tensions between environmental and commercial claims on public space.

During the 1950s and '60s, commerce along the nation's network of highways became more conspicuous, which led to criticism of its negative effects. Spurred by his first lady, Lyndon Johnson's administration attempted to regulate the aesthetics of American roads with the Highway Beautification Act. In Lady Bird Johnson's words, the legislation aimed for "pleasing vistas and attractive roadside scenes to replace endless corridors walled in by neon, junk, and ruined landscape."[2] Included among these eyesores were billboards, which advertisers found an effective form of marketing, and junkyards, which depended on their proximity to cheap and accessible transportation. Billboard advertisers, scrap-metal dealers, and automobile-salvage traders were threatened by this proposed regulation and lobbied Congress to protect their use of the roads.

Historians have framed the highway-beautification debates as a referendum on Lady Bird Johnson's political activism, yet the Act also offers an opportunity to discuss competing visions of America's roads as they collided in a dispute over regulation.[3] The issue of highway beautification pitted business interests against the federal government and environmentalists, foreshadowing the struggle over environmental regulation in the 1970s and '80s and revealing attitudes toward road use that transcend simple notions of recreation, conservation, or exploitation. This essay places the topic of highway beautification in the context of evolving interests, specifically the scrap-material and outdoor-advertising industries, as well as advocates for beautification. For many years these interests all held stakes in how the roads were used, and their conflicts intensified in the decade prior to 1965.

American Road Use Prior to 1965

Concerns about commercial use of the roadside existed well before the Highway Beautification Act; action, however, as with most other environmental matters, was more likely to be taken at the municipal or state level than at the federal level.[4] As Americans' commutes lengthened during the late-nineteenth and early-twentieth centuries (first in trains, then in automobiles), advertisers began to take advantage of the increasing amounts of time people spent in transit. The extension of rail lines at the turn of the century was accompanied by a proliferation of billboards visible from the trains.[5] With that proliferation came resistance; urban reformers representing the City Beautiful movement opposed the billboards, identifying them as nuisances that detracted from the city's natural beauty. Over the first two decades of the new century several municipalities regulated the size and numbers of the signs.[6]

The local ordinances did not eliminate roadside advertisements; indeed, as the automobile became a greater presence in American life, advertising on the roads between cities became commonplace. Americans owned eight million automobiles in 1920, and more than three times that number by

1930. From the thirties onward, automobiles were the primary mode of leisure travel in the United States.[7]

As people spent more time in their cars, advertisers began to pay more attention to the roadsides. Outdoor advertising grew throughout the 1920s, and although the Great Depression curtailed business, the styles of billboards became more sophisticated.[8] Roadside advertising evolved during the 1930s from a slogan painted on the side of a building into more complex formats, such as Burma-Shave's famous series of rhyming messages that the driver read sequentially as his car moved down the road.[9] By the 1950s, advertisers considered billboards to be viable methods of reaching consumers and even, in the words of Burr L. Robbins, president of the General Outdoor Advertising Company, "the art gallery of the public."[10] As the interstate highway system grew, the billboard industry expanded, with annual revenues increasing from $44,700,000 in 1940 to more than $200,000,000 in 1960.[11]

If advertisers viewed the roads as potential showcases, scrap traders saw them as conduits between cities. The scrap-material industry began to grow in the middle of the nineteenth century, when industrial manufacturers demanded larger amounts of affordable secondary materials, initially rags for paper manufacture and subsequently ferrous scrap and other metals. As steel became a standard material for construction, railroads, ship-making, automobile manufacture, and the burgeoning appliance industry, the scrap-metal trade grew, with the number of businesses in major cities almost doubling between 1890 and the end of World War I.[12] Most of the new businesses engaged in the scrap-metal trade; *Scientific American* estimated that annual revenues from scrap iron rose from one hundred million to a billion dollars between 1914 and 1917.[13]

A hundred years earlier, in 1817, New York City began licensing junk peddlers in an attempt to curb theft and other petty crimes associated with their business. As concerns over contagious disease and fire escalated in the late-nineteenth and early-twentieth centuries, scrap and rag shops came to be regarded as threats to public health. By the end of World War I, legislation had pushed scrapyards out of many urban residential neighborhoods and into the unpopulated periphery or into poorer neighborhoods that lacked the political power to oppose their siting. Despite these challenges, the scrap industry grew rapidly and even developed a public-relations campaign in which scrap dealers defined themselves as conservers of valuable economic resources.[14] The industry's two national trade associations, the National Association of Waste Material Dealers (NAWMD) and the Institute of Scrap Iron and Steel (ISIS), adopted the rhetoric of conservation to promote their members' virtues, arguing that the scrap trade was vital to the nation's economic health; and for most of the twentieth century it remained closely linked to increasing industrial production.[15]

Benefitting from a consumer culture that now valued style over durability, junk traders accumulated large numbers of mass-produced appliances that could be resold or processed as scrap. A new, specialized junkyard developed specifically for automobiles. Here customers could purchase obsolete automobiles for scrap or individual parts for use in repairing cars still on the road. Detroit's business directory for 1920 featured listings for thirty-six automobile salvage yards, and by the end of the decade, automobile graveyards full of discarded vehicles and spare parts were to be found in or near most American cities. Scrap-, salvage, and junkyards were typically located on the urban periphery, in part because of zoning regulations, in part because these sites offered easy access to major transportation routes.

By midcentury, both the outdoor-advertising and the scrap industries had responded to increasing municipal regulation by relocating their operations to exurban sites. As they moved outside the city limits, scrap traders not only escaped restrictions but also gained access to the new interstate highway system. The outdoor-advertising industry focused on highways in order to reach the growing number of drivers on the nation's expanding network of roads.

After World War II, the context in which these industries functioned changed. The establishment of the federal highway system signaled both the government's intention to decentralize transportation during the Cold War and the cultural shift from an urban to a suburban population. As more Americans lived and drove in suburban communities, once-rural areas developed traffic problems. Aesthetic and environmental attitudes began to change as the first cases of sprawl appeared. The unprecedented abundance enjoyed by Americans during the 1950s and 1960s generated equally unprecedented waste. This phenomenon was so pervasive that when John A. Kouwenhoven titled his 1961 collection of essays on American life *The Beer Can by the Highway,* contemporary readers recognized the image as an apt reflection of his subject.[16] Human pressures on the environment became dramatically visible, especially in matters relating to buildings, transportation, and energy.[17] Construction sites—of homes, commercial establishments, shopping malls, recreational centers, and factories—were a hallmark of the postwar period, consuming undeveloped land on the urban peripheries as Americans in greater and greater numbers lived, shopped, and conducted business outside city centers.[18] With sprawl came innovations in transportation to accommodate the rising number of automobiles, trucks, and airplanes. These vehicles required ever-greater amounts of fuel to run, and petroleum consumption skyrocketed.[19]

"God's Own Junkyard": Opposition to Roadside Business in the 1960s

In 1951, an estimated 25,000 automobile graveyards were scattered across the nation.[20] By the mid-1960s, over eight million automobiles lay waiting to be scrapped.[21] The proliferation of scrapyards as the nation suburbanized made the industry more visible, and in periods when demand for scrap iron was low, as it was at the end of the 1950s, car bodies piled up. As Americans migrated to the suburbs, scrapyards once isolated from public view were gradually surrounded by new residences, strip malls, and fast-food establishments. At the same time, the billboard industry was thriving.[22]

In 1964, author/photographer Peter Blake, a German émigré, railed against the profusion of billboards and junkyards along the nation's roadsides in an illustrated screed titled *God's Own Junkyard: The Planned Deterioration of America's Landscape*. Invoking the arguments of the well-known urban planner Robert Moses, Blake made a case for highway beautification on the grounds that roadside eyesores are traffic hazards that can cause accidents by distracting drivers. Public safety was not Blake's only goal, however. He also advanced aesthetic reasons for beautification, associating it with the turn-of-the-century City Beautiful movement.[23] Though Blake felt that highway safety was the strongest argument against billboards, he recognized that the aesthetic argument would prove more popular.

Public pressure increased during the years prior to 1965, and the Highway Beautification Act was not the first attempt to regulate the American roadside. In 1958, Senator Richard L. Neuberger of Oregon, supported by other conservationists, proposed that the federal government ban billboards from any highway constructed with federal funds. This proposal met with vehement (and successful) opposition, including a rejoinder from Senator

Robert S. Kerr of Oklahoma, who proclaimed on the Senate floor: "[I]t will be a grave day in this country when we reach so high an [aesthetic] pinnacle that men are willing and able . . . to deprive citizens of their vested rights. . . . What kind of culture [is this?] . . . It is the kind of culture one can find in Russia. It is the kind of culture Hitler went down the drain trying to implement in Germany."[24]

Kerr's comments equated beautification with totalitarianism, implying that unbridled consumption was a vital feature of a free society. In the Cold War context, such characterizations could be intimidating to foreign-born activists such as Blake. Yet advocates for beautification had long continued to press for legislation to regulate billboards. Later in 1958, Congress had passed a law known as the Bonus Act that gave an extra half percent in funding to states that agreed to limit billboards. The incentives did nothing to slow the spread of billboards and junkyards, however, and opponents of outdoor advertising resorted to other tactics, including a mass letter-writing campaign by the Maryland chapter of the American Automobile Association to members of the state legislature there, and in New Mexico the vandalism, by "one or several 'persons unknown,'" of billboards along the highway running between Santa Fe and Los Alamos. Despite these efforts, there were "more billboards . . . more neon-lit hot dog stands, more garish bowling alleys, more glistening diners, more used-car lots, more junk piles" along America's roadsides in 1964 than there had been in 1958.[25]

Because Blake regarded roads as trespassers in the natural environment, he saw roadside commerce as a further violation of the relationship between nature and America's citizens. "The brutal destruction of our landscape is much more than a blow against beauty. Every artist, scientist, and philosopher in the history of mankind has pointed to the laws of nature as his greatest source of inspiration: without the presence of nature, undisturbed, there would have been no Leonardo, no Ruskin, no Nervi, no Frank Lloyd Wright. In destroying our landscape, we are destroying the future of civilization in America."[26]

Blake had an unrelentingly negative view not just of the junk and neon on the roadside but of the nation's highway system itself. Most highways "are hideous scars on the face of this nation—scars that cut across mountains and plains, across cities and suburbs, poisoning the landscape and townscape with festering sores along their edges."[27] According to Blake,

the highway system's primary function was to serve the capitalist impera-
tive: "Detroit needs more highways to sell more cars, and America needs
Detroit to sell more steel, aluminum, rubber and oil. If it ever became necessary to pave over the entire country to keep Detroit humming, Congress
would at least consider appropriating enough money to do just that."[28] He
concluded that the blight of advertising and junk, far from being the art
gallery of the public, was an assault on Americans' sensibilities: "In America today, no citizen (except for an occasional hermit) has a chance to see
anything but hideousness—all around him, day in and day out."[29]

Soon after Blake published *God's Own Junkyard*, Lady Bird Johnson
used her influence to promote political action on the issue, advocating a
series of beautification programs that included one to improve public
spaces in the District of Columbia. The president then instructed his staff
to craft legislation designed to control aesthetic blight. He established the
Task Force on Natural Beauty, naming Lady Bird as its direct liaison with
the White House and charging it to develop policy recommendations on
the subject. By late 1964, the first lady had publicly supported the removal
of billboards and junkyards from America's roadsides.

That same year the task force presented a set of recommendations to
the president, urging him to establish federal regulations for billboards
and junkyards. A few days after the 1964 election, Johnson called his Secretary of Commerce, Luther Hodges, and said, "Lady Bird wants to know
what you're going to do about all those junkyards along the highways."[30]
(Throughout the president's push for beautification, he repeatedly associated his wife's interest with the impetus for producing a law, exclaiming
that he wanted one passed "for Lady Bird" and telling his cabinet, "You
know I love that woman and she wants that Highway Beautification Act,"
and "By God, we're going to get it for her."[31]) In his State of the Union
address on January 4, 1965, Johnson told the nation that a "new and substantial effort must be made to landscape highways to provide places of
relaxation and recreation wherever our roads run."[32]

Like Peter Blake, the first lady viewed beautification as critical to the
health of the nation. "Getting on the subject of beautification is like pick-
ing up a tangled skein of wool," she wrote in her diary on January 27, 1965:
"All the threads are interwoven—recreation and pollution and mental
health, and the crime rate, and rapid transit, and highway beautification,
and the war on poverty, and parks—national, state and local. It is hard to

hitch the conversation into one straight line, because everything leads to something else."[33] Highway beautification was thus in the public interest, and she felt sure that it would have the public's support. "Public feeling is going to bring about regulation," she told reporters, "so you don't have a solid diet of billboards on all the roads."[34]

While his wife led the task force, President Johnson pressed Congress. In a February address, he explained the rationale for beautification to Congress this way: "[W]e need urgently to work towards the elimination or screening of unsightly, beauty-destroying junkyards and auto graveyards along our highways. To this end, I will . . . recommend necessary legislation to achieve effective control, including Federal assistance in appropriate cases where necessary."[35] The president asked Congress to enact a bill that would authorize the federal government to require states to ban the "beauty-destroying" billboards and junkyards within a thousand feet of the pavement, and to screen or remove existing yards. States failing to do so would lose their federal highway funding.[36]

Industry Responses

Proposal of the Highway Beautification Act represented a new chapter in the history of America's highways. The federal government was moving to regulate the location of scrapyards and advertising, and the case for beautification was being made by powerful public figures. President Johnson and the first lady joined the advocates of preserving aesthetic beauty, and the president's recommendations for a law would restrict the established business practices of the scrap and billboard trades. These industries responded with a vigorous lobbying effort. Moshe Oberman, editor of *Scrap Age,* voiced objections to the proposed bill: "What is a processor supposed to do when a new highway passes close to his yard and at a higher level? Put a roof on it? In some areas of the country it would be necessary to grow giant sequoias to screen it effectively with living growth. No fence could be as high as required."[37]

The scrap trade associations, in league with the Outdoor Advertising Association of America (OAAA, the major billboard trade association), launched a concerted lobbying campaign to minimize the potential effects of legislation on their businesses. The campaign employed themes that the associations had used for decades—that scrap dealers provided unique and vital services as agents of conservation, and that their activities, unsightly as they might be, were necessary to the nation's economic well-being.

In defending the work of scrap dealers, M. J. Mighdoll, executive vice president of the National Association of Secondary Material Industries, Inc. (NASMI, the new name of NAWMD after World War II), took exception to having his wares called "junk." Testifying before the Public Works Committee of the Senate in hearings on the Highway Beautification Bill, he stated: "[T]he time has come for our nation's leaders to clarify the terminology relating to an industry that this country found it could not do without during years of war and which it now finds essential to its industrial capacity during years of peace." He noted that the total annual revenues of metals, paper, textiles, rubber, and plastic scrap processors were $5 billion. This could hardly be considered "junk," he said, particularly to the many industries dependent on these secondary sources for their raw materials.[38]

Concerns about the industry's reputation led to a new push among industry leaders to stop using the word "junk" when describing their work. A front-page editorial in *Scrap Age* declared: "The scrap industry should realize now, more than ever before, that the word 'junk' has absolutely no place in it. The nearly 20 state legislatures which considered measures to control the unsightliness of 'junk' yards—and now the U.S. House of Representatives [is] considering a similar bill—made no distinction between 'junk' yards and 'scrap processors.'"[39]

The distinction between "junk" and "scrap" reflected a contrast that ISIS founder Benjamin Schwartz had made three decades earlier between modern scrap traders, who provided a service to the economy, and exalted junk collectors, who were little more than a nuisance.[40] In 1965 *Scrap Age* restated Schwartz's view that *scrap* connotes a utility while *junk* does not, and exhorted dealers to identify their businesses as scrap firms.

> To a great extent, this basic problem arose because of the short-sightedness of many scrap processors who either insist on keeping the word "junk" in their corporate names or persist in listing themselves under "Junk Dealers" in the Yellow Pages of the local telephone directories. There is no justification for continuing either of these practices. They are outdated; they are incorrect; and they are harmful. . . .

> We urge scrap processors to label themselves correctly. Refuse to take advertisements in any publication except under the heading of "Scrap Iron and Metals" or "Scrap Processing." The name of this game is "scrap." Anything else is a disservice to your firm, your industry, and your future.[41]

Anxiety about the industry's image was not limited to questions of terminology. William S. Story, executive vice president of ISIS, told his constituents that many would have to voluntarily change their behavior if they were to avoid federal regulation: "The general public is saying that old abandoned cars which litter the highways and the alleys should be removed; that spreading autowrecking yards be curbed; and that all other operations—including those not in the scrap industry—should take reasonable steps to improve their exteriors. . . . It boils down to this; if the industry does not want to be tagged with the junk label, then it must take the necessary steps where needed to improve its standing in the eyes of the public."[42] While the trade associations advised their members to upgrade the image of their industry, they lobbied Congress to limit the impact the beautification bill would have on their constituents. NASMI and ISIS asked Congress to provide for payment of compensation to scrap processors who were required to screen their yards or to relocate. ISIS also successfully lobbied Congress to stipulate that scrap-processing yards in industrial areas that could not be effectively screened would not be obliged to relocate.[43]

Republican opposition to the bill reiterated the industries' position and also voiced concern that it would divert funds from road construction to beautification, thus "crippling the [highway] system," in the words of Florida Representative William C. Cramer.[44] Opponents also focused on the first lady's role in developing the legislation. In a move meant to criticize her influence on the bill, Representative Robert Dole of Kansas suggested replacing the title "Secretary of Commerce" in the proposal with the name "Ladybird Johnson." Dole's action not only echoed his subsequent ones in derailing the health-care reform proposed in 1993 by the Clinton administration; it also underscored the gendered dimensions of beautification, with women seen as homemakers infringing on the expertise of engineers, businessmen, and elected politicians. Beautification, according to this view, was the first lady's folly, at once totalitarian and frivolous.[45]

Marketers of outdoor advertising complained that the law would not only hurt small businesses reliant on billboard advertising but would also establish the federal government as the arbiter of standards of taste in public art.[46] The OAAA's lobbying strategy was not to kill the proposed legislation but rather to modify it to its members' advantage, supporting provisions that would affect only 1 percent of the total number of billboards managed by large firms. Recognizing that support of a highway-beautification law might improve the outdoor advertising industry's public image, the OAAA lobbied for a bill that ultimately did little to stem the spread of billboards. Once the bill met the trade association's requirements, the OAAA embraced it, stating that "outdoor advertising, will, in the future, relate to the environment of the community, and we will support legislation and engage in voluntary efforts to meet these ends."[47] As the new law did little to restrict the large outdoor-advertising companies, the Highway Beautification Act effectively led to consolidation of the industry.

The trade associations' efforts persuaded their allies in Congress to amend the bill in favor of the outdoor-advertising industry, adding a provision that required "just compensation" for advertising marketers whose billboards were removed, and eliminating proposed penalties for noncompliance. After debate throughout the summer and early fall of 1965, Johnson finally signed the Highway Beautification Act on October 22, 1965, making the following observation: "This bill does not represent everything that we wanted. It does not represent what we need. It does not represent what the national interest requires. But it is a first step, and there will be other steps. For though we must crawl before we walk, we are going to walk."[48]

Effects of the Highway Beautification Act

In the opinion of most historians, the Act did little to limit the spread of billboards along the highways. Efforts made in the late 1960s to strengthen the act proved futile, and environmental groups subsequently recognized it as protecting the very business interests it was meant to regulate. Despite the Highway Beautification Act, the billboard industry flourished in the 1970s. Johnson aide Joseph Califano regarded the act as one of the president's rare legislative gaffes, one in which Johnson underestimated congressional opposition to the bill, a miscalculation that resulted in what Califano and others considered a weak law.[49]

The Highway Beautification Act is significant in the history of the American environmental movement for at least two reasons. While its impact on billboards was minimal, the law did affect the many junkyards lining the highways. The Department of Transportation estimated that by 1979 over thirty-three hundred illegal junkyards had been relocated or screened from view.[50] The Act also represented the first federal legislation to manage the aesthetic aspect of U.S. roadways. Prior to 1965, federal laws affecting the scrap industry related to import and export issues, price controls, and transportation, while aesthetics were regulated at the municipal level. President Johnson targeted junkyards as eyesores, and the scrap industry responded with a lobbying campaign based in part on the strategy it had successfully employed to fight economic regulations.[51]

New environmental regulations complicated the operations as well as the status of the scrap industry. Under the provisions of the Resource Conservation and Recovery Act, manufacturers were not held legally accountable for the potentially hazardous wastes created by their products. Materials in scrapyards, however, were judged to be at the end of a product's life and were therefore designated waste, even if they were to be reused in industrial production. Thus, the liability for improper handling of hazardous wastes fell on scrap processors, not the original manufacturers, and included fines, lawsuits, and criminal penalties.[52] Companies now had to assess how their processing and storage methods affected the land, air, and water, as well as their employees. Trade associations worked with the Environmental Protection Agency to determine ways to recycle salvageable materials while complying with federal regulations. Between 1965 and the end of the twentieth century, the Highway Beautification Act transformed the business practices of the scrap and salvage industries along with the view of public spaces in the United States.

Conclusion

The conflicting visions of the American highway reflect a debate over what constitutes a landscape. Whereas many define it as being free of human effects (and advocates for beautification such as Blake fall into this category), a school of thought founded by John Brinckerhoff Jackson and articulated in a series of books by John A. Jakle and Keith A. Sculle has expanded the definition of landscape to include even commercial development. Such features as gas stations, restaurants, and motels can be seen as aesthetically pleasing even if they are not natural, a "vernacular landscape" rather than a vulgar blight upon nature.[53] Over time these businesses have learned to package places as products. According to Jakle and Sculle, entrepreneurs have successfully commercialized the roadside by making their businesses, trademarks, logos, and color schemes familiar parts of the landscape, thereby minimizing drivers' anxieties.[54]

This packaging, designed to increase commercial activity and serve travelers, refutes Peter Blake's assertion that roadside development represents a violent assault on the driver and may also explain why the beautification movement was not more successful. Billboards were artistic statements and helpful guides for the traveler and could even enhance the highway experience. Junkyards, on the other hand, represented chaos and waste— or, as Mary Douglas put it when defining dirt, "matter out of place."[55] The yard owner had a far more difficult case to make for aesthetic value than did the billboard marketer. Automobile graveyards could provide consumers with replacement parts for their vehicles, and one could argue that junkyards represented an early stage of recycling that benefitted the consumptive society by keeping materials out of dumps and landfills; but such arguments are economic, not aesthetic. Piles of jagged, rusting metal could not easily be packaged as part of an ordered landscape. The screening and relocation of thousands of scrapyards can thus be seen as an ordering of the landscape that blended natural beauty with a homogenized commercialization of the roadside.

Economic vitality was a central tenet of American road design, but the desire to expand commerce did not, in and of itself, distinguish U.S. highways from those of other industrialized nations. Where the American highway was unusual was in the degree to which the roadside participated in economic development. Businesses catering expressly to the driver grew substantially during the period in which beautification was debated. Motels, gas stations, and fast-food restaurants enjoyed rising popularity in the 1960s. The national character of America's highways involved the autonomy of drivers, national security, and the development of commerce by means of accessible interstate roads.

The Highway Beautification Act of 1965 thus engaged two competing visions of America's highways and of American citizens as consumers of those highways. Advertising and scrap firms regarded highways as sites of economic activity. Members of the nascent environmental movement saw highways as conduits between the American people and the country's natural beauty. The tensions between these visions shaped the Act, and as the two factions lobbied Congress, the scrap and advertising industries sought to present themselves in terms that were friendlier—or at least less threatening—to the environment. Outdoor advertisers claimed to place signs in ways that improved scenic views and donated space on billboards for public art, while scrapyards redefined themselves as recycling centers.

The new culture of environmentalism also brought additional political measures at the federal level aimed at preserving the nation's natural resources. A series of regulations regarding solid waste and hazardous materials were enacted between 1965 and 1980, and in the 1980s many scrapyards were designated Superfund sites and closed. For the scrap industry the fight over beautification inaugurated a series of conflicts with the government over environmental accountability. More than four decades after the first federal legislation to curb commercial activities along the highways, Americans are still being exposed to the "hideous" aesthetics Peter Blake railed against in 1964. The battle over beautification exposed tensions between environmental and economic uses of public space, tensions that were resolved in favor of commercial activities as long as they did not include waste storage. Beautification was not so much a failure of environmentalists as an affirmation of an aesthetic sensibility that demanded coherent packaging of natural and built aspects of the national landscape.

SIX

A Rough Modernization

Landscapes and Highways in
Twentieth-Century Italy

Massimo Moraglio

[T]he giant embankment of the roadbed floods and fills the valleys with its enormous mass of earth, brutally altering the appearance of the localities. Elsewhere, the road excavates and destroys hills, slicing into and removing parts of mountains, slashing away and cutting down everything in its inexorable march forward. It then takes wing and soars upward on viaducts built on tall concrete pillars, ugly and clumsy to look at, striding across the valleys. Everything points to a technical, obtuse, engineering-oriented approach that has no regard for any aspects and needs other than the techniques of road-building and cost analysis. It is quite clear that the layout was made in a rigid, abstract manner without the slightest consideration being given to the terrain and formal nature of the areas it traverses, quite apart from the visual impact that comes from the necessary inclusion of the road in the hilly and mountainous landscapes through which it passes. . . .

[It is no better elsewhere, because] the real characteristic [of highways in the plains] is their extraordinary and almost total monotony. The same banal, drab, and insignificant picture can be seen upon entering the highway and then all the way along it, the same in every point.[1]

In the January 1961 issue of *Comunità*, Renato Bonelli used these harsh words to describe the initial stretches of the Autostrada del Sole, the so-called sunshine highway between Milan and Naples. The article, which reflects a particular intellectual environment of liberal-democratic inspiration, gave a decidedly unfavorable assessment of the new roadway and was highly critical of the direction taken by economic development in Italy. Behind the tirade against the nation's highways lay a criticism not so much of the process of industrialization—which most Italians favored—as of its being out of balance with the country's real needs.[2] The verdict was negative on all fronts, but it had a basis in fact and highlighted the limitations of Italian road and highway engineering. Indeed, except in a few rare cases, scant attention was paid to the integration of roads into their environment, and highways least of all. In order to understand better both the reasons for this approach and the motives behind it, we must look at the history of the Italian road system and analyze why a country that had long remained agricultural, and that would experience a period of true industrial growth only after World War II, had built its first highway back in 1922.[3]

What makes careful analysis essential is the patent contradiction between the comparative backwardness of the country[4] and the extensive highway-construction programs that were planned and implemented. As we shall see, this subject is closely linked to that of the landscape, for the economic, cultural, and technical considerations that shaped the first highway projects also influenced the choice of routes, their spatial layout, and their integration into the landscape.

The Politics of Roads in Nineteenth-Century Italy

Italy is divided from the rest of Europe by the Alps and traversed from north to south by the Apennine mountain chain. In the nineteenth-century, its transportation system had to contend not only with geographical obstacles but also with political fragmentation into a number of different states. Italy's exclusion from the most active economic circuits in Europe had been both a cause and a consequence of national decline during the eighteenth century.[5] Once national unity was achieved in 1861, the road system's lack of infrastructure as well as its lack of resources to improve the state of things became more apparent. The issue of linking localities was seen as one of the core aspects of nation-building, but attempts were made to solve the problems of transport by an active and almost paroxysmal railroad-construction policy, part of the train mania that characterized the second half of the nineteenth century.[6] The question of ordinary road links thus became a secondary issue despite the fact that Italy's road system was rudimentary compared to those in countries such as England, Belgium, and France.

Italy at that time had a limited number of engineers and few good engineering schools and administrative organizations able to deal with the problems of road construction. There was also an unfortunate division of responsibilities for the road system among various public offices. The state was committed to laying railway tracks and increasingly tended to reduce its operations and expenses in the road sector.[7] This policy did not mean, however, that other public offices—provincial and municipal local administrations in particular—had greater independence in the management and construction of roads. To grossly oversimplify, whereas the French system relied on centralized technical organizations (the Corps des Ponts et Chaussées, for example, which from the eighteenth century had direct control over forty thousand kilometers of national roads and also took action on smaller roads), and the English system delegated just about everything to various local authorities, Italy's policy promoted neither centralization nor delegation.

It was a hybrid situation that offered no practical advantages, since the work of the local administrations was hampered by a lack of funds and by interference from the central powers, while the state had no intention whatsoever of intervening with the energy that would have been required to produce any real effect. This state of affairs, which widened the gap between Italy and other European countries and dragged on for years, deprived the country of a public service that would ensure unified operations and capable engineers with expertise in the latest road-planning techniques. The introduction of the automobile in the early twentieth century only made matters worse. The challenge of modernizing road networks involved all of Europe and America. In October 1908 the First International Road Congress was held in Paris. The principal aim of this meeting was to coordinate the renewal of unpaved roads; while addressing this topic, however, participants were also laying the groundwork for the extraordinary process of renovating carriage roads that took place during the 1910s and '20s.

In Italy this process occurred very slowly, at least until World War I, which proved to be a turning point. The massive use of trucks for military purposes had demonstrated the value of road transport even in backward Italy. Once peace was made, the use of motor vehicles for commercial purposes and the development of motor-car tourism, domestic and from abroad, made the issue of critical importance for the national economy. In 1914 the total number of cars, trucks, and buses on Italian roads was about 24,000 (1 for every 1,600 inhabitants); by 1920 it had reached 49,500 (1 for every 760 inhabitants); and in 1925 it stood at 117,500 (1 for every 335 inhabitants).[8]

However, the cumulative delays of the past weighed heavily on the present. Discussion focused on finding a new, more effective strategy for publicly administering the roadways, with debate revolving around which of the various governmental authorities—state, provincial, or municipal—should be responsible for overseeing the system's transformation to one that would accommodate automobiles. So while in other countries work was underway to surface all the roads with asphalt, almost nothing was done in Italy, even though the number of vehicles continued to rise and traffic problems continued to increase.[9] The provincial governments, whose resources were quite limited, made the first experiments with tarring and asphalting the roads, but an independent state authority for roads—the Azienda autonoma statale per la strada—was established only in 1928. A program for regulating and improving transport on the main roads was finally initiated in the early 1930s, though it would not be completed until after World War II.[10]

Public Works and Private Enterprise

It is essential to know something about the conditions of the road network during the earliest days of motoring in Italy if one is to have a clear understanding of the country's first highway projects. We have already seen that the system was seriously deficient: except in the largest cities, roads were usually incapable of coping with the automobile traffic of the time, which was growing rapidly even if the pace of growth did not compare to that in other countries.[11] Led by motor-car drivers themselves, the industries involved in the development of motoring all demanded navigable roads. At the beginning of the 1920s, contemporary observers were amazed and concerned by the fact that some highways leading to cities were always packed with vehicles and that progress on Italian roads in general was slow and difficult.[12] The need for faster, broader, and more convenient roadways, from which horse-drawn carriages and carts would be banned, became increasingly urgent. In other words, the nation was enduring a period of infrastructural inefficiency caused by carriage roads that were inadequate for the new phase of industrial growth.

Public institutions and centers of power, engaged in an authoritarian and dictatorial modification of the Italian political system, were suffering from operational gridlock right at that critical phase. This impasse worsened as time went on, providing ample opportunities for those interested in improving the traffic situation to submit proposals that were sometimes extremely innovative if not always perfectly scrupulous.

Among these figures was the Milanese entrepreneur and engineer Piero Puricelli. The owner of a large road-construction company as well as of several quarries, Puricelli was also a supporter of the new Fascist regime, of which he was presumably one of the first financial backers.[13] He had close links to the Italian Touring Club, was involved in the management of Milan's influential trade-fair association, and later became a senator.[14] Recognizing that the road sector was entering an epoch-making period, Puricelli realized that the new roadways offered enormous benefits, in terms of both money and prestige, to those skillful enough to make the right moves at the right time.

A first, tentative scheme for renovating the Italian road system was put forward by the Touring Club, which proposed improving transportation between Milan and Venice by the construction of an *autostrada*—a road reserved for motor vehicles only and subject to a toll.[15] When this suggestion fell through in April 1922, Puricelli again proposed building an autostrada, but this time between Milan and the lakes to the north—in other words, a shorter, more modest route than the link to Venice would have been yet one likely to ensure a consumer base, since the road would lead to the traditional vacation areas of the Milanese middle classes.[16]

Puricelli took the railway system as his model for both administration and management. Like the railways, highways were intended to supplement the ordinary road network. Just as it was necessary to buy a ticket for the train, transit on the highway was to be contingent on the payment of a toll that corresponded to the distance traversed. The revenue would cover construction and running costs.[17]

Despite the approximation of the economic estimates and the highly original, if somewhat risky, funding and organizational plans, Puricelli's highway project soon became operational. With surprising alacrity, just a few weeks after the Fascist dictatorship came into being, Mussolini's government concluded an agreement in December 1922 with a private company incorporated by Puricelli, granting it the right to build and manage the highway links between Milan and the sub-Alpine lakes. The company's revenue would be guaranteed by the tolls received, while the state would guarantee the bonds issued and provide an annual, reimbursable subsidy.

Construction of the highway between Milan and the lakes, covering a total length of eighty-four kilometers, soon started up, and was completed between 1924 and 1925. When the highway was opened to traffic, its concrete paving was a relative novelty for the province of Milan, where the local administration was particularly attentive to the road system. In 1926, the combined length of paved roadways was still no greater than two to three hundred kilometers, most of which were in the north.[18] Puricelli's autostrada was thus something entirely new: it was almost incredible to be able to drive on a road without encountering potholes, jolting bumps, or horse-drawn carts that slowed traffic to a crawl.[19]

Capitalizing on this first success, Puricelli submitted new proposals for building highways, centered mainly around Milan (the city with the highest per capita income in the country and the greatest proportion of motor cars) and along the routes opened up by the railways. In just under a decade, several highways were built, mainly in the north of Italy, all of which were toll roads run by private companies.[20] The absence of any overarching plan that could channel the energies of the factions involved in this sector meant that individual initiatives like Puricelli's had a free hand. Despite their incoherence and confusion, many contemporary highway proposals showed a clear understanding of the problems of motoring traffic. Most of Puricelli's peers were convinced that an entirely new road system would have to be built, one that would replace rather than adapt existing roads, lengthy sections of which were inadequate with respect to banding radius, slopes, and paving. More or less consciously, the plans for this new system followed the model of the nineteenth-century railway.

But apart from several cases of unethical business speculation, which did indeed occur, the chief interest of those designing the highways was not to profit from the companies set up to run them; and in fact almost all of these companies declared bankruptcy.[21] On the contrary, many factions were interested in improving road conditions in Italy in order to foster the growth of industries in which they were working and which constituted their core business. For Puricelli, highway construction was a way to establish dominance in the automotive industries. For Fiat (the largest and ultimately the only Italian car manufacturer), highways were an indispensable means for opening up the stagnant domestic auto market.[22] The same can be said of rubber and cement manufacturers, to say nothing of those involved in the extraction and refining of hydrocarbons, who would benefit from the sale both of fuel and of bitumen and tar. But this economic sector also included associations of hoteliers (then, as now, tourism was one of Italy's most important industries), of motorists, and so on. Each of these groups had its own reasons for wanting better roads and, as in the case of the construction industry, aimed to obtain commissions and make handsome profits.

From the story up to this point, it is clear that, in contrast to those in other countries, the highways in Italy developed not according to a program drawn up by public authorities but rather as a result of actions taken by private groups and without any reference to an established public plan. Nor was the state able to intervene in order to direct resources, whether public or private, in the field of transportation. These circumstances influenced the type and quality of highway construction, which lacked any standard design or engineering guidelines. Each licensed company was free to organize the highway project as it saw fit, while state control was limited to the opinion of the Ministry of Public Works.[23]

A paradoxical situation had thus arisen. Between the wars, average road conditions in Italy were terrible, but rather than taking decisive steps to improve the system, the government delegated responsibility for road construction to the business sector. This meant that private companies received generous public funds to build highways, but these were then subject to tolls and managed along the lines of profit-making businesses. If we look at the low levels of motorization in the 1920s and '30s, we can see that the early success of highways in Italy was due not to a massive proliferation of motorcars but rather to their limited numbers. In other words, while car and truck diffusion did not have sufficient critical mass to trigger a decisive and widespread improvement in road conditions, it was sufficient to encourage initiatives from those parties with direct financial interests in the development of motoring.[24] In 1939, Italy had embarked on neither the mammoth projects drawn up by Puricelli's engineers nor those of the national road authority, yet it still had a network of about five hundred kilometers.[25]

Regardless of its successful progress and its congenital limits, the making of a highway network in the prewar period had two important effects. First, it determined the lines along which the highway system would evolve after World War II: the plans approved by the Italian parliament in 1955 and 1961 drew on subjects and suggestions originally made in the 1920s.[26] After all, Italian highways outlived Piero Puricelli, their much-celebrated, self-aggrandizing "inventor," perpetuating the myth of backward Italian society while supporting with their very existence the start of new development in the postwar period.

In the second place, Italian highways—particularly the first one, from Milan to the lakes—aroused an extraordinary amount of interest in the rest of Europe. Taken alone, no single feature of Puricelli's highway was really new—neither the payment of a toll nor the ban on horse-drawn carts nor the elimination of crossings. But Puricelli's innovation was to join these three elements on a grand scale, as he did with the eighty-four-kilometer highway between Milan and the lakes. Moreover, his genius was to do so at such an early time with respect to Italian and European motoring, which would reach a mass level only in the 1950s and '60s.

The remarkable success of the Italian highway model may be partly attributable to Puricelli's gift for publicity and self-promotion, since he was able to propagandize his initiative all over the Continent: from Germany to Finland and beyond, the idea of autostrade met with great fanfare.[27] It is hardly surprising that the Fascists, largely for propagandistic reasons, had always strongly supported highway construction. Mussolini's dictatorship helped Puricelli to "invent" the myth of Italian leadership in the development of highways, even if the propagandistic commitment was ultimately limited by two factors. First of all, the national road network remained small and anemic, especially in comparison to Hitler's during the 1930s,[28] because more significant growth would have strained Italy's exiguous national resources. In the second place, the role of the government was minor relative to that played by the lobbies, which always held the initiative in their hands. Moreover, the Fascist dictatorship, because of its alliances with wide-ranging industrial interests, had no intention of assuming responsibility for the building of highways.

Highways in the Postwar Period

This dynamic persisted even after World War II ended, creating a period of substantial continuity in the management, design, and even the architects of highways; but in the 1950s and '60s Italy embarked on the construction of a massive highway network based on plans drawn up decades earlier. Due to the considerable destruction it had suffered, Italy found itself in the immediate postwar period with a railroad system that was largely unusable. In 1949, for the first time, the volume of commercial and passenger road traffic exceeded that on rail lines, thanks in part to the large number of trucks abandoned in Italy by the Anglo-American forces at the end of the war.[29] From then on, national transport policies shifted decisively toward modernizing the road system and highways in particular, to the detriment of other forms of transport.[30]

The main executor of this action was the Istituto di Ricostruzione Industriale (IRI), the public agency set up in 1933 to tackle the economic crisis of the early thirties. The IRI, which also controlled the national iron and steel industries; Fiat; Agip, Italy's sole petroleum company and another public concern; Pirelli, the country's leading rubber manufacturer; and a group of cement manufacturers constituted an extremely powerful alliance for highway construction. All benefitted, in one form or another, from the new national policy. After authorizing some sporadic construction work in the late 1940s and early '50s, aimed at combating unemployment, the Italian parliament approved a program in 1955 to coordinate construction, establishing at the same time a set of priorities to be followed. The management model remained that of licensing to private companies— first of all to the IRI through its Autostrade company—and thus of tolls, despite a generous state subsidy.[31] This system worked extremely well: the total number of kilometers in the Italian highway network rose from almost five hundred in 1939 to fifteen hundred in 1961 (when a second highway plan was approved), to forty-three hundred in 1971, and to fifty-nine hundred in 1980.[32] As this gigantic construction program was getting underway, a comparable process of mass motorization was also occurring, particularly in the period from 1958 to 1973.

There was obviously close cooperation between the centers of political and economic power, but such an ambitious highway program should also be interpreted in light of other factors. We should recall that Italy went through its real industrial revolution during the 1950s and '60s, experiencing extraordinary annual growth rates. Highway construction, considered fundamental to the economic boom, was given priority over other sectors of infrastructure. The development of the roads was linked to the output of the auto industry, which introduced a country with an ancestral hunger for material goods to modern ideas of consumption and travel. More than any other object, the car could represent this for everyone, in an almost totemic manner.[33]

The escape from poverty took place in the name of individual mobility, of drastically modified isochrones, and of the reduced time and geographical distance offered by these new roads. Rather than just assisting communication, highways created it.[34] The fact is that the desire to possess a car and travel was not "the result of a plot hatched by a band of capitalists" but symbolized "the pursuit of widely sought-after cultural models and lifestyles."[35]

The Landscape Issue and Environmental Impact

This elaborate process, only the basic elements of which have been discussed here, did not lead to carefully devised landscape policies, because there were no coordination policies and because roads were considered a feature of modernization to which all environmental factors had to be adapted. Overlooking the patient work of construction by nature and by man, which had created fascinating and complex landscapes, Italian engineers regarded the land as no more than a backdrop for the powerful actions of man, devoid of value except as an arena in which modern road communications were to play an important role.

The eighteenth- and nineteenth-century metaphor of the road as a bringer of progress to the backward, ignorant countryside retained all its symbolic potency. The wealth and technological resources of the twentieth century made it possible for roads to have a truly disruptive effect in previously isolated areas. The cacophonous and destructive impact of highways on the landscape of the Apennine valleys, described so masterfully by Renato Bonelli in the article quoted above, was not considered as damaging to the environment but rather as an indication of significant development and progress away from the isolation and poverty of the past. So it is not surprising that in the 1960s and '70s the highway companies' press agencies chose to publish mostly bird's-eye views of viaducts and bridges being built, reifications of the dynamics of the control and subjugation of nature.[36]

Many architects and journalists remarked in harsh terms on builders' failure to integrate these structures more carefully into their environments. Until well into the 1980s, the subject of the landscape was almost never explicitly identified as among the issues to be grappled with when designing and building highways. The typical approach appears to have aimed at continuity with engineering practices of the past—basically, laying down railway lines—without any understanding that the shift to a new means of transport called for a new approach, or any awareness of how much attention was paid to landscape by highway designers in other countries.[37]

The logic behind these planning processes was simple and, from some points of view, obvious. A generation of engineers and architects who had grown up under the influence of the legendary railroads, in a country with neither effective road-planning mechanisms nor landscape-architecture schools, applied to highway projects the same construction theories that had worked in the railroad era. It should be remembered that railroad techniques were already in use and had achieved success: they were considered equally valid and serviceable for building highways, without requiring any serious reconsideration of the model that had given rise to them. For example, ignoring the characteristics of the automobile, one of the objectives of highway planning in Italy right up to the 1970s was to make the longest possible straights; and where there had to be a change of direction, rather than adopting clothoid curves, designers obstinately maintained a planimetric course that followed the arc of a circle—an approach with a highly negative environmental impact and a bad effect on drivers, yet one that in 1946 had been expressly endorsed by the Ministry of Public Works.[38]

Through the national road authority, the ministry prescribed guidelines for highway projects, indicating them quite clearly under the title "Strada" in the *Enciclopedia Italiana*. So that roads might

> achieve economy of consumption, ease of traffic and safety from any danger[,] . . . the ideal objective should be to avoid series of bends or rises and falls. The layout should aim to obtain a *recti-linear* course, excepting in such cases where obstacles might prevent adequate technical means to go above or below them in a suitable manner. . . . When curved connections cannot be avoided, they shall be *preceded and followed by a rectilinear stretch* and shall have the widest radius possible, no less than 100 meters in the plains or in the hills, except in the case of hairpin turns.[39]

This certainly does not mean that the engineering was slovenly or lacking in expertise. Italy had some highly skilled road designers, but in trying to reconcile the precepts of the past with their own age's desire for modernity, they overlooked the environmental aspect of roads in order to concentrate on the efficiency of the route. The idea that roads and highways should follow the shortest and most economic route was paramount: "[I]n Italy, the 'philosophy' of the projects was to draw the straightest possible line between two points. . . . The Padua-Venice highway is a fine example of this, for the stretch up to Mestre consists of a 22-kilometer straightaway."[40]

The subject of the landscape in Italy during the twentieth century is obviously too vast and complex to be covered in a few paragraphs, especially because a substantial body of scholarly literature on the topic does not yet exist. The problem of integrating an infrastructural artifact into the environment is linked to the wider issue of the relationship between tradition and modernization, which in every country reflects a process of economic development. Despite the risk of oversimplifying, it seems worth pointing out that because Italy was a latecomer in terms of industrialization, the modernizing process was taking place in a underdeveloped nation, even if its elites were aware of its standing in relation to countries on the other side of the Alps. The eagerness to bridge, and bridge quickly, the gap that separated Italy from the rest of Europe made the question of the landscape—a landscape built with patience by past generations—of secondary importance. So, in spite of a rich tradition of landscape architecture, modernization occurred without any thought for the preservation of the landscape and the environment—all in the name of a progress to be achieved as quickly as possible. It may seem paradoxical that the nation. that since the eighteenth century had been the main destination of European bourgeoisie's Grand Tour, famous for its landscape's variety and beauty, began to discount completely—or almost completely—its most salient feature, its countryside. And yet, beyond the antiquities, the monuments, the masterworks, and specific sites of indisputable importance (Venice, Rome, Florence), the country was subjected to an intense process by means of which modernity eclipsed tradition. The result was the dissipation of an extraordinary natural and human heritage. As already noted, this shift occurred during the period between national unity and Fascism in the name of progress, considered the guiding principle in developing the nation's infrastructures: in other words, modernization superseded every other consideration. Things were no better under the dictatorship, because even if references to Italy's past were numerous, they were associated only with a very remote antiquity, that of the Roman Empire. For propagandistic reasons, many archaeological sites and ruins of the classical period were excavated, but they were relics of a past too distant to have any link with the present, any real connection with everyday life. Finally, in the post–World War II era, economic prosperity and mass consumption meant that environmental issues worried only a small minority, whose concerns went entirely unheeded by the rest of the nation.

Beyond the interest groups and the political factions, to Italian society as a whole the land appeared able to assimilate any type of building or use (fig. 6.1). The designers and the commissioners, the users and the inhabitants of the areas in question were not even thinking about possible aesthetic links between artifact and landscape. At that time the countryside was no more than a "transparent" aspect of the project, in so far as it was simply ignored both by the designers and by the citizens.

Attention was focused exclusively on the individual artifact, which was referred to as the *opera d'arte*—the "work of art"—a term carried over from the nineteenth century. Bridges, viaducts, and tunnels were considered unique works, artistic creations with a beauty of their own, by no means reproducible, and representing a complete architectural element in themselves. Professional and commemorative publications provided all of the

6.1. A section of the Messina-Palermo motorway as it descends to the harbor in Messina, Sicily. Reproduced by permission from *Le autostrade della seconda generazione,* ed. S.p.A. per l'Autostrada Serravalle-Milano-Ponte Chiasso (1990).

technical specifications, measurements, and construction costs of the most challenging works—those that were the greatest and most daring from an engineering viewpoint.[41] Everything was designed to exalt the incisiveness (and, paradoxically, when one considers the results, the aesthetic capacity) of the human hand and its dominion over the land—crossing rivers, boring through mountains, leaping over valleys to diminish distances and facilitate communication. The terrible effect on the landscape was regarded not as an aesthetic disaster for both the land and the road but rather as a demonstration of man's technocratic power over nature, of humans' ability to subdue the environment, and of our creative genius. This notion has influenced Western society throughout history, but in late-twentieth-century Italy, a country desperate for progress and modernity, it appears to have been accepted without question.

Yet it is unfair to condemn designers' neglect of landscape during this period, or to interpret it as a sign of national backwardness, or even to point a finger at self-serving alliances between politics and business. Instead, we should examine the basic principles that guided engineers in their planning. The numerical and functional limitations of the architectural studies, combined with the need to act quickly in order to keep pace with the economic boom, meant that there was no overall coordinated plan for these public works and that private construction companies were left to bear the costs and meet the engineering challenges of building bridges, tunnels, and viaducts throughout the nation. On the Autostrada del Sole, the work was divided into lots and

> carried out on a roadbed . . . without really knowing how the junctions, crossings, and exits would be made. The [state-drafted] convention was vague about almost all aspects, including the speed . . . that the vehicles would be able to maintain on the new section of road. . . . each licensee company had to make its own designs for the "works of art" and perform all the relative calculations before constructing them. Since no company could obtain more than one lot, twenty-seven different architects worked on the Apennine stretch. This is why the bridges and viaducts all appear different today, in iron, pre-stressed concrete, or arched.[42]

In other words, the design of a highway was based on a standard layout that was reduced to a simple sketch, leaving individual companies free to work as they saw fit, making any necessary additions and changes to the template they had received. One of the criteria that naturally determined their choices was the need to spend as little money as possible, to the detriment of aesthetic considerations—and of the landscape. Since construction work was based on this system of undefined contracts and designs were created as work progressed, the graceless results were entirely predictable.

Coda

There was no single authority establishing standards for and distributing information about the function and style of Italian roadworks, whether in relation to the engineering of an individual bridge or to the design of the road as a whole. Landscape architects—in other countries key figures in the process of designing roads and harmonizing them with their environment—did not exist in Italy. When a state road agency finally was established, no landscape architect was appointed to its staff, while laws meant to safeguard the environment either failed to effectively limit the works carried out in protected areas or were simply disregarded.

Multiple factors led to engineering that largely ignored the issue of integration with the landscape. The problem went beyond inattention or lack of interest, however. The landscape was not considered a design issue, and the true importance of environmental issues was simply not grasped. But fundamental policies were also influenced by Italy's limited economic resources compared with those of other countries. What point could there be in sculpting highways and seamlessly integrating them into the landscape if doing so would merely increase traveling time and fuel consumption, even if only by a little? Highway users—and it should not be forgotten that drivers paid a toll calculated according to the distance they covered—would not have benefitted; on the contrary, it would have damaged their interests. This was the reasoning of the designers and the boards of directors of the highway companies, and officials at the Ministry of Public Works, charged with approving the projects submitted to them, shared that reasoning.[43] Why design beautiful, expensive highways, no matter how thoughtfully planned, when it was so difficult to raise the funds needed to build simple, functional highways? Why slow down heavy trucks that were slow enough already? The number of vehicles on the roads before the 1960s was very small, and if the highways were to be used, then their advantages had to be maximized and drivers given what they wanted: direct, level routes that would conserve fuel.

Nor did drivers have the slightest interest in the landscape. Cars were strictly a means for getting from one place to another, and except for those features that qualified as picturesque or scenic in the nineteenth-century sense of those words, the landscape on either side of the highway possessed no inherent value. The countryside was considered not as an organic whole but rather as a juxtaposition of different elements: some "beautiful," others not. As noted earlier, the motoring and tourist associations, led by the powerful Touring Club Italiano, were advocating a second wave of road construction, without facing the larger question of how new highways and the infrastructure necessary to support them would change the territory they crossed.

Some cultural, intellectual, and technical groups expressed grave doubts about this approach and pointed specifically to the American and German systems as models to be followed. Environmental-protection associations, such as Italia Nostra, as well as some cultural organizations, including the journal *Comunità,* voiced concern but failed to achieve any significant results. Their proposals had limited circulation; the tone of their criticisms was often elitist; and their opinions on the social changes occurring in Italy, including the process of democratization and the rise of mass consumption, could hardly have been more cynical.

The defeat of any alternative was due not so much to the competing interests involved with the highway projects as to the widespread indifference toward the value of the landscape. Presumably these interests were also present in the United States, Germany, and the United Kingdom, where attitudes toward the landscape were quite different. In other words, the concept of environmentally sound land use—which in a broader sense had influenced the entire development of building and urban planning in Italy— became in the twentieth century a minority view, displaced by a distorted idea of modernity and by the immense political and social influence wielded by the construction and automotive industries. To understand how such a major change in the way Italians conceptualized landscape could occur so quickly will require further analysis, and I hope that this essay offers a starting point for future studies of this important cultural shift.

SEVEN

Building and Rebuilding the Landscape

of the Autobahn, 1930–70

Thomas Zeller

Visitors to Germany have always been and remain even today attracted, repelled, or fascinated by that country's highway network, the autobahn. While some American motorists enjoy the absence of a speed limit so much that they would like to emulate it on their own roads, it is safe to assume that just as many foreign drivers are terrified by solidly built German cars whizzing by at 120 miles or more per hour.[1] The German word *autobahn*, like *kindergarten, blitzkrieg*, and *angst*, has entered the English language; and since 1974 it has been associated with the highly aestheticized image popularized by the German electronic band Kraftwerk of an efficient transportation machine. The lyrics of Kraftwerk's international hit "Autobahn," along with the song's hypnotic rhythm, evoke the endless forward motion of a road trip in the direction of a "wide valley" touched by the sun's rays. The scenery includes the road—"The highway is a grey ribbon / White bands, green edge" (fig. 7.1)—and the car radio plays a song about the autobahn itself, thus marking the road trip as a self-reflexive encounter between technology and nature.[2] For regular users of the autobahn, such as the Germans themselves, the most quotidian emotion these days appears to be anxiety over the prospect of a traffic jam.[3]

Whatever their origin, many contemporary images of the autobahn express the often tacit assumption that these roads belong to a rational sphere

7.1. Emil Schult's design for the cover of the 1974 Kraftwerk album *Autobahn*. Reproduced courtesy of Emil Schult.

of economic production, commodity transport, and individual mobility created by disinterested technocrats. Yet the history of these technologies is far more complex and nuanced and therefore much more rewarding to study. Like other large-scale technological systems, these highways both mirror and influence the political, social, and cultural history of which they are a part; they shape society to the same degree that they are shaped by it.[4] This becomes particularly obvious in the case of the landscape of the autobahn: these roadways shape their surrounding landscapes as much as they are shaped by them. Rather than seeing nature and technology as polar opposites and the creation of infrastructures as manifesting either man's dominion over nature or the inexorable decline of a once-pristine environment, historians can examine the ever-changing tableau of topographic features and human perceptions that together constitute landscapes, both real and ideal.[5] The German geographical discourse of the *Kulturlandschaft*—the cultural landscape that emerges from the interaction between humans and their environment—can offer a framework for understanding historical changes wrought by the spread of the automobile during the twentieth century. Pollution, urban sprawl, and public-health issues have rightly made the automobile anathema to environmentalists. Precisely for this reason, it is essential to determine which automotive landscapes gained cultural approval and political currency before the rise of the post–World War II environmental movement.

This essay takes a closer look at the shifting meaning of the autobahn and its landscape in two different political regimes: the Nazi dictatorship and the nascent Federal Republic of Germany. The Kraftwerk song and the images cited above support a perception of the autobahn as a twentieth-century technoscape where speed and efficiency are paramount values. In purposeful contrast to its musical peers, Kraftwerk showcased in its music a specifically German artifact but chose to represent it as devoid of historical content.[6] Historically informed observers will, however, remember the Nazis' enthusiastic sponsorship of the autobahns, which became known as "Adolf Hitlers Straßen"—Adolf Hitler's roads. While extolling these highways as harbingers of future transportation technology in a passionately linear view of history, the National Socialist propaganda machine also claimed that the autobahns reconciled tensions between nature and technology; instead of intruding upon the landscapes, these roads would harmonize with the countryside through which they passed. The contrast between these two symbolic identities could hardly be greater: the utilitarian highway of a market economy and reconstructed liberal democracy of the Federal Republic versus a far-reaching technological initiative meant to demonstrate the visionary, environmentally sensitive nationalism of the Nazi leadership. The questions to be addressed, then, are who created the meanings of the autobahns, what did these creators have in mind when they assigned purpose and significance to these roads, and how did these multiple meanings compete with or reinforce each other?

The first meaning of the autobahn considered here is its derivative relationship to railways and railway design. Almost since the invention of self-propelled internal combustion engines, promoters of roads—such as the Good Roads movement in the United States; the car, tire, and gasoline lobbies; professional organizations of civil engineers; and the occasional writer-driver—have always favored a rhetoric of freedom of movement that is, at least superficially, antithetical to the strict regimen of railways and railway schedules. Some historians continue to accept this paradigm. Wolfgang Sachs, for instance, describes how middle-class car drivers such as the author Otto Julius Bierbaum found equal joy in adventurous motoring and in writing about it.[7]

Yet it is important to note that most of the early interstate highways built in Italy and Germany resembled the railways both in design and in spirit.[8] On one level, this is not altogether surprising, since civil engineers' textbooks focused almost exclusively on how to build railroads. Also, the networks of roads that began to spread across the United States and Europe after World War I were designed to be managed by a central authority that controlled access points and exits, set tolls, and disciplined drivers through policing.[9] Power over all aspects of these roads was centralized in groups of experts akin to those that had directed the railroad companies since the nineteenth century. The shift from local and regional road management to national oversight was not a necessary development but rather the result of political strife and cultural validation. By aligning themselves with state authority, engineers and other professional groups, such as landscape architects, hoped to ensure both job security and social prestige.

Before 1933 a lobby of urban politicians, engineers, and car promoters in Germany tried to put an autobahn project on the agenda of the Weimar Republic. Encouraged by Mussolini's sponsorship of the Italian autostrade, this group introduced the neologism *Autobahn* to designate special tracks for cars. The term played off of *Eisenbahn*, the German word for *railway*.[10] From 1926 on, the Hafraba association (named after three major cities on the autobahn's planned route: Hamburg, Frankfurt, and Basel) lobbied for a cars-only infrastructure system. Their efforts to secure a government charter to operate a toll-road system failed. Apart from legal obstacles to toll roads in the Reich's constitution, the degree of motorization was so low that the Hafraba was constantly put on the defensive. According to Germany's first nationwide systematic traffic count, made in 1924–25, horse-drawn vehicles still outperformed cars; a General Motors' study concluded that Germany's 1929 automotive market was comparable to the US market in 1911.[11] In Germany the ratio of residents to passenger cars in 1930 was 131 to 1, while the ratio in the United States was 5.3 to 1. The Weimar

Republic's transportation priority was the railway system. Roads remained under the jurisdiction of individual German states, whose financial constraints made maintenance difficult.[12]

The Hafraba association advertised its planned toll road as a way to accelerate circulation and modernize transportation, but even some automobile manufacturers and one automobile club deemed the upgrading of existing roads more important than the development and construction of a new road system. While Hafraba's aspirations were lofty, its actual achievement was limited to detailed plans for an autobahn between Frankfurt and Heidelberg.[13] In 1932 a twenty-kilometer-long two-lane highway was opened between Cologne and Bonn, not as a Hafraba project but under the auspices of Cologne's mayor, Konrad Adenauer. The Hafraba blueprints would have remained just another failed proposal had the Nazi regime not seized on the autobahn project as an opportunity to manifest its technological prowess.

Only two years before Hitler's appointment as Reich chancellor, the Nazi faction in the Berlin parliament had voted down proposals to build new interurban roads. Yet, as he rapidly centralized power and established his dictatorship, Hitler touted cars and roads as markers of modernity. In a speech at the February 1933 car-and-motorcycle show in Berlin, the Führer stated that highway kilometers, not railway kilometers, would become the indicators of the relative status of nations. Obedient members of Germany's racially cleansed community were to receive the "Volkswagen" and the autobahns as consumerist rewards from the Nazi regime. While it failed to produce the former in appreciable numbers for civilians, it quickly erected 3,625 kilometers of the latter.

Economic historians still argue over whether the massive push for road-building was folly or a boon.[14] In environmental terms, the four-lane concrete roadway connecting all corners of the Reich and Austria after its annexation constitutes a curious mixture of conservationist rhetoric and engineering arrogance, of ecological concern on the part of some planners and a craving for unmitigated speed on the part of others. The creation and sculpting of roadside landscapes was the often-contested goal of different professional groups with varying agendas.

The Nazi official with ultimate authority over the entire autobahn project, Fritz Todt, worked for a Munich construction company and earned a doctorate in civil engineering from that city's Technical University. In 1927 he had produced plans for a highway from Munich to Starnberg Lake, south of the Bavarian capital. It is safe to assume that this project acquainted him with engineering literature on parkways in the United States, which were then the subject of much interest among German road-builders. When commissioning a landscape architect, Alwin Seifert, to work on the auto-bahn six years later, Todt spoke of a "Parkstrasse," thereby alluding to the parkways in the United States.[15] Todt's department, the Generalinspektor für das deutsche Straßenwesen, or general inspector for German roads, sponsored a translation of *Roadside Improvements* for its employees, a pamphlet by two landscape architects who had worked on the Mount Vernon Memorial Highway, south of Washington, DC.[16] As will be shown, however, the mere fact of this translation should not be seen as an indication of a widespread technology transfer.

In the propaganda literature issued for a wider public, the Nazi regime continually employed the vocabulary of the parkways yet emphasized the German quality of the roads and the landscapes. Todt elevated civil engineering design to the level of art, in the process claiming cultural capital for his profession, and stressed that utilitarianism was not the goal of German road-building: "The road must be an expression of its landscape and of German essence."[17]

Newspaper articles, brochures, novels, and, most importantly, commissioned paintings and photographs sought to demonstrate how successfully the roads blended into their surrounding landscapes.[18] Some engineers even asserted that the roads could enhance their environs. Autobahn designers and their propagandists declared that the curvilinear contours of the roads and the plantings alongside them would integrate these highways into local landscapes, unlike the railroads, which had ruined the countryside with their straight alignment and ubiquitous trenches, dams, and embankments. An outpouring of stories about the successful synthesis of road and landscape provided employment for a legion of writers, painters, and photographers and raised the autobahn's public profile. Yet these representations do not corroborate archival evidence of government activities.

It would, however, be a mistake to assume that the autobahn was simply an adaptation of the American parkway or that German highway design was straightforward and without conflict. For one thing, Germany's road system was built to accommodate truck traffic as well as cars, while parkways in the United States had strictly excluded common-carrier traffic from the beginning. For another, in a confusing jumble of resource extraction, divided managerial authority, and political infighting typical of the Nazi regime, the state-owned railway company, Deutsche Reichsbahn, became involved in the autobahn project and at one point was promised a freight monopoly on the new roads. Reichsbahn officials, as well as Germany's military leaders, had strongly objected to the highway project, but both groups were overruled by Hitler's propaganda instinct.[19] As the influence of the Reichsbahn's senior leadership gradually waned, Todt's agency was happy to utilize the public company's funds and to employ the hundreds of railway civil engineers who were assigned to work on the roads—1,959 of them in 1934 and 1935 alone.[20]

The professional training of these engineers, their previous experience designing railroads, and the reward structure of the civil service offered them few incentives to design roads that displayed the parkway characteristics of sinuous curves, pleasant vistas, and attention to roadside planting. While the propaganda writers of Nazi Germany never tired of pointing out how beautiful and harmonious these roads would become, their chief designers were required to produce plans from scratch at a breakneck speed of one thousand kilometers per year. In order to demonstrate its technological and economic significance, the project known as "Adolf Hitler's roads" had to grow at this annual rate starting in 1934. The dictator himself seems to have called for this strenuous pace, which was unjustified except for purposes of propaganda. For the engineers this translated into a frenzy of surveying, planning, designing, and supervising construction. For the laborers it meant long shifts and hazardous working conditions in isolated parts of the country; strikes arose and were quickly crushed. For the roads the hectic pace of construction diminished attention to the aesthetic aspects of landscaping and design.

It was in this atmosphere of coercion, haste, and pressure that the landscapes of the autobahn were formed. In his effort to endow German highway design with features similar to those of U.S. parkways, Todt authorized a group of some fifteen landscape architects under Seifert's leadership to work on these roads. While the civil engineers were government employees, the landscape architects were merely consultants. Relying on Todt's patronage, the landscape architects (called "*Landschaftsanwälte*," or landscape advocates) joined the fray of planning and construction. Their correspondence with each other and the Generalinspektor shows how fragile the enterprise of landscaping the autobahn was, both conceptually and materially.[21]

Because the landscape architects were in no position to command the career engineers of the Reichsbahn, they had to rely on their persuasive skills. Many attempted to enhance their status by appealing to the higher causes of *Volk* and Nazi ideology. For them, whether a road was to be built in straight or sweeping lines was not just a technical question but a culturally loaded decision (fig. 7.2). Their calls for attention became effusive, even shrill, as the landscape advocates were forced to recognize their subordinate role in the autobahn project. At a particularly critical juncture, Seifert complained to Todt that his men's position was "unclear and undignified."[22]

The landscape architects' insistence on using only "native" plants must be understood in this context. With priorities beyond the parkway idea of enhancing the driving experience, Seifert bluntly asserted that more important than the driver's comfort or pleasure was the conservation of landscape,

7.2. Whether the autobahn of the Nazi years should be built in straight lines or sweeping curves was the topic of vigorous debate between civil engineers and landscape architects in the employ of the Third Reich. This photograph, taken by Wolf Strache sometime between 1936 and 1939, shows a stretch of autobahn in which straight segments are connected by short curves. From the Library of Congress Collection of Prints and Photographs.

and even more important than that was the restoration of lost landscapes. He envisioned mature crabapple trees, "wild" pear and cherry trees, and anemones growing right next to the roads thirty or fifty years hence.[23] When Todt's administration balked at the cost of providing saplings of this supposedly native fauna, which were hard to find in commercial nurseries, Seifert's clique stressed that the national character of the roads necessitated the planting of German vegetation, and they nudged the administration to sponsor phytosociological research to help identify Germany's postglacial landscapes unaltered by human intervention. Yet when Seifert planned to cut down a row of chestnut trees next to a suburban Munich road, a local Hitler crony successfully intervened with Todt. The Reich's lead engineer stopped the felling and scolded Seifert for his extreme interpretation of ecological theories.[24] Earlier, Todt had stated in an internal memorandum that roadside planting's main function was to "invigorate" the driver; blending the roads into the landscape was a secondary objective.[25]

Divisive administrative structures, poor leadership, and ideological perturbation led to most prewar sections of the autobahn mirroring railway rather than parkway design, as even the ebullient Seifert admitted.[26] Certain stretches of the road, in particular the Munich-Salzburg route with its proximity to the Alps, were more elaborately landscaped than others and were thus overrepresented in the photographic record of the autobahn. But the image of German highways presented in newspaper and magazine articles differed substantially from the roads that were built as the result of acrimonious altercations over design. Rather than representing a harmonious marriage of landscape and technology, the autobahn in the Nazi era signified clashing professional aspirations, conflicting ideologies, and a rushed planning process driven by propaganda goals (fig. 7.3).

During the war a series of speed limits and the rationing of gasoline soon turned the autobahn into a network devoid of cars. Bicyclists traveled on the roads, and in 1945 the liberating Western troops used them to penetrate Germany wherever they weren't thwarted by the demolition of hundreds of bridges by the retreating German army. In the initial phase of postwar reconstruction, restoring rail service was paramount, not repairing an extensive road network. Very soon, however, the meaning of the highway system began to change. As the icon of a defeated dictatorship, the autobahn carried heavy ideological baggage in the Federal Republic. Thus its qualities could not remain uncontested in a democratic West

7.3. Instead of a roadway lushly planted with native species, as landscape architects of the Nazi era had imagined it, the autobahn was planted with vegetation selected according to its likely effect on drivers. The administrators who chose these varieties of trees and bushes sought to produce a low-stress driving experience rather than an aesthetic and ecologically sustainable landscape. Photograph taken between 1936 and 1939 by Wolf Strache. From the Library of Congress Collection of Prints and Photographs.

Germany. Politicians and engineers sought to distance themselves from any association with the most oppressive regime in European history, and they did so by pointing to the pragmatic purpose of these roads. This is even more remarkable given that the personnel of the Nazi autobahn, with very few exceptions, integrated smoothly into the federal department of transportation.[27]

This tendency to rationalize the autobahn by stripping it of its Nazi connotations was the most effective rhetorical strategy employed by policy-makers and engineers in the 1950s. A case in point is the stern admonition issued to German road engineers by the FRG's newly appointed secretary for transportation, Hans Christoph Seebohm. In 1950, addressing a meeting of the Society of German Road Engineers, Seebohm reprimanded its members in harsh terms. It would have been much better, he argued, if decisions in the past had addressed immediate transport needs instead of anticipating a distant future. That approach had produced a system teeming with mistakes. Seebohm was, of course, referring to the autobahn, which he deemed dysfunctional and inefficient. The epitome of his critique was the route from Frankfurt to Kassel. The autobahn's avoidance of the main economic centers necessitated long drives to and from the motorway. The transport minister also castigated the steep inclines of up to 9 percent on some portions of the autobahn. Trucks had difficulties climbing the mountains and were often forced to circumvent the autobahn in order to travel on roads that were not as steep. Summing up his evaluation of the Nazi autobahn, Seebohm remarked: "That man, to whom we owe so much evil, made decisive errors in this regard as well."[28] By making Hitler personally responsible (without naming him), Seebohm effectively managed to divert attention from the actions of the road engineers themselves, who would shortly constitute the new federal road-building administration. Attributing the problems with Germany's motorways to a nameless demonic figure reinterpreted the Third Reich as a kind of supernatural aberration. The autobahn remained "Adolf Hitler's roads," as Nazi propaganda had labeled them, but now it was the dysfunctional failings of the transportation network that could be ascribed to the dictator.

Another, even more blatant discrepancy was the extent of the autobahn network in relation to the number of cars. Of the 3,600 kilometers of Nazi autobahn, some 2,100 were laid in what became West Germany, making it the world leader in terms of autobahn kilometers, as Seebohm pointed out. If autobahns are defined as four-lane highways divided by a median strip and without intersections on the same level, the United States in 1952 had only 1,202 kilometers of autobahn-quality roads.[29] Yet in 1950, when the ratio of cars to passengers was 1 to 4 in the United States, in West Germany the ratio was 1 to 104. By 1955 the ratio had dropped to 1 to 31, and only in the early 1960s did the ratio fall to below ten people per car. This imbalance was so gross that the politicians cautioned the engineers.

For Seebohm in the 1950s, referring to America served a dual purpose. On the one hand, using a historical and free-market argument, he could show that the Nazi autobahn was built too far ahead of demand. He wanted the civil engineers to distance themselves from this tradition. On the other hand, and much more importantly, comparison with the United States was seen as a way to evaluate the Federal Republic's progress

7.4. Postwar autobahn design emphasized safety. Building more—and more "modern"—autobahns was seen as the antidote to the rising accident statistics. Guardrails and small median strips were intended to help drivers focus on the road, not the countryside. Reproduced by permission from Hans Lorenz, *Trassierung und Gestaltung von Straßen und Autobahnen* (1971).

(fig. 7.4). Politicians and engineers were quick to point out that a massive interstate road-building program was about to begin in America, supposedly based on scientifically generated projections and mathematical estimates of expected demand, from which engineers would build, quite literally, the roads of the future. In the 1950s and '60s, German road engineers adopted the methodological tools necessary for anticipating traffic. They measured current trends of motorization and extrapolated from the figures they recorded. The engineers were thus able to fashion themselves into road-building experts. They authored extensive programs with a projected time span of ten to fifteen years, which were then subdivided into four-year plans to be approved by the federal assembly, the Bundestag. The planning instruments were part of official efforts to integrate the legacy of the autobahn into the new federal transportation system.[30] By the same token, they allowed the road engineers to pursue professional interests. By adopting "scientific" and "American" methodologies of statistical distribution, they could continue to build highways and still be able to distance themselves from the Nazi autobahn. In this way the autobahn could be transformed from one of "Hitler's follies" into a modern, democratic motorway.

How would this change autobahn design? In his speech, Seebohm ridiculed the steep inclines on the autobahn as dysfunctional. These infamous inclines had not been determined by the topography; on the contrary, hilly routes had been favored over flat ones in the Nazi era, since they offered more opportunities to enjoy the scenery charged with German values. The road-building style of the autobahn thus suffered a remarkable decline in reputation after 1945. The same design features that had once won the engineers praise now drew ridicule. Seebohm's criticisms strongly influenced the rhetoric and methodology of road engineers in West Germany.

In 1954 the head of the road division in the federal Department of Transportation launched an attack on the landscape advocates' design proposals. In a programmatic article entitled "Rational Road Building," he declared that the volume and speed of present-day traffic made it irresponsible to plan roads according to "outdated criteria" or influenced by regional sentiments. Road landscaping had to become more systematic, and it was to be subordinated to the demands of growing traffic.[31] By introducing a rhetoric of demand and rationally planned supply, the author, as an engineer, hoped to bolster his profession's position in postwar road-planning, and he dismissed the landscaping of German roadways as, at best, an afterthought. Speaking for the "driver," whom the engineers imagined as male and for whom they intended to speak, an imagined personality very much like the professional males who took their place rhetorically, engineers stressed that the postwar driving experience should be fast, safe, and economical.[32] One particularly blunt engineer stated that "the autobahn is not a hiking path."[33] Safety became a rallying cry for drivers and for the increasingly powerful car lobbies, politicians, and engineers in the Federal Republic. The numbers of car drivers and passengers killed in accidents rose dramatically throughout the 1950s and '60s. At the beginning of this period the annual rate of traffic deaths was about 8,000; by 1972 that number had surged to 19,000. Building new and safer roads was seen as the best way to reduce this death toll.[34] The topic was prominent enough for Chancellor Konrad Adenauer to mention it in his inauguration speeches of 1953 and 1957.[35]

Fast, safe autobahns were planned using a methodology adapted from an approach developed in the later years of the Nazi regime. The issue of straight versus curvilinear roads had remained contested during the hectic construction phase of the autobahn. As building slowed and finally came to a halt in 1942, civil engineers began to search for a standardized approach to the process of determining road alignments. Rather than hiking through the countryside where a road was to be built, as the landscape advocates advised, engineers preferred to address the issue mathematically. While planning a never-realized transit autobahn from Breslau/Wroclaw to Vienna, an engineer named Hans Lorenz developed geometrical tables that could be used to calculate alignments for any road, not just the one he was planning. These calculations eventually replaced the technique favored by landscape architects and helped to establish widely applicable design parameters for connecting straight stretches of highway with sweeping curves.[36]

Increasingly the engineers offered scientifically generated, deductive proposals to counter the inductive plans produced by the landscape architects. Studying the nexus of the straight line and the curve, engineers concluded that the geometric figure of the spiral transition, or clothoid, curve would best suit the purpose. (A spiral transition curve is defined as a curve in which the radius varies inversely with the distance along the spiral.) This reasoning was based exclusively on abstract mathematical formulae and transformed road design into a matter of predictable, repeatable operations that could be taught as part of the standard engineering curriculum.

Quantification was in this respect a significant professional tool for civil engineers. As Theodore Porter has pointed out, reliance on numbers and quantitative manipulation minimizes the need for firsthand knowledge and personal trust. Nonlocal and impersonal communication becomes easier, and the knowledge produced with the help of quantitative arguments appears more legitimate than that advanced through other rhetorical strategies. Quantification helped autobahn engineers to respond to the landscape advocates' challenge in the 1930s and achieve more "rational" design parameters after the war. The transition curve was both a successful tool and a symbol of civil engineers' control of the autobahn design process in the Federal Republic. By the 1960s the transition curve had become part of the shared engineering vocabulary in many countries.[37] In the case of West Germany, it contributed to putting landscape architects on the defensive, and it reinforced civil engineers' status as the sole experts on road-building. The transition curve promoted construction of safe, fast, and well-designed

7.5 With some hyperbole, a 1971 civil-engineering textbook presents this photograph as an illustration of "the only optically unfavorable" stretch of the Nazi-era autobahn. Reproduced by permission from Hans Lorenz, *Trassierung und Gestaltung von Straßen und Autobahnen.*

roads; engineering textbooks included examples of poorly planned Nazi autobahns as warnings (fig. 7:5).

How did landscape architects react to this shift in autobahn rationales? Seifert himself was not permitted to act on behalf of his fellow landscape architects as he had under the dictatorship. For one thing, the federal structure of the new republic, which delegated design to the Bonn Department of Transportation and the fine-tuning of plans to the individual states, made such a single leader superfluous. The new federalism led to a distribution of power and production of knowledge different from those under the Third Reich. Some landscape architects changed the fundamental approach to their work. Landscape was gradually superseded as the key concept by "space," which could be ordered, dressed, and groomed for the drivers' attention. In the most extreme case, one landscape architect functionalized his work and rhetoric profoundly and used the term *habitat space* where *landscape* would have sufficed some years earlier.[38]

By integrating themselves into the new framework of rationality and safety, however, the landscape architects tacitly accepted the idea that their role in the road-building process was subordinate to that of the road engineers. Since the engineers claimed that their superior methodological apparatus equipped them to design roads better than anyone else, landscape architects were left to decorate highways that had already been planned. One of the former landscape advocates (who continued to use this appellation) assessed a particular stretch of the autobahn for a pilot project on "safety vegetation." Plants were chosen not for their value as roadside adornments but for their effectiveness as a buffer when cars veered off the road and for being low-maintenance and amenable to mechanical cutting.[39] Utility and economy became the chief criteria for landscape architects' designs. Chaotic during the Nazi years, the design process became regularized, standardized, and more uniform in the postwar period. Local concerns and individual personalities mattered far less in this environment.

In the 1950s, quantification offered a dual means for combining autobahn-building with the utilitarian program developed by the administration. First, grounding roadway design on mathematical formulae was a way to distance the autobahn from alleged Nazi romanticism. This process of quantification was portrayed as nothing less than a crusade against irrationalism. Second, road engineers could become undisputed authorities on the alignment of the autobahn. Instead of fighting with landscape architects over where to place the roads, the engineers were now the only experts capable of determining correct road design. Both the antiromantic stance and the advantage of expert status contributed decisively to the dominance of mathematical thinking in postwar German highway design.

That these methods could be labeled as "modern" in the 1950s assisted the ideologically tainted engineers in their political struggle for professional recognition after their alliance with the Nazi regime and its most prominent technological icon had put them on the spot. Without ever expressing these connections openly, Seebohm's oblique hints reflected the engineers' desire to assert themselves socially. Their quantitative rationale enabled them to present a rehabilitated version of the autobahn—a seemingly de-Nazified version of Adolf Hitler's roads, so to speak—and to break the link between their profession and a powerful Nazi propaganda tool. Public demands for safety could also be couched in this new, rational rhetoric.

In the reevaluation of the autobahn during the 1950s, the old roads were labeled as dysfunctional. In an exculpatory effort, their unsuitability for the number of cars and other design failures were attributed to Hitler himself. Transportation as a means to economic prosperity became the West German agenda for road-building, and the highway system was assigned a new rational and democratic character. This proved to be an effective strategy for garnering support and obtaining access to resources and allies in the political sphere, and it is tempting to quote Immanuel Kant's assertion that "We shall be rendering a service to reason should we succeed in discovering the path upon which it can securely travel."[40] Apparently the path in this case was the mathematically based engineering of roads. Yet, apart from the question of reason, professional politics contributed to discovering this path as well.

The path of science delineated here raises questions about the politics of science and technology in autobahn-building. The example of engineering—of using deductively generated formulae to determine autobahn alignment—seems to contradict notions about science and technology in Nazi Germany: that individual scientists and engineers were seduced, either by bureaucrats or by Hitler's fascinating personality; that their work was pseudoscientific and bore little relation to legitimate Western science; and that Nazi technology must, by extension, be regarded as a perversion of modernization.[41] This example speaks in favor of a historical evolution that was both more continuous and more contingent. Especially seen in the light of its postwar fortunes, the technology developed to build the autobahn was neither fascist nor democratic nor neutral (to paraphrase Kranzberg's law).[42] It gained currency in both political environments while remaining contested within the disciplines of civil engineering and landscape architecture, which were themselves divided by competing professional and scientific agendas. Clearly a technological artifact such as the autobahn can acquire different cultural meanings for different societies.

Not seduction but rather self-mobilization characterized the careers of both civil engineers and landscape architects who participated in Nazi Germany's building craze. Rather than merely an emblematic icon of Nazi ideology, the autobahn can be understood as a set of complex negotiations over design, meaning, and professional status. Technology was a key element in the Nazi pursuit of modernism, which required catching up with the Western world while reconstructing German cultural identity. Nature, technology's antithesis, was united with it in an organic rhetoric overshadowed by a growing emphasis on race as the critical factor. After 1945, engineers attempted to preserve a professional continuity by presenting a methodological discontinuity. Stressing quantification helped them to present technology as a neutral, rational Western tool for ensuring safe designs and fostering economic growth. While the Cold War background was a prerequisite for this change, the orientation toward objective scientific values can also be seen in a context of professional self-interest. An often unspoken reference in these discourses and practices was the state of the autobahn in East Germany. West German civil engineers' competitive efforts to maintain and expand a freeway system superior to that of the GDR made the orientation toward Western and especially American values all the more significant and powerful. Social freedom, in this version of the conflict of systems, had to include automotive freedom.[43] As technology, environment, and their interstices were renegotiated and redesigned, landscape as a concept was declining in importance. In order to assert automotive freedom during the Cold War, all speed limits on the autobahn were abolished in 1955. Thus the idea of carefully tended roadside vegetation blurred into an indistinguishable mass of shrubbery in drivers' rearview mirrors.

Landscapes, at least in the case at hand, are hardly the mechanical antithesis of civilization envisioned by the Romantics. Far from it: they are both the arena for and the outcome of constant conflicts over the cultural meaning and social politics of beauty. Therefore, and paradoxically, Kraftwerk's stylized 1970s "Autobahn" image, Seifert's aesthetically landscaped autobahn, Todt's consuming vision of the autobahn, and the more mathematically grounded autobahn of postwar West Germany have much more in common than just their name.

EIGHT

Socialist Highways?

Appropriating the Autobahn in the
German Democratic Republic

Axel Dossmann

It is only a human being who assigns meaning
to a landscape by allowing it to trigger off in
him certain thoughts, feelings or associations.
Their nature is not fixed for all time but is
mediated by symbols, needs to be learned
and has its own history.

KARL SCHAWELKA[1]

Introduction

"Modern expressways require good integration into the landscape," as an
advertising brochure of the VEB Autobahn Construction Company, the
German Democratic Republic's nationalized highway-construction firm,
claims in four languages.[2] On one page of this brochure, with which the
company sought to attract foreign investors in the early 1980s, are two
aerial photographs of the Berlin-Rostock highway, built between 1970 and
1978. Looking at the photos with Schawelka's words in mind, one reacts
with irritation, at the very least. The top photo shows the highway making
a wide curve through flat, open countryside. Presumably this image was

intended to illustrate the famous "sweep of the highway through the land-scape," which was the main principle of German roadway design in the 1930s.[3] Next to a patch of woods is a small picnic area. But in order to stop there, the driver would have to brake sharply when coming off the high-way, since the long lanes for acceleration and deceleration, already common in Western Europe at this time, are absent here. The bottom photo shows an absolutely straight section of the highway cutting through a wooded area. At one time, before the building of the highway, this forest had obviously been undivided. How well this picture illustrates the modern highway's integration into the landscape is questionable. The viewer notices imme-diately that the rest stops (picnic areas) have no sanitation facilities. Further-more, there are no crash barriers, either on the sides of the highway or on the median strips. Despite these significant differences from the "inter-national standard," which for GDR highway builders was a political as well as technical standard, the advertising brochure presents this highway as an epitome of modern engineering. The landscape remains undifferentiated but appears to be "central European."

The highway also sweeps through forest and field in the picture on the brochure's front cover (fig. 8.1). Here, the lanes do not even have a hard shoulder. As in the other photographs, only a few cars and trucks are on the highway, so its functionality as a road for traffic is secondary. Rather, these aerial views depict the highway as an artificial ornament of the land-scape. The perspective of the driver behind the windshield does not emerge in these representations, but the view from above promises a rapid and pleasant drive through nature.

This tension between the symbolic and the functional characterizes the entire history of the highway system in the GDR.[4] It also demonstrates once again that artifacts do have politics, and politics do produce arti-facts.[5] The history of highway-planning in Germany tells us much about the transcultural exchanges and political agendas that informed road de-sign and construction in the postwar period.

The Autobahn in the Years of Reconstruction, 1945–61

The autobahns as instruments of national and social integration (and sepa-ration) received special governmental attention several times during the

VEB Autobahnbaukombinat · DDR

Straßenbau
Road building · La construction de routes
Construção de estradas

8.1. Cover image of a brochure developed for potential foreign investors in East Germany's highway-construction cooperative, the Volks Eigener Betrieb Autobahnbaukombinat.

period of the Soviet Zone/GDR. The closing of the autobahn route from Helmstedt to West Berlin during the 1948–49 Berlin blockade is well known. Helmstedt-Berlin was the only route on which allied (and military) vehicles had been permitted to move through the Soviet Zone/GDR. After 1949 the politics of traffic and customs checks along this Interzonen-Autobahn (later the Transit-Autobahn) served as a barometer for the general political climate, especially during the Cold War years of the 1950s.

Just after the end of World War II, infrastructural politics were dominated by a sense of pragmatism. The autobahn system, at that time unique and new, had been perceived almost as a gift from history. In fact, this legacy of the Third Reich to post-Fascist Germany was far from perfect. Because many large bridges had been destroyed, the autobahn no longer functioned as a system and demanded enormous investment for rebuilding. But by its mere existence the autobahn enjoyed a privileged position among the state's infrastructural networks. The Soviet military government tried to integrate into new positions those civil engineers and architects who had made their extraordinary careers with the construction of the *Reichsautobahn*. Senior civil engineers let there be no doubt that "their" autobahn had to be reconstructed as soon as possible. Yet the majority of these figures sought to establish themselves in the Western zones—often with success and in many cases without any repercussions from their involvement with National Socialism.[6]

In contrast to West Germany, very few of the civil engineers who had been employed by the Third Reich continued working in the GDR. But it was these few men who most criticized the neglect shown by the state's road administration (Hauptverwaltung Straßenwesen). This central office was heavily dependent on political programs and short-term reconstruction campaigns designed by the heads of the Socialist Unity Party (SED). According to its political vision, the Communist Party would be able to successfully manage all aspects of economic and societal development, including those relating to traffic and transport. During the GDR's forty-year existence, railways were the most privileged sector of transportation policy.[7] Moreover, the Communist leadership favored public transport over individual mobility. But among both experts and the country's citizens, consciousness of how private and commercial road traffic could promote economic development continued to grow. Yet until 1958, no such recognition appeared in official projections, which were based only on rough extrapolations of traffic patterns in highly industrialized Western European countries or the United States. Senior urban planners and civil engineers began to argue for more financial investment in the reconstruction of outdated cross-country roads and in the completion of the autobahn network.

The empirical data for their arguments were drawn from rather insufficient sources and reflected the "big-industrial nostalgia" typical of the GDR political economy.[8]

The different traffic estimates generated intense discussions between civil engineers in the Ministry of Transport and Communications (Ministerium für Verkehrswesen) and economists on the State Planning Commission (Staatliche Plankommission), an organization whose members worked closely with the Central Committee of the SED. Their discussions were kept unofficial and had only a slight impact on road-construction policies. Much more important was the ongoing economic rivalry with West Germany. This competition of political systems (*Systemkonkurrenz*) molded a cultural pattern that profoundly influenced political agendas and, not least, the planning and building of the autobahn.

The prevention of traffic jams, for example, emerged as one of the SED's chief political aims because it demonstrated the superiority of socialism over market capitalism. The socialist government was able to provide the necessary infrastructures for future traffic in a timely manner, in contrast to the so-called capitalist chaos on the roads ("Verkehrs-Chaos"). This science-fiction autobahn, with its divided lanes and without crossroads, would represent a modernity very much in the people's interest and compatible with the Communist future that was expected to arrive any day. The acceleration of industrial development could be synchronized with the acceleration of traffic and transport. Acceleration was established as both goal and metaphor for the social dynamic. In 1958 the SED used an expression associated with driving to describe the chief objective of the East German economy for the coming years in language associated with driving: "einholen und überholen" (to catch up and overtake). The phrase was coined in relation to West Germany's growing consumerism during its *Wirtschaftswunder,* or economic miracle.

It was also in 1958 that the government of the Federal Republic for the first time allotted more public funds for road construction, including plans for the new Bundes-Autobahnen. For the SED party this was yet another reason, although one kept secret, to put the construction of new roads on the political agenda—overnight, and without any public discussion. The route from Berlin to Rostock, on the coast of the Baltic Sea, would be built as the first section of a huge autobahn system (fig. 8.2). In the euphoria produced by the implementation of an agreed-upon and realistic plan,

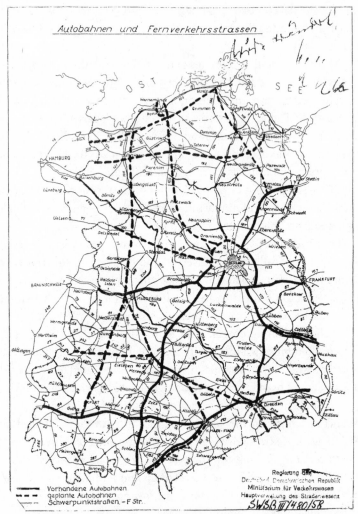

8.2. Map of existing and planned autobahn routes in East Germany, ca. 1958. The handwritten notation in the top right-hand corner—"wird verändert"— indicates that the plan "will be changed." From the archive of the GDR's Ministry of Transportation, Bureau of Highway Administration.

engineers also recognized the officially endorsed option of reunification with West Germany. No consideration of existing landscapes can be discerned in records of this stage in the planning. The drive to integrate dominated; the actual landscape was treated strictly as available empty space between the cities and concentrated industrial areas.

In a speech in September 1959, the state and party leader Walter Ul-bricht publicly announced the Seven-Year Plan (1959–65) for the first time; the Ministry of Transport, unknown to the public, had prepared it a year earlier. In 1963 the building of the autobahn between Berlin and Rostock would be designated a "Bau der Jugend," or young people's construction project.[9] The autobahn thus became a large propaganda project of the Freie Deutsche Jugend, the state-sponsored youth organization. The younger generation would mark their new homeland with an immutable imprint through the construction of dams, ports, and factories, as well as the new autobahn. The goal was a "cultural landscape" that would display the am-bition of the first generation of socialists to build a new world.

The new autobahn would not only improve the north-south transporta-tion in the GDR but would also, in the words of Walter Ulbricht, "represent an important link for the transportation of goods at the Rostock port. This link will also be of great importance for international transportation between Scandinavia and southern and southeastern Europe. This autobahn will bring the working people in comfortable travel buses or in their own motorcy-cles and cars quickly and safely to the beautiful vacation and recreation areas on the coast and in the heart of Mecklenburg."[10] Such a formulation recalls images that had already stimulated the desire for individual mo-bility in National Socialist propaganda about the *Reichsautobahn* and the Volkswagen.[11] But, in contrast to the Third Reich and its empty promises, the GDR—the workers' and farmers' state—would soon fulfill its promises.

Just as the state leader had done in his speech, journalists could also create fantasies of the socialist future. A story in the popular *Das Magazin* imagined a leap into the year 1965, exactly the end of the Seven-Year Plan. In this story, a GDR astronaut returns to his homeland after a seven-year mission in outer space.[12] To his surprise, time appears to be no longer a limiting factor; everything is oriented toward speed by means of "modern technology." His car rolled down the

> metropolitan majesty of the Stalin Boulevard astonishingly quickly and easily through unusually heavy traffic. . . . our hero made the trip to the airport conveniently with the high-speed train, which brought him to his destination faster and more safely than any car, with fewer stops in between. A charter plane—one of the many cheerfully colored "air-cabs" of Czechoslovakian make—stood ready

for him. Minutes later they set off on the route home. . . . Out of the dark patches of woods new industrial complexes appeared, gigantic installations assembled "at a single blow," there was nothing of the confused, dark factories pasted together over many decades. The bright bands of the new roads cut through the open land. And this land was no longer the old one: the move toward closer spatial integration really brought out a greater unity. . . . [T]he landscape . . . was undeniably brought to a higher, more rational order, a clearer structure, and therefore revealed a more colorful hygiene than he could remember.[13]

In this science-fiction fantasy more and ever-faster means of individual transport harmonize with still-more rapid and safer public transportation, and domestic flights offer extraordinary comfort to rushed travelers. The astronaut sees from his bird's-eye view industrial complexes set down "at a single blow" next to generously designed workers' quarters, surrounded by recreational areas, and everything accessible by new roads and rail connections. This conception of a homogenous, well-ordered, and literally supervised world replicates the imagined gaze of the state over its possessions: in *Seeing Like a State,* James C. Scott analyzes this perspective as an example of the authoritative claim of the "high-modernist state."[14] This spectacle of a completely altered landscape would evoke emotions consistent with the positive connotations of modernity. "Ten thousand kilometers of new rail lines and streets in use. That will be technologically advanced, useful, beautiful, and modern in the best sense of the word."[15] Such visions were certainly attractive to many citizens of the GDR, for whom factories, high-speed trains, zeppelins, automobiles, highways, and new cities were already being designed and built in the 1920s and 1930s. Around 1960, "modernity as a state of transportation" ("Moderne als Verkehrszustand") also became a very influential concept in the GDR, helping authorities to promise a new order.[16]

For the state, this new order appeared above all as "rational," since it offered the perspective of social and cultural integration of the population while enhancing opportunities for political education and control. In this respect, the autobahns as orderly channels for rapid, safe transportation fit perfectly into the picture that the GDR leadership had constructed of the nation's future. In 1961, the editors of *Das Straßenwesen* attempted to illus-

8.3. Cover of a 1961 issue of *Das Straßenwesen*, a government bulletin produced for highway engineers, construction crews, and other road workers in the GDR.

trate this future graphically on the magazine's cover (fig. 8.3). For most of the early sixties the cover image of this professional journal for GDR highway engineers showed the outline of a deserted autobahn winding away into the distance. The emptiness invited interpretation: for whom was the highway open? The destination of the journey, however, was much clearer:

on the horizon, chimneys and power-station smokestacks indicated the highly industrialized future. To the left of the autobahn, three caterpillar tractors plowed the broad fields toward the horizon in evenly spaced furrows. Their battle formation referred to the collectivization and industrialization of agriculture, which had long been programmatically connected with the "neutralization of the opposition between city and country" ("Aufhebung der Stadt-Land-Gegensätze"). While the Third Reich's folk-nationalistic propaganda photos show farmers tending the fields next to the autobahn, in the GDR pictures from the 1960s, a formation of combines drives parallel with the autobahn into the future. The GDR's technological modernity strove toward technological acceleration. If even agricultural machinery that resembled tanks could promise freedom, it was evident that no harmonizing of the pastoral ideal with modern infrastructure was sought.[17] This image does not indicate the autobahn's utility as a transportation route, but it offers a seductive perspective on modernity. The imaginary landscape, lit up by the sun, also displays the symbol of the Seven-Year Plan: the GDR coat of arms with a hammer shaped like the number 7 and a circle with a garland of corn.[18]

Fantasies about the new autobahn system were wide-ranging. Yet in the spring of 1961, in the midst of economic and political crisis, the State Planning Commission had to defer the autobahn project. Only few months later, in August 1961, the Berlin Wall was built. At that time Berliners sardonically told each other that the SED had decided that instead of building the Berlin-Rostock route, it would set up sections of that autobahn vertically between the Soviet and Allied sectors of Berlin—just in order to dry the concrete.[19]

The Autobahn as Tool for the Neue Ostpolitik, 1960s to 1970s

Behind the Wall, however, the economy of the GDR seemed to flourish. This economic upturn was accompanied by better consumer options in response to rising public demand.[20] Growing consumerism also led to an increase in automobile tourism. In fact, the rate of motorization (the ratio of cars per inhabitants) since the late 1950s had nearly matched that of the Federal Republic, though with a big difference in absolute numbers.[21] By the end of the 1960s it was no longer the Auto-Suggestionen (projections of

cars) but existing traffic, especially in the industrialized south, that legiti-
mated road construction in the GDR and set the pace for constructing new
autobahns and other cross-country roads.[22] In 1969, Walter Ulbricht, at that
time still the head of the SED, coined a new slogan that proposed an even
more challenging maneuver: "überholen ohne einzuholen" (to overtake but
not catch up).[23]

Once again a big autobahn construction program was launched. The
first plan projected a total of 1,375 kilometers of new autobahn before 1990,
of which 800 would be completed before 1980. This meant almost a doubling of the length of the roads, which in 1966 totaled 1,390 kilometers, in
a period of only fifteen years. Before 1990, thirteen of the GDR's fourteen
regional capitals would be linked by the autobahn system, and 85 percent
of the industry and 75 percent of the population would be within reach of
a major highway. This vision of an autobahn network connecting the entire territory of the GDR promised widespread integration of economic, social, and even political perspectives. The autobahn would be the model of
infrastructural suppositions for an East German "transportation land" that
would be equal to its neighbors, above all its Western ones.

Because the so-called *Bedürfnisstruktur*—East Germans' need for and
views of the good life—could and should be only slightly influenced, the
problem had to be confronted head-on: steps were taken to link the burgeoning road traffic with connecting train routes through the autobahn.[24]
In this period, when not only engineers were fascinated with cybernetics
and automation, it was clear that the model of smooth-flowing traffic
would particularly influence the planning of infrastructure. Instead of
drivers having to deal with big problems, such as traffic jams, everything
should be "quick and easy," like the consumption of food in self-service
restaurants off the autobahn or mobility with one's own car. But how should
this vision of car mobility be realized? The catchphrases for acceleration of
the building pace corresponded to the central concepts of national economic reform: automation, specialization, mechanization, motorization,
and, not least, brighter prospects. The enthusiasm for politically controlled
self-regulation of the economy through computer-operated systems offered
freedom of opportunity for technocratic inclinations among engineers,
technicians, and functionaries.[25] After 1969 autobahn construction was a
national budget priority—to the disadvantage of more numerous, no less
urgent road-construction projects, which were either downsized, deferred,

or eliminated altogether.[26] In October 1971, the GDR's first autobahn, stretching from Dresden to Leipzig, was completed almost according to the SED's original schedule.

In 1971, with the change of party leadership from Ulbricht to Erich Honecker, a new pragmatism determined most of the political decision-making. The core of the SED's new agenda of "unity of economic and social policy" ("Einheit von Wirtschafts- und Sozialpolitik") in the mid-1970s was a large housing program. In order to finance this program, execution of the autobahn plans made in 1968 was first scaled back and then, in 1978, just after the Berlin-Rostock route was opened to traffic, suspended altogether.

This was not the last autobahn constructed by GDR construction crews, however. Because trade between the two German states was of both economic and political importance, access and traveling conditions to and from West Berlin continued to be a key issue. The Transit-Autobahn played a decisive role in the policy of détente and the Neue Ostpolitik, the liberal foreign policy adopted by West Germany in the mid-1960s toward East Germany and especially East Berlin. In September 1971, the famous Quadripartite Agreement was signed and became the basis for a number of subsequent agreements and treaties advancing more intensive cooperation between East and West Germany. In 1972, the Transit Agreement between the two German states was finally signed. Among its points was a commitment to improve the autobahn from Berlin to Helmstedt at the border of West Germany, followed by an agreement in 1975 to construct an autobahn route from West Berlin to the West German city of Hamburg.

The rule of this domestic deal was simple but effective. It was an open secret that the GDR economy was dependent on foreign currency (*Valuta*). According to the Transit Agreement, East Germany assumed responsibility for constructing, while West Germany consented to cover the major part of the building costs and also accepted a road toll to be paid in a lump sum. Between 1975 and 1978, the Helmstedt-Berlin route was reconstructed by GDR road crews, and in 1982 the new Transit-Autobahn from Berlin to the West German border, in the direction of Hamburg, was opened to traffic.

The car had long been the "the East German's most beloved child."[27] At the same time, road conditions in the GDR deteriorated and traffic grew heavier. East German car drivers became familiar with traffic jams in the 1970s, especially in the industrialized south. The scarcity of new and used automobiles as well as spare parts meant that cars were rarely used for traveling to work but were used mainly for leisure pursuits.[28] Cars offered the ideal means for the weekend "trip to nature" (*Fahrt ins Grüne*), freeing their owners from the Deutsche Reichsbahn's timetables and its often dirty and unheated trains. Such possibilities for escapism were limited within the reality of socialism: by the availability of cars, by the bad roads, and not least by the impenetrable borders of the country itself. For the citizen of the GDR, every carefree trip on the autobahn ended somewhere at the "wall," on the border of the Federal Republic. Desire for acceleration and the freedom of the unrestricted journey culminated, surprisingly enough, in popular criticism of the constrained life enforced by the East German secret police, the infamous Stasi. In June 1989 a report by the state security service estimated that many East Germans perceived the successful management of traffic flow and maintenance of the autobahns as validations of the socialist system.[29] Nonetheless, nobody expected that the "first autobahn" erected in the GDR, the Berlin Wall, would fall, as it did on November 9, 1989.[30]

Bridges as Monuments, Dedicated to the Socialist Productive Forces

I turn now to the question of how civil engineers applied professional knowledge gained in the construction of the *Reichsautobahn* to the practices of road-building in the GDR. With the formation of postwar politics, new views of landscape were again possible. Reconstruction was a "magic formula" for a large percentage of the "generation of reconstruction" (*Aufbaugeneration*), born in the 1920s. This generation "was young enough to take up the challenge of a new beginning in post-war Germany, but at the same time it was extremely hurt by the experiences of war and defeat, and more sensitive and vulnerable to the possibilities of a new political involvement than their beaten parents."[31]

For many of them reconstruction meant building up a clear alternative to National Socialism. But what did this mean for the practical task of reconstructing the destroyed bridges of the former *Reichsautobahn*? In the early 1950s, civil engineers of the GDR undertook many initiatives to ensure authentic reconstruction (*originalgetreue Rekonstruktion*). This architectural program led to a partial renaissance of monumental natural-stone bridges.

The reconstruction of bridges in the 1950s took place under material conditions similar to those in the later phase of bridge construction during the period of National Socialism, when there was a shortage of steel and of qualified workers. Therefore, it was not only aesthetics but also the lack of modern building materials that led civil engineers to use natural stone and concrete for bridge construction. In the GDR, however, this preference for stone bridges was a boon to all those civil engineers and architects who wanted to maintain the aesthetic principles of the 1920s and '30s. They could do so because East Germany's master architects (*Baumeister*) collaborated with politicians of the SED leadership who had put the doctrine of classic design (*klassische Bauweise*) on the political agenda. With this architectural program, which was in fact a set of rather vague ideas, the SED adopted theories favored by Soviet cultural politics since the 1930s.

Within this Soviet theory, classicism was held to be a progressive epoch of art, which should be appropriated critically under the new socialist conditions.[32] Already in 1943, the National Committee of Free Germany (Nationalkomitee Freies Deutschland), a gathering of German Communists in Soviet exile preparing the socialist reconstruction that would take place after Nazi Germany's defeat, had oriented itself toward "national traditions." Holding onto the "sources of national pride" was a political tactic to win as many supporters as possible for a socialist Germany, along with the people who had voted for the NSDAP or belonged to national-conservative wings of German society.[33]

With regard to architecture and art, the formula of integration was "to be national in form and democratic in content" ("national in der Form, demokratisch im Inhalt"), a slogan vague enough for the goal of social and political integration. For architecture this meant first of all that buildings integrating constructive elements were discouraged under the rule of the Neues Bauen.[34] The shift to "national heritage" coincided with a rejection of the International Style. One had to resist American cultural influence, it was claimed, to guarantee the continued existence of the German people ("für den Fortbestand des deutschen Volkes").[35] According to the architect Kurt Liebknecht, president of the Deutsche Bauakademie (which had been reestablished in 1951), classicism was "the last important realistic period of construction" and therefore ought to be perceived as a positive legacy of national culture with the postwar reconstruction in Germany.[36]

The doctrine of *klassische Bauweise* encouraged civil engineers and architects to rebuild the damaged bridges of the *Reichsautobahn* in a manner as faithful to the original as possible and discouraged any substantive debate on national architectural styles.[37] This lack of serious public reflection on architectural legacies was mirrored in how reconstruction was reported in a 1963 publication commemorating the establishment in 1948 of the foundation of the Ministry of Transport and Communications.[38] While discussing the manifold efforts to reconstruct the autobahn, no hint was given about the original construction of these very bridges in the 1930s. All were presented as unique and as fitting superbly into the natural scenery, but no information that might help to historically conceptualize them—date, location, or name—was mentioned. That history was simply effaced. Paradoxically, there was only reconstruction and no original construction anymore. This rhetorical strategy made it easier to integrate the bridges into the "national architectural heritage." Only by ignoring their history of National Socialism could *Reichsautobahnen* become "*Our* Autobahnen," as the Ministry of Communication and Traffic called them in one of its publications.[39]

The reconstruction of the autobahn bridges also offered self-portraits of artisan skill from the prewar period. Stories told by stonemasons underlined engineers' determination to make it impossible to distinguish between old and new masonry, creating implicit proof of the continuity of "German high-quality craftsmanship." *Deutsche Qualitätsarbeit* had been one of the most vivid concepts for both manual and industrial workers during the nineteenth and twentieth centuries, and as an integrative idea it has transcended all political systems and ruptures up to the present.[40] The autobahn bridges built during this period were meant to assert the "beauty of the homeland" in the socialist GDR, without striking a directly nationalistic tone. The appropriation of the autobahn bridges can be understood as part of the politics of separation from the Third Reich, as former members of the National Socialist Party were simultaneously absolved and integrated into the socialist work of reconstruction (*sozialistische Aufbauarbeit*). This was part of the "politics of amnesty and integration"—that is, the politics of the Nazi past in the GDR or, as Norbert Frei has termed it, "*Vergangenheitspolitik.*"[41]

By the 1960s, senior engineers could only with some hesitation consent to build the autobahn bridges from prefabricated parts. Their claims to give the "socialist highways" a distinct character with these conspicuous bridge constructions foundered on the state-promoted ideal of "radical standardization" of architecture. Under such an architectural premise, the autobahn could not actually become a positive symbol of the GDR.[42] At the same time, designers attempted to confer symbolic status on them. After the route from Leipzig to Dresden was completed, civil engineers celebrated a new bridge built across a river as an extraordinary construction because it combined steel with concrete and featured *Freivorbau* (cantilever construction), an avant-garde technology used for the first time in the GDR.[43] In 1984, the Gesellschaft für Denkmalpflege (Society for Preservation of Historical Monuments) suggested recognizing this bridge as a monument to the GDR's *Geschichte der Produktivkräfte* (history of productive forces).[44] "For cultural and national identity in the GDR," one of the members argued, "it is necessary to include those latest material witnesses to the history of technology."[45]

There is no doubt that the construction of this bridge was a great challenge for the GDR's civil engineers. But cantilever technology had already been used in bridge-building in the 1930s; for example, in the Muldetalbrücke near Siebenlehn.[46] Designating the fifteen-year-old bridge a monument to the "development of productive forces in the GDR" was an attempt to silence the history of the 1930s. The ecological costs of this new bridge were also ignored, as this new route directly crossed the Döbener Wald nature preserve. In 1967, although road planners voiced distress about this, it seemed inevitable.[47] In the 1980s, however, an autobahn bridge in the midst of a nature preserve could serve as a means for shaping national identity. Could one imagine a more potent symbol of the ambiguous relations between industry, ecology, and identity politics in the GDR?[48]

The appropriation of nature as an exploitable resource for industry and agriculture is not in the least apparent in the construction of the Transit-Autobahn from Berlin to Hamburg. While the GDR sections of this roadway were built at high speed and without any great attention to nature, ecology, or the interests of individual inhabitants, the construction of the sections in the territory of the Federal Republic was often delayed well beyond the dates agreed upon for their completion. In the Federal Republic, environmental-impact studies had long been standard practice. In contrast, under the central-planning authoritarianism of the GDR, no such possibilities for a democratic discussion of road construction existed.[49]

Transformations of Experience: "Sweeping Roads" and Median Strips

Which landscapes should be presented to drivers in the GDR? And did the highways of GDR socialism ever offer a particular view of the landscape around them? In order to answer the first question, we must first explain how the aesthetic concepts of shaping landscapes had been handed down in the GDR.

Rolf Näser, a civil engineer born in 1930, is representative of the engineers who belonged to the GDR's generation of reconstruction. In the 1950s, Näser and others found a mentor in civil engineer Franz Roesmer, who must have been a charismatic man. Years earlier, in the 1930s, Roesmer had been a close colleague of the architects Friedrich Tamms and Paul Bonatz, both important advisors to Fritz Todt, the general inspector under the Third Reich. From 1935 to 1945, Roesmer worked in Berlin as a bridge architect in the Supreme Building Organization of the *Reichsautobahn*. One of the few engineers who continued to earn a living under the authorities of the Soviet Zone and, after 1949, under the SED, Roesmer was recognized in 1957 as "Technician of Outstanding Merits to the People"; and in the 1960s he was named the GDR's "doyen of bridge-building."[50]

In a 1998 interview, Näser recalled Roesmer's influence on junior engineers during the 1950s:

> The engineers constructing autobahns in earlier times had accumulated enormous knowledge, drawn not from books but from experience. And most of them shared their tacit knowledge with us [the younger generation]. To give you one example. . . . Together with Mr. Roesmer and all the other guys—we walked or drove by jeep the entire route from Berlin to Rostock. In the North there are a lot of lakes. . . . And there, Mr. Roesmer told us time and time again: "Change the route! . . . But not in such a way that it would pass close to the lake. If there is a forest, then take care that there are always fifty to a hundred meters of wooded land between the lake and the autobahn, because it is much more beautiful if one can gaze at the water through the trees." . . . This was not because of nature conservation or something like that, you know. . . . Well, the man was right. There were thousands of such small matters in which Roesmer kept us up to the mark.[51]

Apparently, Franz Roesmer taught nothing other than the perspective on nature from the drivers' point of view. The presentation of a "natural" landscape with lakes and woods could be made "appealing" for the driver through carefully orchestrated road-building. Nature was a performance piece, to be played like a romantic nature film in front of the windshield. The driver should be offered not close-ups, but panoramic views. Roesmer's eager protégé, Rolf Näser, who by the 1960s was already highly placed in the administration, took care that such visions of landscape consumerism would continue to be relevant for the practice of road design in the GDR. Autobahns should be built in areas where beautiful scenery was to be found. In the late 1950s, for example, one plan proposed an autobahn route along the Ruppiner See in order to guarantee the driver a view of this lake.[52] In regions without pleasant scenery, the landscapes should be made more bearable for travelers by the creation of scenic parks.[53] A 1960 document of the planned Berlin-Rostock route states that this roadway would provide access to recreational areas, such as the Plauer Lake, the Müritz Lake, and the Petersdorfer Lake: "When deciding on the route, we attempted insofar as possible to achieve constant change in the scenic view. At some points the route is laid out in such a way as to offer views of lakes and other delightful objects."[54]

In 1960, even Erwin Kramer, then the minister of transportation, sent civil engineers to Western European countries to gather information about the latest technologies and concepts of highway and road construction, as part of the means of reaching the goal of *Weltniveau* (a world-class level).[55] Road-planners realized during their visits to England and France that route designs in those countries were largely determined by economic considerations. Therefore, they stated with surprise, this way of planning "would not fit with the conditions presented to us in the GDR concerning aesthetics and the question of how roads fit best into the landscape."[56]

GDR engineers maintained the attitudes toward landscape design that had been developed before the war. These views were established as common sense among the elder and younger generations, a common sense validated both by shared experience and by textbooks on road construction. The textbooks published in the GDR during the 1950s repeated verbatim the words and phrases from those of the 1930s. Johannes Kastl, born in 1905 and in 1949 appointed head of the road-construction administration in Saxony, authored most of the few textbooks on road construction for civil-engineering students in the GDR. In them he accepted without question the aesthetic principles formed during the 1930s on the harmony of roads, bridges, and landscapes.[57] "The wide strip of the autobahn should be integrated as a new element of landscape design; otherwise the scenery will be reduced considerably. Because the routes through the landscape do not run in accordance with mathematical laws, it is necessary to analyze systematically all the experiences and the knowledge gained in the past construction of the autobahn."[58]

In contrast to this statement from 1960, republished in 1968, other sources indicate that the mathematical principle of the clothoid was at that time as much favored in the GDR as it was in West Germany.[59] GDR civil engineers drew most of their information about the state of the art of their profession from West German technical literature, although this was difficult to obtain after 1961. The harmonious integration of nature and technology by the mimetic principle of road construction was taught in technical universities of the GDR as it was in West Germany, engaging with "good" and "bad" images of the *Reichsautobahn*. The "bad" examples displayed long straight sections, sharp curves, and zig-zagging paths. The "good" examples showed, in contrast, the gently rolling sections of the *Reichsautobahn* that had been built in the mid-1930s.

The Soviet textbook *Aesthetics of Road Construction* (1967) also argued for harmonizing road design with nature. In this book the "good" examples are photographs of what appear to be (West) German autobahns during the 1930s *and* the 1950s, but the exact locations are never actually identified in the picture captions. The photographs show the roads' sweeping lines with trees and bushes along the margins.[60] These images are contrasted with photographs of "bad" roads, which show American inner-city highways during rush hour. These are classic images of utilitarian civil planning: featureless, treeless lanes of concrete cutting through residential and industrial areas.

In theory, then, the desire to harmonize roads and nature for the pleasure of car drivers was clear. In practice, however, the major political and economic claims for fast, efficient, and cost-effective construction were at long last overriding these minor questions of aesthetics—very much to the regret of some young East German engineers of the *Aufbaugeneration*, who had tried to save and develop the practical knowledge of their mentors and masters. Questions of money and security had been more relevant than those of landscape architecture. Sometimes, however, issues of safety and design were bound together. Civil engineer Rolf Näser recalled how he and other engineers considered adopting aspects of highway construction that they knew were used in the United States:

> There was the question of how to design the median strip. You can't imagine the discussions we had then! There are median strips in America that are much broader than those in Europe and have a trough. Those median strips are planted very lushly but only with bushes—not with trees. The advantage is that you don't need crash barriers. . . . Such ideas we discussed again and again. But they wouldn't work out! Our land is too valuable here in the GDR—or [was] at that time in the GDR.[61]

It was not environmental issues but matters of agricultural outsourcing and speed of construction that drove decisions about route design in the GDR. When the route from Berlin to Rostock was eventually built, crash barriers were installed only next to the bridges, and there was not a single gas station along the 270-kilometer stretch. This autobahn was not much more than a paved concrete double line running in smooth curves through the landscape.[62] As was the case with the Leipzig-to-Dresden route in 1971, there was not much public celebration when the new autobahn was opened to the traffic. The road construction left barren strips of land about thirty meters wide on both sides of the autobahn, which party authorities demanded be planted with fast-growing trees and bushes. A green roadside should help to meet "international standards." About three million Ostmarks were budgeted for landscaping, although in the end only one million were actually spent for this purpose.[63] In order to have the green roadside "ready" as quickly as possible, highly diluted Agent Orange imported from Great Britain was used. While application of this chemical would change the natural growth cycles of the plants, it would also accomplish the visual aim: getting something "green and pretty" along the autobahn—no matter what the ecological costs.

To be sure, this is an extreme example of landscape-design practices along the autobahn in the GDR. But all available records lead to the conclusion that landscape design was mentioned in the programs only because senior civil engineers knew very well that it was essential to modern road construction, along with high standards of services and driving safety.[64] In all these respects the GDR autobahns displayed deficiencies when measured against established standards. It was these discrepancies with the West German model that gave socialist highways their distinctive character.

The Autobahn as Showroom of Socialism?

The everyday experience of the driver demonstrates that East German autobahns were unsuited to the construction of a positive self-image. The disrepair of the infrastructure was in fact a cause of psychological alienation within the GDR. Many East Germans turned to the road-building authorities with petitions and complaints, reporting on conditions of the socialist autobahn with displeasure and even fury. A small sampling of such letters from 1987 and 1988 illustrates the experience of the autobahn from its users' perspective.[65]

In a general petition, shift workers complained about the "unbearable noise pollution" on the autobahn from Berlin to Dresden.[66] A Dresden motorist gave vent to long-suppressed anger over the autobahn from Dresden to Bautzen: "The word *autobahn* shouldn't even be allowed to be used here. These ongoing repairs are just stopgaps."[67] The quality of gastronomy and the condition of the toilets at the rest stops was criticized repeatedly. One woman, writing of her experience at a rest stop in Köckern, summed it up in words that also seem to describe the general state of things in the GDR: "Everything is so forlorn."[68] This driver, observing that acceptable toilets were available only to Western travelers just passing through the GDR, asked: "Should we East-German women just sit ourselves down on the Autobahn, like the men stand around?" At the Teufelstal rest stop she preferred the woods to the public toilet. A stand of trees on the GDR-autobahn, while offering little by way of a romantic vision of nature, could nevertheless provide privacy in a moment of need. "But so many foreigners come by there that one is ashamed."[69]

This expression of shame in front of travelers from the West is repeated in these letters,[70] but their authors are also angered and bewildered by the apparent discrimination against citizens of the GDR in their own country. "Why are acceptable facilities built only for Westerners? In what categories do our citizens fall?"[71] This letter, from a dentist who described himself as "representing countless 'sufferers,'" was apparently signed by many of his fellow East Germans. His protest linked the disrepair of the autobahn between Dresden and Bautzen with the issue of car maintenance: "This 'hiking path' absolutely cannot be described as an autobahn! In parts one doesn't know how to avoid 'car traps.' There even 20 km/h is too much! Does this bear any resemblance to an autobahn? Especially considering that we have to keep our cars running as long as possible, with the waiting periods for new ones and the situation with service and spare parts!"[72] The driver of a Trabant, the most widely sold car in the GDR, inquired angrily about the potholes on the section of the autobahn near Jena: "Does the responsibility for taking precautions rest only with the driver, or do you also have responsibilities? . . . Who will repair my vehicle when it is destroyed by these hair-raising conditions?"[73]

In the answering letters from authorities, East German citizens had to read sentences such as this one, written in 1988: "On account of other building projects the central building authority is not responsible for this construction. . . . Repairs to the road between Dresden and Bautzen cannot be expected before 2000."[74] Such reactions could hardly have satisfied the authors of these petitions, as they just revealed once again the well-known situation of economic crisis. As "showrooms of socialism," the GDR autobahns broke down. With these difficulties in the foreground, a drive on the autobahn left the beauty of the landscape by the wayside. An impression of nature was not conveyed as part of the driving experience. Anyone who had to worry about shock absorbers and the next toilet certainly had no feeling any longer for the beauties of the landscape on either side of the autobahn.

And how did Western travelers passing through the provinces of the GDR perceive the trip on the autobahn? Owing to the lack of other sources, the comments of two writers must suffice as representative of this transit experience: the unpleasant crossing over the borders, the strict speed limit on the autobahn (one hundred kilometers per hour), and the monitoring of traffic by the police and state security were for Western travelers like a "school of dictatorship."[75] As the West Berlin writer Friedrich Christian Delius summarizes it: "The Western sense of freedom, what would it have been without this transit journey?"[76]

The difference between East and West was physically discernible even at the border crossing to West Berlin: the rhythm of the dull stretches between the plates of concrete followed the driver to the next checkpoint. Peter Schneider, a writer from West Berlin, wrote pointedly in 1982 about his feelings as he approached West Berlin after driving for two hours through East Germany: "Sighting the wide taillights of the cars, the pale showroom lights, the turning Mercedes star above the Europe-Center, I was overcome by the desire that seizes the car driver after two hundred kilometers in transit on the Berlin AVUS: to step back, to let the beast inside run wild. Once again to order a beer at midnight, to buy a newspaper, to hold a hand-written menu in your hand, to gaze into the dissipated face of the West."[77]

As clichéd as such pictures may be, they make clear what Delius himself knew: "The country through which we pass barely interests us."[78] The Western gaze through the car window during the journey across the GDR was politically inscribed. It showed the GDR in sharp contrast to the West, as a charmless state of total surveillance. Images of its political alternatives posted intermittently along the stretches of autobahn had just as little appeal as the recurring but unobtrusive advertisements on the autobahn bridges or, during the Leipzig Fair, on the median strips (fig. 8.4). There was no demand for "plastic and elastic from Schkopau" and "machines from Bulgaria"; nor did alternative products exist for East Germans. Instead the ads left an impression of constant political indoctrination in an otherwise barren landscape.

8.4. A section of the Leipzig autobahn with road signs declaring the GDR an internationally recognized trade partner. Photograph by Jürgen Dossmann, 1969.

Conclusion

The mathematical curve theory employed by engineers in the late 1930s became established only in the two postwar German states, where it came to influence the aesthetics of the German landscape. Not only the construction of curves in the Federal Republic but also the "sweeping" of new highways in the GDR "buil[t] geometrically and geodesically upon Schürba's Tafelwerk [i.e., guidelines]" of 1942.[79] This adaptation of road architecture to the dynamics of high-speed automobile traffic, which until 1945 was accompanied by *völkisch* and national arguments, also demonstrated a great deal of continuity, in that the inventors of clothoid curve design were able to take up leading positions in the agencies of the Federal Republic soon after the war. In the GDR as well, engineers who had been involved in construction of the autobahn during the Third Reich passed on the doctrine of the adaptation of roadways to the landscape—a doctrine that was neither genuinely National Socialist nor offered any guarantee that ecological considerations would be taken into account. The history of the sweeping curve is a fascinating example of the complex interactions and negotiations that took place under varying political regimes between champions of a technical idea and the cultural interpreters of landscape and *Heimat*.

A desire to be able to travel freely in one's own automobile had been stimulated among Germans in the 1930s under the National Socialist regime. After a delay of more than a decade, many East Germans could also fulfill this desire—not with the "strength through joy" automobile (*KdF-Wagen*) or the Volkswagen, but rather with the Trabant or Wartburg. Under National Socialism, in the Federal Republic, and in the GDR, German society's efforts at acceleration found in the autobahn a fitting visual and technical medium. As a symbol of unchecked progress, the highway also remained attractive for the GDR's would-be socialist utopia and was supposed to serve as a memorial to the era of postwar reconstruction.

As a purportedly ideal technical instrument of social, political, and cultural integration and for the harmonious flow of economic energy, the autobahn today remains an issue employed by politicians seeking to appeal to (motorized) voters. As the first free elections in the GDR approached, German Chancellor Helmut Kohl, the "architect of German unity," promised East German voters that he would soon establish "blühende Landschaften," or blossoming landscapes. One element in this political vision of a cultural landscape had been the Neue Verkehrsprojekte Deutsche Einheit (New Traffic Projects of German Unity), including the construction of several autobahn routes that had been in the works since the 1920s. Kohl's party, the CDU, won the election with a decisive majority in East Germany.

In Germany political freedom and automobility are inextricably linked with one another, especially in the East, where until 1990 the hoped-for *freie Fahrt* (open road) ended, in the best case, at the state border. For many desperate citizens of the GDR who attempted to flee, travel ended with death at the final steel barrier of the state security services.[80] Without a doubt it is also for this reason that traveling on an American interstate highway figured prominently among the longings of many East Germans after 1990. Unlimited speed and new highways are, however, anything but the route to political freedom, as the experience of the present has finally demonstrated.

NINE

"'Beautified' Is a Vile Phrase"

The Politics and Aesthetics of Landscaping Roads
in Pre- and Postwar Britain

Peter Merriman

Introduction

In this chapter, I examine the debates that emerged in the 1930s, '40s, and
'50s about the landscaping and planting of Britain's roads and motorways.[1]
Landscape architects and other design professionals assumed a prominent
role in the landscaping and planting of the German autobahns and American parkways during the 1930s,[2] but British architects, horticulturists,
preservationists, and landscape professionals had little or no formal, routine involvement in highway *design* until the government began to execute
their postwar reconstruction plans in the mid-1950s and '60s.[3] I explore the
disagreements that emerged between preservationists, horticulturists, and
landscape architects about the most appropriate styles of designing and
planting Britain's roads and motorways. I examine the early work of the Roads
Beautifying Association (RBA) during the 1920s and '30s, when the association advised local authorities on the planting of several hundred miles of
arterial and bypass roads. I then study the work of planner-preservationists
on the Council for the Preservation of Rural England who criticized the
RBA for its predilection for ornamental flowering trees and shrubs, and argued that Britain required a national network of carefully designed, orderly,

functional, modern roads and motorways similar to those being constructed in Germany and Italy. Next I consider the arguments promoted by modernist landscape architects, including Brenda Colvin, Sylvia Crowe, and Geoffrey Jellicoe, who criticized the RBA for concentrating on the relatively superficial issue of roadside planting rather than focusing on larger concerns, such as the layout, design, and landscaping (as well as planting) of Britain's roads and motorways. Then I address arguments made during the mid-1950s by Ian Nairn and others who saw the nation's new motorways as a solution to the spread of a universal suburbia, or subtopia, that was blighting the British landscape. Finally I examine commentators' reactions to the design and landscaping of Britain's first major motorway, the initial sections of the London-to-Yorkshire motorway, known as the M1, which were opened to the public on November 2, 1959.

The Roads Beautifying Association and (Sub)urban Aesthetics

The Roads Improvement Act of 1925 empowered local authorities to purchase land bordering roadways for amenity purposes, but few councils exercised their powers.[4] In a 1928 letter to the *Daily Express,* Dr. Wilfrid Fox—a businessman, amateur horticulturist, and retired physician—expressed his dismay at the ongoing neglect of Britain's roadsides.[5] After a meeting with Minister of Transport Colonel Wilfrid Ashley, Fox founded the Roads Beautifying Association. The association's first meeting was attended by prominent politicians, county-council officers, and arboricultural, horticultural, and transport experts. Within days they announced their intention to beautify the Kingston Bypass with plantings.[6] As this new bypass was located in suburban Surrey, the association proposed avenues of cherry trees; flowering shrubs, such as broom, laburnum, and roses; wild flowers, to include bluebells, primroses, and cowslips; as well as chestnut, hornbeam, scarlet oak, and copper beech trees. Almost at once, however, commentators expressed concerns about the association's choices. First, despite assurances that no trees with heavy foliage would be planted, journalists and members of the public pointed to the dangers of skidding, listing this as one reason why vandals had destroyed some of the new trees on the bypass.[7] Horticultural writer Edwin Campbell presented the situation as one of "art *versus* utility," asserting that the association had completely ignored the views of motorists and that, "on principle, we are opposed to roadside tree planting."[8] The second set of criticisms involved the types of species being planted. It was suggested that the planting proposals were "too exotic," were unsuitable for local conditions, and contained too few "characteristically British" trees—charges that would be leveled at the work of the Roads Beautifying Association well into the 1950s.[9] Wilfrid Fox referred to those who held these views as critics from "the pure English school . . . who think that the scenery of England is so beautiful that if you make any changes or additions you are ruining the picture and that only trees and shrubs indigenous to England should be employed to adorn roads."[10] In Fox's opinion, these commentators lacked historical knowledge and horticultural expertise, as many of England's most successful and well-loved species had been introduced into the landscape by progressive and enlightened landowners and landscape gardeners. At a time when the landowner's power was in decline following the breakup of many large country estates after World War I, the need arose for "some other authority" that could continue the "*constructive* beautification of the countryside."[11] Supporters argued that, in the case of roadsides, this authority should be the Roads Beautifying Association.

The English landscape was seen as a dynamic achievement expressing different senses of tradition and modernity; and while an organization such as the National Trust focused on the preservation of "old inherited charms," the RBA committed itself to "the reconstruction of English scenery" and "the growth of a new character, reflecting modern life":[12]

> The truth is that the scenery of England has changed throughout the ages and is always in a state of transition, never static, . . . and what we have got to do is to hand on to posterity something which is worthy of our present knowledge. . . . It is impossible to stand still in either science or art, and landscape horticulture is surely a combination of both. . . . Why should the architects be the only revolutionaries? For good or ill they have in this era definitely left their stamp on our cities, but they deny the horticulturists the right to do the same thing on our roads.[13]

The Roads Beautifying Association's horticulturists were styled as progressive modernizers of the English landscape: planting species suited to the surroundings, introducing foreign species where appropriate, planting "garden hybrids and varieties" in urban or semiurban spaces, yet ensuring that only "wild species" appeared in open countryside.[14] The German autobahns and American parkways offered instructive models to the British highway engineer and horticulturist. Photographs of both were placed alongside English examples in Roads Beautifying Association booklets such as *The Highway Beautiful*,[15] but Fox also looked to such diverse sites as Alpine passes and Japanese suburbs when formulating a vision of picturesque roads adorned with flowering trees and shrubs: "I should like to see as much as possible of the small leafed flowering tree, of the cherry type. . . . I see no reason why the outskirts of London should not be as beautiful as [those of] Tokio."[16] While horticulturists engaged in discussions about the relative merits of planting "indigenous" and "exotic" species, the urban or rural character of individual roads was also vigorously debated. In 1944, three prominent members of the Roads Beautifying Association stressed that many of their most notable and controversial schemes—including bypasses at Crawley, Henley, Winchester, and Kingston—had been planted with flowering shrubs and trees because they were fast roads in the vicinity of towns, a circumstance that "to our way of thinking calls for colour schemes which readily strike the eye."[17] The landscapes surrounding these roads were seen to warrant an urban or suburban horticultural treatment. This was a time when suburbia was "a contentious English landscape, valued by some as essentially English in its modest scale, domestic values, and humdrum life, and castigated by others for the same characteristics."[18] The RBA envisaged detailed, colorful planting schemes for urban and suburban areas, but landscape architects and planner-preservationists countered this view by arguing that fast-moving roads necessitated functional and unobtrusive designs that would calm rather than distract or excite drivers.

The Council for the Preservation of Rural England and Roadside Order

While the Roads Beautifying Association regarded itself as progressive and its detractors as conservative, ill-informed, and antimodern in their approach to roadside planting, many of its critics were associated with organizations that presented their own designs as forward-thinking, innovative, and modern. During the late 1920s and the 1930s, prominent planner-preservationists affiliated with the Council for the Preservation of Rural England—including Clough Williams-Ellis, H. H. Peach, and Noel Carrington—turned their attention to the state of Britain's roads, where unplanned growth, laissez-faire capitalism, and the (in)actions of local authorities were blamed for the resulting ribbon development, roadside clutter, and visual disorder.[19] Planner-preservationists contrasted the haphazard development of British roads with the order and efficiency of motorways and gas stations they had observed in Italy, Germany, and the United States.[20] In 1937, a delegation of 224 British politicians, engineers, motoring enthusiasts, and landscape architects toured Germany in order to study the national highway system there. In its subsequent report the German Roads Delegation praised the autobahns' comprehensive planning, modern design, and extensive landscaping.[21] Other commentators suggested that the German government's ambitious construction programs could not, and should not, be emulated in a democratic country like Britain. As the editor of the *Geographical Magazine* explained in a preface to Alan Brodrick's January 1938 article "The New German Motor-Roads":

> Dictatorship expresses itself naturally in grandiose public works, of which the German *Autobahnen* afford a striking example. Democratic governments, subject to critical opposition and accountable for every item of expenditure, cannot afford to burden the exchequer from motives of self-advertisement, still less for the sake of unavowed aims. . . . Fascinating, therefore, as the new German motor roads undoubtedly are to a people so motor-conscious as our own, the extent to which they offer a model to be imitated in Great Britain can only be assessed after full consideration of the circumstances in which they were built; and for this purpose Mr Brodrick's article supplies valuable material.[22]

Motorways became equated with extravagance and self-advertisement, and despite the campaigning of such groups as the German Roads Delegation, British Road Federation, and County Surveyors' Society, the British government decided against the construction of motorways for traffic-related and economic reasons.[23]

The CPRE worked hard to influence government policy. In November 1936, it established a Trunk Roads Joint Committee in an attempt to shape the horticultural and design policies that would be applied to the forty-five hundred miles of highways brought under government control with the Trunk Roads Act of 1937.[24] The Roads Beautifying Association saw this new committee as an unwanted competitor, but the ensuing arguments died down after the Ministry of Transport appointed the RBA to act as its official adviser in 1938.[25] Very little work was undertaken during World War II, and in 1947 the Ministry of Transport replaced the Roads Beautifying Association with a single horticultural adviser, W. G. Sheat. The choice of Sheat was unpopular with both the RBA and the CPRE. The RBA was incensed that its own experts had been superseded by "a young New Zealander, a boy in his early twenties at the outbreak of war, prior to which he had completed 15 months at Kew."[26] P. A. Barnes, secretary of the Lancashire branch of the CPRE, expressed dismay that the ministry had chosen "an expert on herbaceous borders" who had spent most of his career in Australia; while the well-known planner-preservationist Clough Williams-Ellis, in a letter to *The Manchester Guardian,* criticized not only Sheat's appointment but also the Roads Beautifying Association, disparaging the RBA's "incorrigible addiction for little exotic timidities."[27] Williams-Ellis and other planner-preservationists feared that the nation's roads would be transformed into fussy suburban or urban gardens through the use of "foreign" plants. To avert such a danger, the CPRE revived its Roads Joint Committee in 1949. The Committee included representatives from the CPRE, the RBA, the Automobile Association, and the Royal Forestry Society of England and Wales, as well as a prominent figure from the Institute of Landscape Architects (ILA), Brenda Colvin, who joined the CPRE in criticizing the work of the RBA.

Landscape Architects and the "Modern" Road

In the 1940s, leading lights in the Institute of Landscape Architects—including Geoffrey Jellicoe, Brenda Colvin, and Sylvia Crowe—actively sought to construct and promote a role for their profession at the heart of postwar planning, architecture, and design policy and practice. The involvement of an increasing number of influential planners, architects, and geographers in the institute during World War II—including Lord Reith, Thomas Sharp, Clough Williams-Ellis, and Dudley Stamp—helped to provide opportunities for landscape architects in the postwar period, while new academic posts and courses at British universities provided the educational base for this expansion.[28] With these and other developments, the Institute of Landscape Architects began to distance itself from its prewar image as a "domestic garden society."[29] Suburban landscapes and private gardens became associated with domesticity, amateurism, and triviality; and senior members of the institute contended that professional landscape architects, planners, and engineers should be charged with shaping nationally important public *and* private spaces. As Brenda Colvin commented in 1951: "In matters concerning landscape and gardens in Britain, it seems that the advice of the gardener, or of some commercial firm, or even an amateur is still considered good enough by self-respecting Public Bodies who would quite appreciate the need for professional advice in matters concerning architecture, engineering, or health. The profession of Landscape Architecture has yet to reach the point where it is felt to be indispensable in its own field."[30]

During the 1940s, '50s, and '60s, government departments, public bodies, and private organizations began to employ landscape architects on a regular basis in the design of forestry plantations, new towns, housing estates, schools, factories, power stations, universities, airports, and reservoirs. However, the continual postponement of the government's roads program led to few changes in policies on the landscaping of roads. In the 1940s, landscape architects had joined planner-preservationists in berating the Roads Beautifying Association and local councils for their concentration on roadside planting to the neglect of "a more fundamental" approach to the landscaping and design of roads.[31] The planting of vegetation should form just one element in the landscaping of a road, with the primary goal being to construct what American landscape architects and engineers termed a *fitted highway:* a road shaped to the surrounding landscape and suited to future traffic conditions and speed limits.[32] Landscape architects, like horticulturists and planner-preservationists, looked abroad for inspiration. Sylvia Crowe had met New York landscape architect Gilmore D. Clarke on a tour of the United States in 1958, and she praised the Connecticut Turnpike for its "clean lines," "beautiful gradients, well-shaped embankments, and graceful bridges."[33] Jellicoe upheld the parkways as "one of the three great contributions" America had "made to modern landscape," while he expressed surprise that with the autobahns "the military mind should have put so much value on landscape."[34] Foreign motorways could inspire British landscape architects to do great things, but Jellicoe and others were quite clear that the design of English roads and motorways must reflect the Englishness and regional character of English landscapes.

In the latter years of World War II—when a broad range of institutions and individuals were lobbying the British government to place a national network of motorways at the heart of postwar reconstruction plans—the British Road Federation commissioned Geoffrey Jellicoe, then president of the Institute of Landscape Architects, to design an exhibition entitled *Motorways for Britain*.[35] At the heart of the exhibition were photographs of twelve well-known British beauty spots onto which Jellicoe had sketched his vision of future landscaped motorways. The theory behind the illustrations was outlined in the *Wartime Journal of the Institute of Landscape Architects:* "The twelve imaginary roads shown in the exhibition are intended to suggest that the modern motor road not only need not spoil the landscape, but should enhance it. It is essential that we all retain this sense of positive planning, for it is our tradition, extending over many centuries of history."[36] The exhibition was one of several wartime commissions that provided Jellicoe with a break from designing standardized government housing projects, while the British Road Federation was keen for this distinguished architect and landscape designer to show how the modern motorways it advocated would blend into "different types of English scenery" and improve the view.[37] No exhibition catalogue was published, but the images were reproduced throughout the 1940s and '50s in numerous British Road Federation and landscape-architecture publications. In 1948 Jellicoe's sketch of a motorway running alongside the Malvern Hills in Worcestershire appeared on the cover of a BRF booklet titled *The Case for Motorways* (fig. 9.1).[38] In a lecture delivered at the Institution of Civil Engineers in 1944, Jellicoe had described how this picture, showing the alignment of the two carriageways on "either side of an existing hedge," demonstrated a "very simple but very subtle" feature that would integrate the motorway into the surrounding hills.[39] Detailed explanations of this kind were notably absent from *The Case for Motorways,* which contained one short paragraph suggesting that Britain's new motorways would "provide opportunities for landscaping which will improve the countryside."[40] While visions of attractive modern motorways might convince skeptical preservationists of their possible advantages, *The Case for Motorways* was designed to persuade members of Parliament to approve the 1948 Special

The case for

MOTORWAYS

BRITISH ROAD FEDERATION

9.1. Cover of a 1948 pamphlet published by the British Road Federation and featuring a photo montage by renowned landscape architect Sir Geoffrey Jellicoe. Reproduced by kind permission of the British Road Federation.

Roads Bill (legislation that would authorize government construction of limited-access motorways). It is not surprising, then, that at this time of fiscal crisis, the primary focus of *The Case for Motorways* was on the economic benefits of construction. The approach was largely successful. The British Road Federation's booklets and lobbying activities were widely praised in parliamentary debates, but despite the almost-routine enactment of the bill in 1949, Minister of Transport Alfred Barnes admitted that the prevailing economic situation would prevent motorway construction for the foreseeable future.[41]

In his writings, Jellicoe stressed that different senses of tradition and history must be reflected in visions of modern, British motorways, and he advised landscape architects to examine the successes and failures of England's past and present landscapes. In a lecture delivered to the Town Planning Institute in October of 1958, Jellicoe argued that while motorways *could* bring an end to a century of badly designed roads in Britain, the precedent for modern motorway design might also be found in the history of British roads. Jellicoe suggested that landscape architects might find inspiration in a nineteenth-century watercolor titled *The Shadowed Road,* by the Norwich School painter John Crome (1768–1821).[42] The painting depicts a small country lane, and while Jellicoe acknowledged that this road was not comparable in terms of scale to any modern highway, the framing of the view and the representation and composition of the landscape could hold the key for postwar motorway designers:

> A complex of tree foliage, the incident of a cottage, the glimpse of a distant view, and an overall play of light and shade. It is precisely these elements, so powerful in their effect upon the imagination, that basically comprise each of the pictures that should unfold before a traveller today. It is merely a matter of planning technique that the pictures are to be broadened and lengthened to adjust themselves to greater widths, greater speed, and to all those factors of safety that are accepted without question by the designer.[43]

Jellicoe invited highway designers to transpose the composition of the lane in Crome's painting to the scale of the modern motorway, emphasizing the fluid, ever-changing visual experience of the driver, as Sylvia Crowe would do in her book *The Landscape of Roads:*

> Driving down a fast traffic road should be a continuous experience of visual pleasure combined with the sense of effortless speed. Safety and pleasure demand that every change of direction or speed should be foreseen well in advance, and every change of scenery

and passing landmark should be appreciated to the full. The same
planting which serves to bind the road into the landscape should
also make the road read like an unfolding scroll before the driver.[44]

The task of the landscape architect and engineer is, then, to provide the
driver with a pleasurable, safe, and enlivening (but not distracting) experience of the landscapes of the road, knitting its forms into the surrounding
countryside.[45] New roads should follow the undulations of the terrain.
Carriageways can be separated horizontally or vertically. Excessive parallelism and monotony should be prevented by planting vegetation and incorporating irregularly shaped pieces of land into the verges. Trees and
shrubs can emphasize curves, prevent dazzle, screen unsightly features, or
frame attractive views. Planting emerges as a functional tool, contributing
to the overall design of the road's landscapes while helping to shape drivers' perceptions, behavior, and actions: "Good planting contributes interest
and variety to the road, which helps to keep the driver alert and vigilant."[46]
Planting may be very simple or sparse, and should be limited to species
found locally (whether or not they were originally introduced from elsewhere). Indeed, Colvin suggests that a well-designed motorway passing
through open country may require little or no planting, as the "dramatic
variations" in topography, geology, or vegetation in the English countryside "can too easily be blurred and lost to the motorist by a lavish use of
trees and shrubs of exotic or garden type."[47] Rural roads and motorways
should not be planted with the colorful flowering trees and shrubs typically
found in urban or suburban gardens, as these require too much maintenance, do not blend in with a rural landscape, and may distract drivers
traveling at high speeds. Silhouettes, a limited palette (essentially, shades
of green), simple textures, and informal arrangements are more effective
tools than detailed, formal arrangements and bright color.

In analyzing examples of good and bad highway design and planting
in her 1960 book *The Landscape of Roads*, Sylvia Crowe compared a number of modern English bypass roads built in the late 1930s with what were
then considered the best highways in America and Germany.[48] Among her
English examples is the Mickleham Bypass: "one of the most pleasant
main roads constructed during the 'thirties . . . curving delightfully under
the wooded slopes of Box Hill" and preserving some "magnificent trees"
between its two carriageways.[49] Crowe felt that this was a modern road laid

out and engineered with considerable expertise, but while careful landscaping could have improved the appearance of this bypass—enhancing distinctive features of the terrain and composing striking views—the plantings had clearly been "put in as an afterthought" rather than as an integrated part of the design, with "strips of *Lonicera nitida* hedge and . . . solid bands of *Buxus*" suggesting "an urban park rather than the countryside."[50] The urban and the decorative, like the suburban and the ornamental, were seen to be out of place, acting as disordering presences in the English countryside. Crowe identified the Bix-Henley Road in Oxfordshire as another example of the same problem. As Crowe and most of her readers were well aware, the planting schemes for both of these roads had been prepared by the Roads Beautifying Association, although she mentioned the RBA by name only in an opening section of the book, where she described its concern for the "cosmetic rather than organic" as not "radical" enough to solve the problem of Britain's ugly roads.[51] Just as Wilfrid Fox had earlier contrasted the RBA's progressive horticultural solutions with a backward-looking preservationism linked to the CPRE, so Crowe would compare the shortfalls and superficiality of the association's "cosmeticism" with the more fundamental, comprehensive, and avant-garde designs of landscape architects. Contrasting planting practices and styles are variously viewed by these different organizations as radical, conservative, progressive, modern, or conventional, highlighting the complexity of debates about modernist aesthetics.

"Subtopia": Landscape and Visual Disorder in 1950s Britain

The ugliness, visual disorder, and "suburban" planting that Crowe observed on Britain's roads constituted just one aspect of an aesthetic blight that appeared to threaten the English landscape. At a time when modernist and functionalist design philosophies dominated discourses of architecture and landscape architecture, Ian Nairn put together a landmark special issue of Architectural Review titled "Outrage," published in June 1955.[52] In it Nairn diagnosed a national disease which he called "Subtopia": a universal suburbia, a "mean and a middle state, neither town nor country," where difference has been eroded through "the *mass application* of *misunderstood principles*" (italics in original):[53] "The difference is between the standardization that makes all places look alike and the standardization that looks right for all places: the difference between Subtopia and the Functional Tradition."[54] Both the problem and its solution were seen to rest with the visual education and skills of the public and experts.[55] While Nairn cast the local-authority engineer and borough surveyor as enemies of order who lacked "visual training" and knowledge of modern functionalist planning and design principles, he identified the architect, the landscape architect, and the observant citizen as potential saviors of a threatened nation.[56] The landscape architect possessed the expertise to prevent these problems from occurring, and the "man in the street" could be guided by Nairn's "checklist of malpractices" as he sought to bring about change in his own neighborhood.[57]

Nairn emphasized the pervasiveness of subtopian forces in a discussion of the spaces most noticeably affected by them: the spaces of the street or road. Ugly lampposts, redundant and poorly designed signposts, rundown cafés and garages, and mutilated trees peppered the landscapes of England's roads—eyesores that planner-preservationists associated with the CPRE had been complaining of since the 1920s.[58] According to Nairn and his colleagues at the *Architectural Review,* a style that they identified as "municipal rustic" was spreading from the desks of municipal engineers and generating the "small-scale," "fussy" embellishments that landscape architects and planner-preservationists associated with the Roads Beautifying Association (and with its clients, the local authorities).[59] Municipal rustic confused the "private and [the] public" and resulted in the proliferation of incongruous "flower garden[s]" and "herbaceous border[s]" along rural dual carriageways from the urban roundabout: "The planting should have been decided by trained landscape architects when the road was cut or the roundabout made. Instead, it has been left to the local authorities."[60] Architects, landscape architects, and planner-preservationists appeared united around visions of an "ordering modernism," in which a functionalist aesthetic could prevent or correct the errors of the local planner or engineer.[61] Indeed, leading advocates and practitioners of the arts and sciences of landscape design and preservation met regularly at conferences and symposia, sat together on committees, and engaged in dialogue through such fora as the *Architectural Review* and the *Journal of the Institute of Landscape Architects.*[62] In February 1956, Crowe, Nairn, and others discussed the issues raised in "Outrage" at a "Symposium on Subtopia" organized by the

Institute of Landscape Architects, and in December of that year another special issue of the *Architectural Review,* titled "Counter-attack," was published.[63] Nairn's "Counter-attack," like Crowe's *Tomorrow's Landscape* (also published in 1956), proposed solutions to the problems of subtopia, remedies that had been missing from "Outrage," his "prophecy of doom."[64]

As carefully planned, designed, and controlled spaces for high-speed movement, Britain's motorways were in many ways a positive counterattack on subtopia. Reflecting on "Outrage" in 1975, Nairn observed that the growth in "motorway land" comprised "the only drastic change in 20 years" along the four-hundred-mile route between Southampton and Carlisle that he had surveyed in 1955.[65] What's more, "motorway design and landscaping" had emerged as "one of the few genuinely collective and genuinely hopeful parts of design in Britain."[66] These highly ordered landscapes were complex, ongoing achievements. The Royal Fine Art Commission had played its role, but it was the government's establishment of the Advisory Committee on the Landscape Treatment of Trunk Roads (or Landscape Advisory Committee) in July 1955 which constituted probably the single most important advance, bringing together individuals who were committed to ensuring order in the design of these modern landscapes of mobility.[67] The Landscape Advisory Committee's policies reflected the prevailing views of representatives from the CPRE and the ILA, while the appointment of Sir David Bowes-Lyon (President, Royal Horticultural Society, 1953–61) as committee chairman effectively muffled the voice of the Roads Beautifying Association's representative, Wilfrid Fox.[68] Sir David set the tone at the committee's first meeting, in April 1956, when he stated the importance of visualizing "the effect of road landscape treatment as seen by the driver" and expressed the hope that his colleagues would "advocate the use of indigenous trees and discourage the use of foreign trees . . . which were uncharacteristic of the region."[69] Sir David's call for the exclusion of "foreign trees" may appear to echo the Nazis' policy of planting the autobahns with native German species, but while the latter sometimes entwined exclusionary nationalist ideologies with discourses of race, ecology, and landscape, the Landscape Advisory Committee grounded their planting policy in horticultural and aesthetic debates about which species would both *look right* and *grow well* in the British landscape.[70] The majority of committee members supported Sir David's views, and in September 1956 Wilfrid Fox resigned, citing the "fundamental difference in outlook" between "the

Chairman and other vocal members of the committee, and myself" as his reason.[71] In 1957 and 1958, the committee focused its attention on extensive landscaping schemes, and internal disputes between committee members were soon replaced by disagreements with other organizations and individuals.

"A new look at the English landscape":
The Landscaping and Planting of the M1 Motorway

The Landscape Advisory Committee's first significant task was to advise on the design and planting of Britain's first major motorway, the initial sections of the London-to-Yorkshire motorway, known as the M1. The exact line of the motorway had been fixed by engineers prior to the committee's first meeting, and the desire to prevent further delays prompted civil servants in the Ministry of Transport to limit the committee's remit to relatively superficial aspects of the motorway:

> In the case of the London-Yorkshire Road . . . it has taken . . . several years to find a satisfactory line. If a road of this description were then to be submitted to a Committee who would no doubt want to go over it from end to end and criticise it from an aesthetic point of view and the consultants had then to examine their alternative suggestions, I am afraid that the making of the scheme and the actual construction would have to be very considerably postponed.[72]

The motorway had been designed by the well-known engineering firm of Sir Owen Williams and Partners, but the absence of any qualified landscape architect to help formulate or coordinate the designs induced prominent members of the profession to lobby for a change in the government's policy. In his role as a Royal Fine Art Commissioner, Geoffrey Jellicoe persuaded Godfrey Samuel, the Secretary of the Commission, to meet Sir Owen Williams and request that the ministry appoint landscape consultants for all major highway schemes, including the London-to-Yorkshire motorway.[73] Ministry officials and representatives of Sir Owen Williams and Partners held a meeting with Jellicoe and Richard Sudell (president of the ILA from 1955 to 1957) to discuss the appointment of consultants for the London-to-Yorkshire route, but while the institute suggested the names of five qualified candidates—Brenda Colvin, Sylvia Crowe, J. W. M. Dudding, Richard Sudell, and L. Milner White—the high fees they quoted led the minister to instruct the motorway's engineers to employ their own consultants.[74] Accordingly, in February 1957, Sir Owen Williams and Partners employed a well-known forestry expert, A. P. Long, along with a junior officer named A. J. M. Clay; but as neither was a professional landscape architect, the Royal Fine Art Commission, Institute of Landscape Architects, Royal Institute of British Architects, and their allies in Parliament continued to argue for the appointment of landscape architects to advise on all major road schemes.[75] By now the president of the ILA was Sylvia Crowe, who, while overseeing the institute from 1957 to 1959 and penning letters to the *Times,* was also writing *The Landscape of Roads,* in which she would detail her concerns about the design of the M1, which she felt compared badly with German and American motorways on which engineers and landscape architects had collaborated.[76]

Crowe was not alone in her criticisms of the M1. Members of the government's Landscape Advisory Committee, Royal Fine Art Commission, and numerous architectural and design commentators of different aesthetic persuasions—including Brenda Colvin, Geoffrey Jellicoe, Ian Nairn, John Betjeman, and Nikolaus Pevsner—voiced their concerns about the design and landscaping of the bridges, service areas, and the motorway itself.[77] Crowe described Sir Owen's rather bulky two-span overbridges as "rough knots" that interrupted the flow of the landscape both along and across the motorway (fig. 9.2).[78] She contended that the poor alignment, excessive parallelism, and unfortunate landforms adjacent to the motorway could have been prevented if engineers had consulted with landscape architects at the design stage. Crowe used cross-sectional diagrams and aerial photographs to show how unfavorably the harsh lines of the M1's embankments and cuttings compared with Germany's latest motor roads (notably the Ulm-to-Baden-Baden autobahn), although the situation in Britain was recognized as markedly different due to the necessary provision of fences and the high cost of agricultural land (which made steep banks, strict boundaries, and parallel lines unavoidable).[79]

Crowe considered the landscaping of the road unsatisfactory, but she argued that strategic and functional planting could help to integrate the "clumsy shapes" of the embankments and bridges into the English landscape.[80]

9.2. Two-span bridges over Britain's M1 motorway, designed by Sir Owen Williams and Partners. Reproduced by kind permission of Laing O'Rourke Plc.

Opinions on what constituted appropriate planting varied widely. As Brenda Colvin stated in a review of the M1 for the *Geographical Magazine,* it was only the interjection of the Landscape Advisory Committee which prevented Sir Owen's consultants, Mr. Long and Mr. Clay, from planting a "ribbon of Forsythia and other garden shrubs on the central reserve."[81] Sir Owen's consultants had submitted their initial planting proposals to the Landscape Advisory Committee in June 1957,[82] but it soon became clear that the consultants and the committee held very different views about roadside planting. The proposals were subsequently rejected and modified by the committee over a period of two years, and their contrasting approaches were highlighted in a meeting of February 1958, at which ministry horticulturist L. E. Morgan stated that the decorative, fussy, ornamental, and exotic flowering shrubs proposed by the consultants would be out of place on this rural motorway.[83] In reply, Mr. Clay cited the Roads Beautifying Association's celebrated schemes for the Winchester bypass as an example of effective planting that could be adapted to the M1. Morgan, however, responded by emphasizing that the Winchester bypass "was actually a flagrant example of unsuitable treatment and was one to be avoided."[84] Even Madeleine Spitta, secretary of the RBA and Fox's replacement on the Landscape Advisory Committee, was highly critical of the planting proposals submitted by Long and Clay. Brenda Colvin condemned the choice of fuchsia, Sir Eric Savill questioned the planting of forsythia and pyracantha (evergreen thorn), and Sir David Bowes-Lyon and the committee "agreed that flowering plants of a semi-garden character were misplaced in real countryside."[85] Motorways in "real countryside" must be designed and planted as part of this "real" English countryside: interurban motorways were neither urban, semiurban, nor suburban spaces. Trees such as copper beech, purple sycamore, and whitebeam should be sparingly used, as "the Committee did not favour colour variations in foliage other than shades of green."[86] Concerns were also expressed about the use of "ugly conifers," the ability for species of trees to grow individually, and the fact that the plans failed to take geological variations into account.[87] The result was that the plans were simplified; while some species remained on the planting schedule, many others considered unsuitable were deleted. After a visit to the motorway in May 1959, Clough Williams-Ellis argued that the huge scale of the motorway meant that the landscaping must be bold and uncomplicated, rather than "niggling and irritating," and that no roadside detailing and very little planting was needed in open country.[88] As Sir Eric Savill had stated in February 1958: "A fast motorway is not a place for the encouragement of interest in flowering shrubs. 'Eyes on the road' should be the motto!"[89] The committee succeeded in removing almost all garden varieties or introduced species from the planting schedule, while limits were also established for the use of poplars (which pose a danger to foundations), elms (which are susceptible to disease), and sweet chestnuts.

Despite their minor involvement in the landscaping of the M1, the Landscape Advisory Committee managed to overrule the planting proposals of the Ministry's consulting engineers; and by joining forces with the Institute of Landscape Architects, Royal Institute of British Architects, and Royal Fine Art Commission, it ensured that landscape architects would be employed on all future schemes and that the committee itself would be consulted on landscape matters at the planning and design stage.

Conclusion

During the late 1920s and the 1930s, the Roads Beautifying Association advised local authorities on the planting of arterial roads and bypasses, but the association's preference for decorative and exotic species of trees and shrubs drew criticism from preservationists and landscape architects. In 1937, as the government took charge of a national network of trunk through-routes, the Council for the Preservation of Rural England saw an opportunity to influence national policy on the planning, design, planting, and administration of Britain's roads. It accused the RBA of suburbanizing the nation's roads, bringing an inappropriate domesticity, fussiness, and superficiality to Britain's roadsides. Leading members of the CPRE and the Institute of Landscape Architects called for a more fundamental and comprehensive approach, one that would take into account not just the planting but also the design and engineering of Britain's roads; and both organizations aimed to bring an "ordering modernism" to the landscapes of roads and motorways.[90] Planning and design professionals looked abroad to Germany, Italy, and the United States for inspiration and precedent, but all agreed that British roads must reflect distinctively British (or English) design and horticultural aesthetics. As politicians and planners approached the reconstruction of Britain's transport network after World War II, planner-preservationists, engineers, and organizations such as the British Road Federation argued that modern motorways could bring a sense of modern order to the British/English landscape. Motorways could provide a pleasant contrast with the chaotic suburban landscapes and cluttered roads observed and documented by Ian Nairn, Sylvia Crowe, and their colleagues at the *Architectural Review* and the ILA. Modernist-inspired visions of landscape became largely accepted by government committees and official bodies, providing an antidote to Subtopia; but with Britain's first major motorway, M1, these intentions were overlooked by the highway designers. The government's newly formed Advisory Committee on the Landscape Treatment of Trunk Roads was allowed no involvement in the routing or detailed designs of the M1, and when the motorway was completed, a significant number of landscape architects, engineers, and architectural commentators criticized the engineering of its landforms, the design of its bridges, and the species of vegetation that had been proposed by the consultants' landscape advisers. The M1 nearly became a linear strip of suburban or subtopian England, and professional bodies pressed the government to appoint landscape architects to work with engineers on all future road schemes, resulting in the appointment of the Ministry of Transport's first full-time landscape architect, Michael Porter, in 1961.

TEN

Physical and Social Constructions

of the Capital Beltway

Jeremy L. Korr

The Capital Beltway has entered the American vernacular as a synecdochic figure for the national center of federal power. The American media report daily on what is happening "inside the Beltway," a phrase popularized in the early 1980s by former *Washington Post* reporter Mike Causey.[1] At the same time, however, this highway is a key social institution in Washington, DC, and its suburbs, as well as a critical East Coast transportation artery. Although the Beltway passes through the District of Columbia for only a few hundred yards, compared to forty-two miles in Maryland and twenty-two in Virginia, it is indelibly associated in the national consciousness with the capital city. And like Washington, a city obliged to serve both national and local interests, the Capital Beltway has juggled responsibilities to multiple and often competing groups since it was first proposed in 1950. Yet some of these constituencies have had and continue to have no meaningful voice in the debates about this highway's future, despite shifts in federal policy over the past four decades designed to include them in the transportation-planning process.

This essay, based on ethnographic and documentary research undertaken between 1996 and 2002, evaluates the extent to which residents of the Washington metropolitan area have been included in the planning of the

Beltway. I focus particularly on the voices of individuals who, from their perspective, were excluded from the Beltway's planning in the 1950s and again in the 1990s and early 2000s. While I find that local residents have had a minor role in the planning of the *physical* construction of the road, they have nonetheless exerted strong influence over the *social* construction of the Beltway—that is, how the road is perceived and conceptualized by the public. Partial or full exclusion from the Beltway's planning process does not, it seems, preclude individuals' ability to influence the highway in other ways.

Inclusiveness and the Planning Process

In 1980, the consulting firm of Payne-Maxie published for the U.S. Departments of Transportation and Housing and Urban Development an extensive analysis of the land-use and development impacts of American beltways.[2] The firm's report explicitly recognized the dynamics of the original planning process that led to beltways—including the Capital Beltway—becoming at once a boon to drivers and a scourge to the communities through which they passed. The 1980 report states:

> Oriented to engineering, the Interstate program initially did not include rigorous planning requirements. . . . Not until the Federal-Aid Highway Act of 1978 was legislated were transportation planners forcefully encouraged to tie their planning to land-use planning and to recognize the socioeconomic, environmental, and energy implications of particular transportation projects. As a result, beltway planning in the 1940s and 1950s mainly involved coordination with local agencies and little analysis of the effects of highways on urban areas: alternatives rarely were evaluated comprehensively, and land-use and infrastructure impacts for the most part were given little attention. Further, effects on central cities and urban-revitalization programs were not examined, nor were impacts on development patterns assessed.[3]

In short, beltways, along with other interstate-type highways, were regularly construed by their designers as decontextualized engineering projects. Engineers' primary concerns were to create roads that would handle traffic as efficiently and as safely as possible; any additional effects, for better or worse, were incidental and outside their purview.

Payne-Maxie's assessment of the planners' and engineers' mindset is written in the passive voice (thereby deflecting responsibility from any specific individual or group), but that mindset produced social and environmental effects that were anything but passive. The Capital Beltway was designed primarily between 1952 and 1964. Although much of the highway went through sparsely developed woods and farmland (particularly in Virginia's Fairfax County and Maryland's Prince George's County), some did not (passing through the city of Alexandria in Virginia, for example, and through both residential and commercial sections of Montgomery County in Maryland). How the planning and highway authorities responded to the challenges of constructing a road through developed communities went a long way toward determining how residents and business owners reacted. Consistent with Payne-Maxie's analysis, engineers and planners gave minimal attention to the effects that the highway would have on these groups.

Officials in both states downplayed the displacement caused by the Beltway's construction. Lester Wilkinson, who reserved the right-of-way for the Beltway in Prince George's County, confirmed that "[t]here were some [displacements]. Obviously. It's almost impossible for a highway that big to go all the way through a county without displacing a few homes. But essentially at that time it was all undeveloped land."[4] Virginia engineer F. L. Burroughs, writing in 1961, also noted that "[s]ome public inconvenience has been caused because of the displacement of people and their homes. However, I think it is remarkable that fewer than 100 houses had to be taken."[5] Both Burroughs and Wilkinson speak about the matter in technical, pragmatic terms; focusing on the positive, they note that relatively few people were affected and do not address the effects of their displacement on those individuals.

In my examinations of three major newspapers, over a dozen county or community papers, and numerous documents from planning and transportation agencies, I found records of only two public hearings on the Beltway's construction, one in Virginia and one in Maryland. Before 1956, when the interstate-highway program was inaugurated, engineers and planning officials across the country designed and built highways with little input from the public. After 1956, federal law required states to hold hearings that would permit public participation in the highway planning process. Despite this change, I found no mention of any other public hearings for the Beltway—let alone any changes made in response to concerns that might have been raised in such forums—held during the entire planning and construction period from 1952 to 1964.

Local newspapers announced in April 1957 that Virginia's Department of Transportation (VDOT) would hold a public hearing at Annandale High School on the nineteenth of the month. The announcement itself suggested that the hearing's purpose was not so much to solicit residents' suggestions as to reveal to them decisions already made by the state's highway administration. A small announcement in the legal notices of the *Fairfax Herald* read, in part: "In accordance with provisions of the 1956 Federal Highway Act, a public hearing will be held by a representative of the State Highway Department . . . for the purpose of considering the proposed location of the Interstate Highway . . . known as the Virginia Metropolitan Area of Washington, DC, Circumferential Route, 22.1 miles."[6] A community newsletter highlighted the point that residents would be seeing previously developed plans, noting that at the hearing, "presumably, the proposed location of the entire 22.1 mile highway will be unveiled."[7] A passing reference in the April 26 edition of another local paper indicates that community representatives who attended the hearing lobbied for as many interchanges as possible in their respective jurisdictions in order to bolster commercial access and development.[8] Beyond this, however, no printed mention appears of the April 19 hearing or of any others that may have occurred in Virginia.

In Maryland the record is more silent still. Fulfilling legal obligations under the Federal-Aid Highway Act of 1956, Maryland's State Roads Commission (SRC) invited residents to a hearing at Glen Echo Town Hall on December 17, 1959. Although this meeting went unreported by the press, a transcript leaves no doubt that there was some heated opposition to the Beltway's proposed route through Montgomery County.

At least a dozen residents of Cabin John and Bethesda strongly objected to construction of the Beltway leg through their communities; residents of Cabin John were especially irate, convinced that the new road would decimate their quiet, cohesive neighborhood. Representing their concerns was A. M. Dodson of Cabin John, who insisted that he and his neighbors "would not hold still for being carved up in any manner that would ruin our community as aplace [*sic*] to live in."[9] But what frustrated Dodson and the other attendees even more was the absolute intransigence of highway officials, who offered neither sympathy for nor even any acknowledgment of the distress they were hearing again and again. The transcript shows State Roads Commissioner John Funk and other officials responding to each speaker by repeatedly dismissing their concerns by reference to a greater good or by moving to the next speaker without comment.[10] Local residents may have had their hearing, but in their view they were not truly heard.

As it turns out, this public hearing closely resembled those held across the nation to discuss the building of interstate highways. Transportation officials, unaccustomed to having their plans reviewed, much less altered, used these federally mandated hearings to publish plans they considered final; these bureaucrats were not yet prepared to incorporate the public in more substantial ways. This was apparent even at the time. Landscape historian Grady Clay, writing from his own experience, offered this contemporary account in 1958:

> What about public hearings? I cannot speak of the thousands of hearings I have not seen, but from *some* personal observation I am forced to conclude that the public hearing is a carefully staged performance designed to show the audience why the route officially agreed upon in private cannot be changed. As one of the British motor magazines recently described it, these are affairs where "at worst, aggrieved persons may hear very sound reasons why things cannot be altered." The burden of proof is placed on the private citizen, who often is poorly informed and easily buffaloed by technical mumbo-jumbo. . . . In other words, don't make any fuss about the route we've already picked. Just be thankful. And if not, be quiet.[11]

Since there were no formal mechanisms whereby residents or others could express their concerns about the Beltway and have them seriously addressed, officially there was no substantive opposition to the Beltway. But it was there.

A large share of this resentment was directed at highway officials not for the actions they took regarding the Beltway but for their callousness in disregarding the consequences of those actions. In Maryland, for example, the SRC gave some families and businesses only thirty days' notice to vacate their premises before the state took over their properties. Near the U.S. 29 interchange, the SRC had assumed ownership of a shopping center and fifty-three houses between 1955 and 1959, and had leased them to tenants on terms that provided for mandatory abandonment on one month's notice. But few of the tenants believed the state would actually give them such a short deadline. When on October 6, 1959, the SRC told the tenants of thirty homes and the Fairway Shopping Center merchants to vacate by November 6, after which demolition would begin, the shopkeepers felt "consternation," according to a report in a local newspaper. Walter Moyer, a pharmacist at the Fairview Drug Store, said that "SRC officials earlier led him and other merchants to believe that at the earliest they would have to evacuate by the beginning of next year."[12] SRC officials insisted that they had stressed the thirty-day termination clauses, but merchants felt ill-treated nonetheless.

From a different perspective, the Fairway retailers and the tenants of the condemned homes were the lucky ones. Because their buildings stood directly in the Beltway's path, the state compensated them for their property and enabled them to move elsewhere. Those living near the highway's alignment, however, were not as fortunate. These neighbors became what today might be called collateral damage, for several reasons. Nearby residents found their lives suffused with noise, later mitigated partially by sound barriers but described in 1964 as "the constant din that permeates our yards and houses even with all windows shut. It disturbs our conversations, our sleep and ordinary enjoyment of life."[13] The Beltway disrupted community life in the areas it passed through (including Cabin John, as its residents had feared) and generated heavy traffic on the local roads used to access it, making it difficult for residents even to leave their homes. In these and other scenarios, residents were frustrated not just by the Beltway's effects but also by the sense that officials were oblivious to the decline in residents' quality of life as a result of those effects.

From their perspective, those living near the Beltway received little or no compensation for their losses, even though every minute of their lives at home was permanently affected. Silver Spring residents Isidore Elrich and his daughter, Lisa Loflin, whose family bought a house adjacent to the future Beltway in 1960, months before the highway was built, tell a story similar to those of many of their neighbors and fellow Beltway abutters. In a 2001 interview, Elrich and Loflin detailed a catalogue of concerns about the Beltway's impact on their lives:

> *Elrich:*   It changed our lives.
>
> . . .
>
> *Elrich:*   The real estate man who sold us the house, he was supposed to tell us that the Beltway was coming in, and he didn't. And I could have killed the sale if I had known, but I didn't know.
>
> *Loflin:*   We were told there was going to be a small road back there, kind of like Forest Glen [then a two-lane country road].
>
> . . .
>
> *Loflin:*   Our house was broken into twice [from off of the Beltway]. . . . You'd park, pull up a truck behind the houses, and put on your flashers like there's something wrong, and leave the truck there. Nobody can see what's happening this side of it, from the Beltway. You just walk into someone's backyard, break in at ground level at the back door.
>
> . . .
>
> *Elrich:*   And it knocked down the value of the house. They're harder to sell on this side of the street than they are on the other side of the street.
>
> . . .
>
> *Loflin:*   And it's also the maintenance. Outside maintenance became a joke. Because, I mean, it just gets covered with soot. When you look at the house you can see what it's doing to your lungs, and why care? . . . We don't use the backyard anymore.
>
> *Elrich:*   Well, we used to grow stuff out there. And then, they—

Loflin: They ruined the yard.

. . .

Loflin: I know that [my parents] could not afford to sell the house and move. But we would have been much happier, all the way around; if those bastards had bought our house.

Korr: Did they even offer?

Loflin: No.

. . .

Loflin: (Softly) I hate the noise. I hate, I hate all the memories. I'd have nightmares as a kid of accidents. I *still* have them. They interrupt—they go into my dreams. I will wake up in a cold sweat and then I'll hear the sirens go by or stop back there for an accident. I don't like that. It's not fair. They took away everything. (Very softly) This was a nice place.[14]

Paul Foer, who as a child lived within a mile of the Elrich family and within two blocks of the Beltway, echoed Loflin's memories of a sylvan childhood shattered by the arrival of the highway:

Numerous times I was awoken by crashes. Severe, horrible crashes. You'd hear screeches and squealing, and then this *huge* impact, glass shattering and of course sirens and all a little bit later. And being awoken from that and the fear and the scare of that. On at least one occasion I very clearly remember going down through the woods and to the edge of the Beltway, to the guardrail, almost, with . . . both my older brothers, and seeing the glass and bloody bandages and wrappers thrown about, and seeing where this had been this horrible crash where probably someone died.[15]

Neither Loflin nor Foer attributes the negative experiences to the engineers who designed the Beltway or to the highway itself. In my interviews with them, Loflin, Foer, and other current and former Beltway neighbors all supported the Beltway and the convenience it provides. What they objected to was *how* Maryland developed the Beltway:

> I don't blame the engineers. I don't. But the planners. It's just, you have to have some kind of vision. If you look at the Disney cartoons from the '60s, there's a Goofy cartoon about him on the highway, and showing more and more and more cars will be coming. All you needed to do was look at the stupid cartoon, and you'd know that what they originally envisioned wasn't going to do it. You had to have better planning. You *have* to.[16]

Apart from a few sound barriers, little if any consideration was given to the impact the highway would have on residents' property values, their environment, or their quality of life. Some of the anxiety Foer and Loflin experienced might have been mitigated if, for example, state representatives had met with them and their neighbors, before the Beltway was opened, to acknowledge the changes the road would bring to their communities, to thank them in advance for their patience and assistance in helping accident victims, and to offer instructions on how to deal with the pollution and crime that would ensue. By remaining silent when it could have done otherwise, the SRC sent the message that the Beltway's neighbors did not matter. "It's like they didn't care about the people," Loflin said.

That attitude was not limited to Maryland's State Roads Commission. In fact it can be traced back to the original definition of the term *freeway* given in a 1930 article by attorney Edward M. Bassett, then president of the National Conference on City Planning. Bassett specifically defined the freeway as "a strip of public land devoted to movement over which the abutting property owners have no right of light, air or access."[17] Ethical or not, Bassett's conception of freeways prioritized the interest of the drivers, not the abutters, and highway officials followed suit.

Similarly, the SRC's procedures of the 1950s were entirely consistent with those of other states. Especially after the creation of the interstate system in 1956, state highway departments tried to build their hundreds of miles of new highway as efficiently as possible, which meant following established procedures and not worrying about the local context of every section of highway. "Asked to build an enormous network of highways in a short time," Clifford Ellis writes, "engineers sought to standardize the production of highway mileage, not convert it into an unwieldy urban design project requiring careful molding of each urban segment to meet local needs."[18]

While Lisa Loflin, Paul Foer, and A. M. Dodson represent very specific cases, my written and oral sources corroborate the presence of a discontented constituency with concerns and stories similar to theirs.[19] Taken together, letters to the editors of local newspapers after the Beltway's opening, brief mentions of residents' unhappiness in newspaper reports, the contentious and now-forgotten 1959 public hearing in Maryland, and personal interviews collectively indicate that a significant contingent of people living near the Beltway had similar apprehensions about the highway, yet did not feel they had a venue to express those concerns and receive serious responses.

After the Beltway opened in 1964, the Federal Highway Administration (FHWA) changed its policies to raise the level of citizen participation in the planning process. The FHWA's *Public Hearings and Location Approval* guidelines, revised in 1969, replaced the single public hearing occurring late in the planning process with two hearings: a "corridor public hearing," to be held before highway departments made their route location decisions; and a "highway design public hearing," to emphasize the specific location and design elements of the road. Later that year, the FHWA amended the guidelines yet again to mandate "citizen participation in all phases of the planning process, from the setting of goals to the analysis of alternatives."[20] No longer would highway officials be permitted to make their key decisions in advance and without consideration of residents' concerns. Requirements for public participation were further enhanced by the 1991 Intermodal Surface Transportation and Efficiency Act (ISTEA) and the 1998 Transportation Equity Act for the Twenty-First Century (TEA-21).[21]

How effective have these policies and legislation been? Analysis of Capital Beltway planning studies between 1994 and 2002 in Maryland and Virginia, focusing on strategies for improving traffic conditions on the Beltway, suggests that although the planning process is substantially more inclusive than it was for the same highway in the 1950s, the updated process is not necessarily inclusive in a meaningful way for all those involved. My own participant-observation fieldwork at planning workshops from 1996 to 2002, together with review of public-hearing transcripts and written comments, indicate that some suburban Maryland residents appreciate their state's attempts to incorporate their voices into the planning process, but that some Northern Virginia residents remain as upset by their state's current planning approach as Marylanders were in 1959.[22]

But Virginians' frustrations are not apparent in any of the literature published by the Virginia Department of Transportation, which describes a far more inclusive process than that of the 1950s. VDOT's Web site for the study (overseen by the coordinating engineering firm, Parsons Transportation Group of Virginia) makes this clear:

> Your participation in the study process is critical to identifying solutions that balance the need to improve the Capital Beltway with minimizing impacts to adjacent communities and the environment. VDOT and the study team welcome and encourage your input.
>
> There are a number of ways for you to get involved and learn more about the Capital Beltway Study. We urge you to attend the study's public meetings to obtain the most up-to-date project information. At all of these meetings, you will have an opportunity to talk with study team members and provide comments. You can also learn more about the project and let us know you are interested by adding your name to the project mailing list or calling the project hotline.[23]

Over the first seven years of the Capital Beltway Study, while officials were considering options that ranged from adding lanes to creating a multilevel segment of the Beltway, VDOT distributed newsletters to thousands of individuals and many organizations, and held public hearings in September 1995, September 1996, June 1999, and May 2002. These hearings were well attended: the three that took place in May 2002, for example, drew over a thousand residents and eighteen hundred written and oral comments.[24]

These figures appear to demonstrate that the public is well represented in the Capital Beltway study's planning process. Yet the level of inclusion described by local residents themselves differs markedly from that described by VDOT. In an interview, VDOT engineer Bahram Jamei spoke proudly about the thick volumes of collated written comments collected at the public workshops, using them as evidence that the public has adequate means and opportunity to communicate with VDOT authorities, and that the public plays an important role in the planning process.[25] But within those volumes themselves are hundreds of angry letters accusing VDOT of being secretive, unresponsive, and unsympathetic to residents. VDOT's own summary of comments received at the June 1999 public workshops alone includes twenty-six categories relating to the environment (including forty-one comments about minimizing impacts to adjacent communities) and twenty-five categories of concerns related to public involvement (including ten comments under the category "VDOT does not listen or take into consideration what the public says" and seven under "Expand opportunities for public involvement in planning and decision-making process").[26]

Most notably, dozens of comments from these public meetings speak to VDOT's tendencies to make critical decisions before holding public sessions and to ignore the effects of transportation projects on individuals, as planning officials routinely did prior to the 1969 FHWA legislation.

> It seems this is just a process and you don't care what we think. It's symbolic.[27]
>
> . . .
>
> When my wife saw all these proposals, she cried. Our beautiful new home we bought in March will probably be destroyed. Thank you for ruining our lives![28]
>
> . . .
>
> We have been shocked by the blithe dismissal of our situation by the VDOT employees who have had an opportunity to respond to questions about it. The houses directly impacted by the proposed changes to the roadway are referred to as "facilities." What an easy way to dismiss the human impact this kind of project has on a community! VDOT, regardless of the lives affected by this proposal, has declared that these new roadways will have "no significant impact" on the adjacent communities. It is stunning to witness how inhumane this system is and the ease with which it dismisses the time, money, and emotion committed by residents to turn their houses into homes and their neighborhoods into communities.[29]
>
> . . .
>
> I think VDOT is completely unresponsive to the destruction you are causing in people's lives. If you want to build this kind of

monstrosity then you should be prepared to offer compensation to those whose homes will be within 200 feet of the highway—not just those whose house you take—they are the fortunate ones. I am a widow, who has serious health problems. I can't afford to move because houses in this area are so expensive and mine probably wouldn't sell. I truly feel that I am being raped by VDOT—no, worse. Victims of rape actually have some rights—unlike victims of VDOT.[30]

Virginia residents are upset over the impact that proposed plans for widening the Beltway may have on their communities and on the local environment, but like their counterparts in Maryland during the late 1950s, they are especially aggravated by state officials' reluctance to acknowledge and enter into dialogue about these potential effects. A different approach by VDOT, one that includes more effective and responsive communication, could do much to improve residents' view and experience of the planning process, even if its results end up being similar to what they would have been anyway. As it is, those residents who feel excluded from VDOT's study and consideration will almost certainly continue to feel aggrieved.

In an example cited earlier, Isidore Elrich in 1960 purchased a house adjacent to the Beltway's right-of-way in Maryland only after a deceptive real-estate agent failed to tell him about the highway's imminent construction, a practice common at the time.[31] The experience of a Northern Virginia resident suggests that this practice continued unabated four decades later:

[M]y wife and I purchased our new home roughly nine months ago. We were very cautious in our decision since this was the home that we would raise our children in (if we are so lucky). . . . Of equal importance was the fact that we were not directly against the interstate and were separated by a buffer-zone of woods. Before we purchased, we checked with our real-estate agent and the builder's agent about any plans to expand the proximate interchange. We were subsequently assured that there were no such plans. But, as time would soon tell, the plans were well underway and soon to be revealed in public hearings. . . . "Conceptual plans" were apparently unveiled several months ago showing my neighborhood; well not really since the aerial photo underlying these plans is from 1995 and thus my new community is not depicted.[32]

While Elrich had dealt only with a shady sales agent, in this 1999 episode the state planners and the seller effectively colluded in, and were equally responsible for, the deception. At a separate public hearing in 2002, another Northern Virginia resident voiced an identical accusation, noting that her community was "also one that is not shown in its entirety" in VDOT photos, because "our community was only built five years ago."[33] Her comment suggests that Virginia officials had not responded to this issue in the three years since it was first voiced at a 1999 public hearing.

In fact, it is not clear to which concerns Virginia officials *have* responded substantively, despite their explicit attempts to solicit as much public comment as possible. In departmental literature and at public hearings, VDOT officials repeatedly praised the extensive input from the public. But to find records of specific input actually influencing VDOT's planning in any way is much more difficult. At a 1999 public meeting, a Northern Virginia resident pointed this out in a prepared speech: "Whereas we appreciate the ability to submit verbal and written inputs, and feel that close communication is a positive step, there is still no quantifiable means for us to determine whether the desires of our citizens are having an effect on the Beltway design decision-making process. . . . [C]ommunity input is meaningful only if its effects are clear and measurable."[34] For residents it is not sufficient to have the chance to offer input; they also need quantifiable evidence that their input has any real value in the planning process.

At the public hearing held on May 29, 2002, in McLean, Virginia, for example, none of the many visual displays on the Capital Beltway Study itemized specific public concerns that were substantively incorporated into VDOT's planning, together with the action VDOT took in response. While the displays and speakers pointed proudly to the extensive public comments collected at the 1999 public hearings, they failed to present any substantive decisions made in response to those comments. Nor did the speakers clarify the role of public input. VDOT engineer William Cuttler opened and closed the hearing by commending the large turnout at earlier public meetings and reiterating that public input is an important part of the process. Environmental project manager Ken Wilkinson summarized the previous seven years of the study. But neither Cuttler nor Wilkinson offered a single concrete example of a comment or concern offered by the public influencing the transportation study between 1994 and 2002.[35] Nor did the Capital Beltway Study's official Web site list any instance of such an influence at the time. These omissions imply that state officials welcome comments from the public but do not actually give them serious consideration when making key decisions.

It is important to note that in the face of residents' anger, and despite many public comments to the contrary, VDOT has made significant progress in incorporating the public into its planning process. Like other states, Virginia had through the twentieth century developed "a professionalized and politically insulated Highway Department, which was able to reduce transportation decision-making to a computational problem. Disagreements about outcomes and cause and effect were resolved within the department, and engineering solutions were imposed on most transportation problems."[36] Initiatives by Virginia governors Charles Robb and Gerald Baliles in the 1980s explicitly attempted to increase the power of citizens (and legislators) in transportation planning. But involving the public has not been enough. Comments from the public workshops and opinions expressed at the McLean meeting echoed the concern of a Northern Virginia resident who declared, "VDOT doesn't have any public involvement process. VDOT now has a process in which they tell the public what they're up to."[37]

Both VDOT and the public have legitimate cases. When VDOT engineers share their pride about how thoroughly input from residents has been integrated into the planning process, their feelings are well founded: Virginia transportation officials have consciously revamped their previously insular institutional culture, dating back nearly a century, to provide unprecedented access to residents. When angry Virginia residents claim that VDOT is not giving them a meaningful role in transportation planning, they too are correct; they continue to feel marginalized because they want a kind of access and an approach to their concerns that differs from what VDOT is offering. Planning in Virginia is *both* inclusive (from state officials' perspective) and exclusive (from residents' perspective).

A study conducted for the Metropolitan Washington Council of Governments in 1998 reached a similar conclusion. The ICF Kaiser Consulting Group studied the extent of public participation and satisfaction of all relevant parties, focusing on several specific studies including the Virginia and Maryland projects cited above. The consultants concluded that "[t]here is no shared or common understanding regarding the meaning or practice of public involvement between members of the public and transportation decision-makers in Virginia, Maryland, and Washington." In particular, the consultants noted, many people without decision-making authority view public involvement as a participatory exercise, while many transportation officials view the public's role as consultative with less direct input into the creation of plans and projects.[38]

In his study of meetings that took place during the 1960s to protest highway development in Boston, Gordon Fellman has concluded that the public participants may have had greater success in achieving catharsis than they had in influencing policy.[39] At protests and at public hearings, Fellman argues, residents had a role to play, but it was effectively only an emotional one, or, in ICF Kaiser's terms, a consultative one: "Anger, impotence, and frustration are vented verbally and harmlessly, in the company of like-minded neighbors and sympathetic outsiders."[40] Virginia's current structure seems to cast residents in a similar role: engineers and planners will invite and even encourage them to speak and offer suggestions, but then fail to address those frustrations meaningfully or incorporate those suggestions into the actual planning. The public's function is distinctly consultative rather than participatory. As a result, VDOT's planning process in the early-twenty-first century satisfies no one.

Shaping the Beltway's Social Construction

While Virginians may have little say in the planning of the Capital Beltway, they and other Washington-area residents are by no means powerless with respect to this highway. It is the area's residents, not its planners and engineers, who most directly generate its social construction, the myriad ways in which it is perceived and understood.[41] This point is not trivial, for the significance of any landscape depends as much on how it exists in people's minds as on how it appears in the physical world.

The power of thought is the key here: Landscapes are both conceptual and physical. How people regard a given landscape—as "wild," "dangerous," "beautiful," and so forth—can have "tangible consequences for how that space is used, which in turn affects the behavior of those perceiving the landscape in that particular way."[42] Highway engineers can do everything in their power to make a road safe or visually appealing, but if drivers collectively perceive it as dangerous or ugly, then it *is* dangerous or ugly, even if more objective measurements would never validate such an opinion.

Drivers on the Capital Beltway experience it largely as an obstacle to their daily pursuits. Some respond by avoiding the highway altogether; others allow it to play a decisive role in their choices of residence and employment. "I resent the hell out of its dangerous volume of traffic," a Columbia resident writes, "because it dominates my visits to my grandchildren."[43] Like this indignant grandparent, many Washington-area residents express frustration about the influence the Beltway exerts on their daily lives. One Chevy Chase resident has "planned virtually all my activities, and my children's activities, to avoid the Beltway."[44] Rather than have their behavior determined by traffic flow, some drivers dismiss the Beltway as a viable transportation route and restructure their personal lives. On this phenomenon, an Alexandria resident writes: "I know many people—even those from this region who will not go anywhere which would require them to travel on the Beltway—which I believe causes a sectorization if you will. The intimidation factor of driving on it serves as an isolation factor for many."[45] People consciously opt out of pursuits that would require driving on the Beltway. "As a local who has to use the Beltway to shop, visit friends, etc.," a Greenbelt resident writes, "it cramps my style and discourages me from doing things I need to do at certain times of day or night."[46] A resident of Baltimore, some thirty miles north of the Capital Beltway, rejects out of hand the idea of driving south: "Anytime I think of something I'd like to do in DC, I immediately remember I'll have to travel the Beltway, and usually decide not to do whatever it was that I wanted to."[47]

Others choose to live or work beyond the Beltway's reach. On the scale of intensity of responses to the Beltway's frustrations, the next step up from avoidance is deliberately choosing to live or work somewhere beyond the road's reach. Some locals will take only jobs that preclude Beltway driving, including the Greenbelt resident who "promised [him]self never to have to commute on the Beltway, i.e., take a job where [he] would have to drive there every day."[48] "I won't even look at certain jobs," an Alexandria resident writes, "if it means extensive Beltway travel."[49] Others look, then turn away: "I have turned down several jobs for more pay over the years to avoid the Beltway," says a respondent from Round Hill, Virginia; and a resident of Prince Frederick, Maryland, declares, "I have not taken jobs because a great part of my commute would take me on the Beltway. The aggravation and unpredictability of the traffic flow is not worth it."[50]

Decisions about where to live can also hinge on the Beltway. "I purchased my house," a McLean resident writes, "specifically so that we don't have to go near the Beltway, except on rare occasions"; and an Alexandria resident states, "I picked my home in a location that would not require its use."[51] "When purchasing a home five years ago," a Waldorf resident echoes, "part of my decision was based on finding a location that would minimize Beltway usage."[52] These drivers cope by choosing homes and jobs that keep their travel on the Beltway voluntary rather than necessary. Choices that might otherwise be preferable are not worth "destroying [one's] soul," as an Alexandria resident puts it.[53]

The most drastic response to the Beltway, however, is to sever ties completely with the Washington area. A 2001 poll conducted by the American Automobile Association (AAA) of 451 drivers living between Baltimore and Richmond found that approximately 15 percent—or about 67 respondents—had considered leaving the region because of the traffic.[54] Respondents to my own survey offer support for this finding, including, for example, a Baltimorean who "moved to Florida for a while partly because of the overcrowding manifested in Beltway traffic."[55] Similarly, a long-time resident of suburban Washington, who once drove the Beltway daily, left behind his chest pains and dread of driving by moving to Tracy's Landing, Maryland: "I fled the Beltway. . . . So, I would say the Beltway has played a big part in my life and still does. It made me change my life and I love it for that."[56]

The Beltway also affects area residents' social decisions in more subtle ways. Engineers designing the highway in the 1950s and '60s did not consciously plan for it to become a dividing line; in fact, they intended the opposite, as the Beltway was meant to connect Washington's suburbs. Yet according to some locals, people living inside the Beltway think, act, and interact differently from people who live outside it. An Alexandria resident who lives inside the circumferential explains: "Most people I've talked to who live 'outside the beltway' look at 'inside the beltway' as something scary. People outside don't like to travel in. It's a separate culture."[57] A Washington resident perceives distinct cultural milieux on either side of the highway:

> [The Beltway is] a cultural boundary. When I was single I wouldn't date anyone from outside the Beltway because it was like they had

a totally different existence (I did give them a chance). They refused to come into the city—in fact hadn't been in in years—and
constantly refused to do cultural events such as the Kennedy Center, the opera, museums, and the like. They always wanted me to
go out there, and to partake in things like bowling, the park, going
to the mall . . . and so forth. They also had no clue about issues of
race and poverty, or the urban experience, but were opinionated
about it anyhow, and they were also overwhelmingly conservative.
I have found the inside-the-Beltway crowd to be a much better fit
for my personality.[58]

While this cultural contrast seems to be an issue of urban-versus-suburban
preferences, the Beltway functions as a border between the two. A former
resident of Bowie, Maryland, some ten miles east of the Beltway, confirms
the perception of the Beltway as the line between city and suburbs: "I
know that my friends who live in the District [of Columbia] definitely feel
the Beltway is a boundary. When I lived in Bowie, no one wanted to visit
because it seemed so far, and was 'Outside the Beltway,' but it was only
20–30 minutes away. They would rather go across town, which could
sometimes take longer than going to Bowie. As soon as I moved 'inside,'
there was more of a willingness on their part to visit."[59]

The Beltway thus operates as a psychological boundary for those who,
for various emotional reasons, feel a need to live on one side or the other.
According to one resident of Arlington, Virginia, some people "are as
horrified at living inside the Beltway (implying an area that's too urbanized) as . . . [others] are horrified at living outside the Beltway."[60] Yet again
the urban/suburban dynamic seems to be key here, this time as the parameters of an emotional tug-of-war. A second Arlington resident explains: "I
lived outside the Beltway in Gaithersburg [Maryland] for a while, and I
hated it because I felt totally out of the loop. The physical distance was a
part of it, but mostly it was just an emotional distance I felt. I love being
'inside.'"[61] This sense of "being 'inside,'" she suggests, is more than simple geographical location.

While the Beltway constitutes a social boundary and, as a physical object, compels residents to structure their lives around it, it also unifies area
residents by providing a set of shared experiences and a common language.
Before the Beltway, the Washington area was less unified socially; after its

construction, a new sense of community developed among residents of the capital city and its suburbs. Demographer Alan Henrickson defines a community as "a territorially and socially differentiated group consciousness. . . . [T]he subjective reality of the place must be taken into consideration along with its objective contents and contexts. A 'place' is not only a site. Besides the physical-geographical, economic-geographical, and social-geographical settings that structure the Washington community, it is organized by the *mental maps* held by its inhabitants."[62] The Capital Beltway restructured area residents' mental maps and, in the words of journalist Larry Van Dyne, led them "to think of DC and its suburbs as a single metropolitan area."[63] The road has created a "regional unity," a "cohesive whole," "one large metropolitan community," "almost one state, affectionately known as the Area."[64]

Increased access created by the Beltway contributes to this regional unity. "I've found," a Greenbelt resident explains, " . . . there are certain terms and references that locals are privy to. It's like you are instantly judged by the vocabulary you choose to use in talking about the Beltway. There's a certain amount of pride that goes along with learning the lingo, conquering the Beltway, etc."[65] Despite its annoyances, an Odenton, Maryland, resident considers the Beltway to be

> part of the fabric that makes us Washingtonians and Marylanders. It is a rite of passage for teenagers after they get their licenses to be able to navigate the Beltway. It is a common link between two strangers. For example, I can have a conversation about the Beltway with someone from the area, and another person not from the area wouldn't be able to follow it. Plus, we can laugh at that same person who got lost in the area and wound up driving in circles for hours![66]

Community members become acclimated to the presence of certain characters; the regular appearances (on radio, television, and the Beltway itself) of traffic reporters and emergency-response personnel reassure drivers that normal routines prevail and that their world is functioning.

The Beltway serves as a community site in other ways as well. Motorists whose vehicles have broken down are often surprised to find strangers stopping to assist and refusing any compensation.[67] A small collection of jokes, poems, songs, and melodies inspired by the Beltway further underlines its role in maintaining a sense of community.[68] But the strongest social bond derives from the Beltway both as a common denominator, a reference point, in the lives of Washington-area residents, and as a physical unifier that shrinks portions of two states and the District of Columbia into a 257-square-mile "Beltland."[69]

A last, but very different way in which individual residents rather than engineers and planners shape the social construction of the Capital Beltway is in their oppositional driving practices. At the start of this volume Rudy Koshar explains how, through what he calls oppositional practices, drivers effectively appropriate roads for their own purposes; in the process, roads become sites of dissidence and resistance to cultural norms.[70] In this sense the Beltway was a locus of subversion from its very beginning. During its construction from 1955 to 1964, it was a site of dynamic but unsanctioned social activity for children and teenagers, as well as a meeting place to bring them together from around the region. Highway officials neither planned nor condoned this use of the partially completed roadway, but they do not appear to have gone to great lengths to prevent it, either. Before becoming a commuter highway and a bypass expressway, as intended, the Beltway was, in essence, a playground.

That is the term used by many residents with fond memories of playing on the construction site. A man who moved to Silver Spring at age eleven offers this recollection: "The Beltway right-of-way between Georgia Avenue and Sligo Creek was our 'playground.' We were approaching driving age when the Beltway opened, so our new 'playground' became a highway for our new 'toys,' our cars."[71] A woman who grew up in Annandale recalls, "The area was our playground. We spent many afternoons in the cisterns."[72] A former Silver Spring resident is more effusive: "Great fun. . . . road [*sic*] my bike home and made go kart on the highway . . . met kids from nearby neighborhoods that did not go to my school . . . raced, played . . . what a great playground."[73] These remarks suggest that before the Beltway connected adult drivers from around the region in 1964, it brought together children and teenagers from different social networks.

These social gatherings were not limited to children. One woman recalls seeing "greasers" taking part in drag races on unopened parts of the highway, which apparently occurred all around the loop and in some locations on regular schedules.[74] A man who grew up in Silver Spring remembers "going to the weekend drag races on the Beltsville section," while a former Alexandria resident writes: "Back when the Beltway had not opened yet, . . . [s]ome of us Alexandria teenager[s] (back in the 60s) used to sneak on to the new Beltway and have drag races—until of course the Alexandria police would show up and run us off."[75] The formality and regularity of the drag races is apparent from the account given by an Arlington woman who participated in drag races "nearly every night of the week. And some of those races were really serious, people came from all over the DC area, some raced for car titles, some raced for what at the time was very big money."[76] That this woman and her friends raced almost daily, in spite of the police surveillance that made such activity "very difficult," attests to the allure the empty road must have had for these would-be racers.

In addition to serving as a gathering place, the construction site was for some a private playground. One woman, whose family home was adjacent to the highway then being built, felt a sense of ownership, saying it was "as though that section of the Beltway that was next to our house did in some way 'belong' to us." She took full advantage: "While [the Beltway was] under construction, my brother and I had a great time taking our bikes down the hill and riding on all that endless pavement that was completely free of cars! It was great! We made little forts underneath the bridge that went back over the Beltway next to our house. I remember how incredibly QUIET it was back then. We had a lot of fun before it was opened to traffic."[77] Others found solitude by climbing out on the bridge spanning the Northwest Branch of the Anacostia River in Montgomery County; one man recalls that he and a friend "used to just hang out on the bridge, throwing objects off the bridge, climbing on it, looking out over the river."[78] In 1964 this option, along with the biking, drag-racing, and go-karting, disappeared when the Beltway was opened. But for a few years the construction sites in Maryland and Virginia inadvertently formed, in one longtime Silver Spring resident's words, "a child's dreamland."[79]

Other oppositional practices were more risqué. A Silver Spring resident, for example, recalls that "a friend who grew up here said when [the Beltway] was new, they used to drive all the way around it smoking pot."[80] This story is echoed by a former Kensington, Maryland, resident, who not only smoked marijuana on the Beltway but grew it there in the road's early years:

> I actually tried growing pot inside of the big curve of the cloverleaf
> at Kensington Parkway. And [the plants] grew, and I'd go and visit

them once in a while, and then one time I visited and they weren't there. I don't know what happened to 'em. . . . But when you're twelve and thirteen—well, actually more like fourteen and fifteen— and you're smoking pot a lot of times, believe me, you smoke whenever you can. And to a certain extent the Beltway provided us with opportunities to do it.[81]

In fact, the Beltway has been a venue for both drugs and sex. In their study of the New Jersey Turnpike, Angus Gillespie and Michael Rockland observe "there is something about the Turnpike that seems to excite sexual desire."[82] Perhaps the same "something" holds for highways in general, or at least interstates, given that approximately 10 percent of the respondents to my Web survey reported having had a sexual and/or romantic experience on the Beltway. Those who provided details suggest that sexual activity on the Beltway skews toward romantic kissing and oral sex. "This is very personal," a Falls Church resident writes, "but [I] perform[ed] oral sex on the driver in a convertible with the top down—maybe not too unusual, but the top down part might be."[83] Others write of giving, receiving, or witnessing oral sex on the Beltway; truckers, in particular, who have a clear view from above of what happens in the cars below, report "quite a bit of sexual activity from passing motorists."[84] Since the highway is a public place—or at best semiprivate, within the confines of private vehicles—those who choose to engage in sexual activity while traveling on it clearly subvert expected social behavior.

In another example of oppositional practices, various groups have appropriated the Beltway at different times as a means to promote their political or religious agendas. Demonstrators on foot used the Beltway for this purpose as early as 1966, when in June of that year a group of demonstrators organized by the Action Coordinating Committee to End Segregation in the Suburbs (ACCESS) spent several days circumnavigating the Beltway in a protest march. The Fairfax County Board of Supervisors, mindful of the shooting one week earlier in Mississippi of civil-rights activist James Meredith that was the march's immediate cause, directed police to let the demonstrators walk on the left shoulder despite laws prohibiting pedestrian travel.[85] Other demonstrations on the Beltway have tended to rely mostly on motor vehicles, including motorcycles: "I've ridden in blockades (farmers to DC in the '80s), often done the Toys for Tots motorcycle rides, ridden in Rolling Thunder—and I can tell you, it's wild to ride your 'bike' with hundreds of other people—the car traffic goes nuts, the adults are usually pretty irritated, but damn, the kids love it (includes the adults [who] can still dredge up the wonder of childhood)."[86] One week after the death of auto racer Dale Earnhardt in February 2001, more than a hundred vehicles took a ninety-minute memorial lap around the Beltway, organized by Elkridge resident Ronald Leizear. The event was publicized in newspapers, radio, and television and condoned by Maryland state troopers.[87] Later that year the Beltway and highways nationwide became showcases for displays of patriotism, as American flags and similar symbols were draped from overpasses in the wake of the September 11 terrorist attacks.

It would thus be inaccurate to conclude that because residents sometimes have little chance to influence transportation planning, they consequently have little effect on the roads that are created as a result of that planning. While the federal and state governments have in recent decades consciously sought to incorporate the public more directly in the planning process, several steps remain to be taken before residents can truly play an active and participatory, rather than consultative, role. But if residents have minimal input into the physical construction of roads, they do hold the power to shape the social construction of those roads. Engineers did not compel Washingtonians to conceptualize the Capital Beltway as a social boundary, a drag-racing strip, a sexual turn-on, or a protest venue. This is not to suggest that drivers or transportation officials should be satisfied with a de facto power-sharing arrangement in which one group controls roads' physical construction and another their social construction. But these observations do indicate that no single group holds all the power in determining how a given road will actually be designed, built, used, and perceived.

Notes

Introduction

1. Kris Lackey, *RoadFrames: The American Highway Narrative* (Lincoln: University of Nebraska Press, 1997), xi. With its focus on nonfiction accounts, this analysis complements that of highbrow travel writing in Cynthia Golomb Dettelbach, *In the Driver's Seat: The Automobile in American Literature and Popular Culture* (Westport, CT: Greenwood Press, 1976).

2. Bill Bryson, *The Lost Continent: Travels in Small-Town America* (New York: HarperPerennial, 1990), 33.

3. Cf., for instance, William Leach, *Country of Exiles: The Destruction of Place in American Life* (New York: Pantheon, 1999).

4. John Brinckerhoff Jackson, *Discovering the Vernacular Landscape* (New Haven: Yale University Press, 1984), 3. For reflections on the ideal landscape, see Denis E. Cosgrove, "Landscape and *Landschaft*," *Bulletin of the German Historical Institute* 35 (Fall 2004): 57–71.

5. D. W. Meinig, introduction to *The Interpretation of Ordinary Landscapes: Geographical Essays*, ed. D. W. Meinig (New York: Oxford University Press, 1979), 1–7, esp. 1.

6. William G. Hoskins, *The Making of the English Landscape* (London: Hodder and Stoughton, 1955).

7. Leo Marx, *The Machine in the Garden: Technology and the Pastoral Ideal in America* (New York: Oxford University Press, 1964).

8. John Brinckerhoff Jackson, *A Sense of Place, A Sense of Time* (New Haven: Yale University Press, 1994), 189–205.

9. For first intrusions, see John Jakle, "Landscapes Redesigned for the Automobile," in *The Making of the American Landscape*, ed. Michael Conzen (Boston: Unwin Hyman, 1990), 293–310.

10. Jackson, *Discovering the Vernacular Landscape*, 21.

11. Jackson, *A Sense of Place*, 192.

12. Cf. George Rogers Taylor, *The Transportation Revolution, 1815–1836* (New York: Rinehart, 1951); John Lauritz Larson, "'Bind the Republic Together': The National Union and the Struggle for a System of Internal Improvement," *Journal of American History* 74 (1987): 363–87. For a survey of the recent literature, see Robert C. Post, *Technology, Transport, and Travel in*

American History (Washington, DC: Society for the History of Technology and American Historical Association, 2003).

13. For a sociological analysis of roads as social spaces, see Hans-Jürgen Hohm, ed., *Straße und Straßenkultur. Interdisziplinäre Beobachtungen eines öffentlichen Sozialraumes in der fortgeschrittenen Moderne* (Konstanz: Universitätsverlag, 1997).

14. Robert A. Caro, *The Power Broker: Robert Moses and the Fall of New York* (New York: Vintage, 1975), 318; Langdon A. Winner, "Do Artifacts Have Politics?" *Daedalus* 109 (1980): 121–36; Steven Woolgar and Geoffrey Cooper, "Do Artefacts Have Ambivalence? Moses' Bridges, Winner's Bridges, and Other Urban Legends in S&TS," *Social Studies of Science* 29 (1999): 433–49; Bernward Joerges, "Do Politics Have Artefacts?" *Social Studies of Science* 29 (1999): 411–31; Clay McShane, *Down the Asphalt Path: The Automobile and the American City* (New York: Columbia University Press, 1994.)

15. Michael O'Malley, *Keeping Watch: A History of American Time* (New York: Viking Penguin 1990); Carlene Stephens, "'The Most Reliable Time': William Bond, the New England Railroads, and Time Awareness in Nineteenth-Century America," *Technology and Culture* 30 (1989): 1–24, esp. 5.

16. Greg Laugero, "Infrastructures of Enlightenment: Road-Making, the Public Sphere, and the Emergence of Literature," *Eighteenth-Century Studies* 29, no. 1 (1995): 45–67. Cf. also Wolfgang Behringer, "Der Fahrplan der Welt. Anmerkungen zu den Anfängen der europäischen Verkehrsrevolution," in *Geschichte der Zukunft des Verkehrs. Verkehrskonzepte von der Frühen Neuzeit bis zum 21. Jahrhundert*, ed. Hans-Liudger Dienel and Helmuth Trischler (Frankfurt am Main: Campus, 1997), 40–57; Wolfgang Behringer, *Im Zeichen des Merkur: Reichspost und Kommunikationsrevolution in der Frühen Neuzeit* (Göttingen: Vandenhoeck and Ruprecht, 2003). For the United States, see Richard R. John, *Spreading the News: The American Postal System from Franklin to Morse* (Cambridge, MA: Harvard University Press, 1995).

17. Jackson, *Discovering the Vernacular Landscape*, 24; cf. also Leach, *Country of Exiles*, 33–34; and Phil Patton, *Open Roads: A Celebration of the American Highway* (New York: Simon and Schuster, 1986).

18. Philip Bagwell and Peter Lyth, *Transport in Britain: From Canal Lock to Gridlock* (London: Hambledon and London, 2002), 45, 48.

19. Simon P. Ville, *Transport and the Development of the European Economy, 1750–1918* (New York: St. Martin's Press, 1990); Albert O. Hirschman, *The Strategy of Economic Development* (New Haven: Yale University Press, 1958).

20. For a revisionist argument, see Theo Barker and Dorian Gerhold, *The Rise and Rise of Road Transport, 1700–1900* (Cambridge: Cambridge University Press, 1995.)

21. Eckart Klessmann, *Die deutsche Romantik* (Cologne: DuMont, 1979). Stanton is quoted here from *The Colorado River Survey: Robert B. Stanton*

and the Denver, Colorado Canyon and Pacific Railroad, ed. Dwight L. Smith and C. Gregory Crampton (Salt Lake City: Howe Brothers, 1987), 254; cf. also, David E. Nye, "Remaking a 'Natural Menace': Engineering the Colorado River," in *Technologies of Landscape: From Reaping to Recycling,* ed. David E. Nye (Amherst: University of Massachusetts Press, 1999), 97–115, 104–6.

22. Cf. Wolfgang Schivelbusch, *The Railway Journey: The Industrialization of Time and Space in the Nineteenth Century* (Berkeley: University of California Press, 1986).

23. Alfred Runte, *Trains of Discovery: Western Railroads and the National Parks* (Boulder, CO: Roberts Rinehart, 1990); Carlos Arnaldo Schwantes, *Going Places: Transportation Redefines the Twentieth-Century West* (Bloomington: Indiana University Press, 2003).

24. Marguerite S. Schaffer, *See America First: Tourism and National Identity, 1880–1940* (Washington, DC: Smithsonian Institution Press, 2001), 130–68; see also Paul S. Sutter, *Driven Wild: How the Fight Against Automobiles Launched the Modern Wilderness Movement* (Seattle: University of Washington Press, 2002).

25. John A. Jakle and Keith A. Sculle, *Fast Food: Roadside Restaurants in the Automobile Age* (Baltimore: Johns Hopkins University Press, 1999); Jakle and Sculle, *The Gas Station in America* (Baltimore: Johns Hopkins University Press, 1994); Jakle and Sculle, *The Motel in America* (Baltimore: Johns Hopkins University Press, 1996).

26. Cf. Diane L. Krahe, "Keeping American Indian Lands 'Roadless' and 'Wild': A New Deal Bureaucrat's Scheme to Preserve the Primitive," lecture delivered at the GHI's Landscapes and Roads in North America and Europe: Cultural History in Transatlantic Perspective conference, October 11–13, 2002. See also Diane L. Krahe, "Last Refuge: The Uneasy Embrace of Indian Lands by the National Wilderness Movement, 1937–1965" (PhD diss., Washington State University, 2005).

27. Bruce Seely, "Visions of the American Highway, 1900–1980," in *Geschichte der Zukunft des Verkehrs. Verkehrskonzepte von der frühen Neuzeit bis ins 21. Jahrhundert,* ed. Hans-Liudger Dienel and Helmuth Trischler (Frankfurt: Campus, 1997), 260–79. For an analysis of a particular highway, see Matthew W. Roth, "Mulholland Highway and the Engineering Culture of Los Angeles in the 1920s," *Technology and Culture* 40 (1999): 545–75.

28. Ruth Schwartz Cowan, A *Social History of American Technology* (New York: Oxford University Press, 1997), 233–48, 236. Cf. also John B. Rae, *The Road and Car in American Life* (Cambridge, MA: MIT Press, 1971); Mark H. Rose, *Interstate: Express Highway Politics, 1939–1989* (Knoxville: University of Tennessee Press, 1990); Bruce E. Seely, *Building the American Highway System: Engineers as Policy Makers* (Philadelphia: Temple University Press,

1987); James J. Flink, *The Automobile Age* (Cambridge, MA: MIT Press, 1993).

29. Leach, *Country of Exiles,* 34.

30. "Public Road and Street Mileage in the United States by Type of Surface," Annual Report of the National Bureau of Transportation Statistics, Washington, DC, 2004, http://www.bts.gov/publications/national_transportation_statistics/html/table_01_04.html. According to the table "Total Length of Motorways" in *Eurostat Yearbook 2004* (Luxembourg: Office for Official Publications of the European Communities, 2004), 211, in 2000 there were 54,434 kilometers of interstate highways in the twenty-five member countries of the European Union, compared to 89,426 in the United States. http://epp.eurostat.ec.europa.eu/cache/ITY_OFFPUB/KS-CD-04-001-6/EN/KS-CD-04-001 -6-EN.PDF.

31. Tom Lewis, *Divided Highways: Building the Interstate Highway System, Transforming American Life* (New York: Penguin, 1999); Raymond Mohl, "Stop the Road: Freeway Revolts in American Cities," *Journal of Urban History* 30, no. 5 (2004): 674–706.

32. David G. Havlick, *No Place Distant: Roads and Motorized Recreation on America's Public Lands* (Washington, DC: Island Press, 2002).

33. Cf. Nancy J. Volkman, "The 'Roading' of Texas: Spanish and German Traditions in Historic Road Preservation," lecture delivered at the GHI conference on Landscapes and Roads in North America and Europe: Cultural History in Transatlantic Perspective, October 11–13, 2002.

34. See the essay by Massimo Moraglio in this volume.

35. Joachim Wolschke-Bulmahn, "Political Landscapes and Technology: Nazi Germany and the Landscape Design of the *Reichsautobahnen,*" in *Nature and Technology: Council of Educators in Landscape Architecture 75th Anniversary, Selected CELA Annual Conference Papers* (Washington, DC, 1996), 157–70; and the essay by Thomas Zeller in this volume.

36. D. W. Meinig, "Reading the Landscape: An Appreciation of W. G. Hoskins and J. B. Jackson," in Meinig, ed., *Interpretation of Ordinary Landscapes,* 195–244, esp. 234.

37. Stephen Spender, *Love-Hate Relations: A Study of Anglo-American Sensibilities* (London: Hamish Hamilton, 1974), 47, quoted here from Meinig, ibid.

38. Sam Bass Warner Jr., *The Urban Wilderness: A History of the American City* (New York: Harper and Row, 1972), 4.

Chapter 1

1. Larry McMurtry, *Roads: Driving America's Great Highways* (New York: Simon and Schuster, 2000), 206.

2. Ibid., 11.

3. Ibid., 21.

4. Clay McShane, *Down the Asphalt Path: The Automobile and the American City* (New York: Columbia University Press, 1994); R. J. Overy, "Cars, Roads, and Economic Recovery in Germany, 1932–1938," in *War and Economy in the Third Reich,* ed. R. J. Overy (Oxford: Clarendon Press, 1994), 68–89; Phil Patton, *Open Road: A Celebration of the American Highway* (New York: Simon and Schuster, 1986); Mathew Roth, "Mulholland Highway and the Engineering Culture of Los Angeles in the 1920s," *Technology and Culture* 40, no. 3 (1999): 545–75; Georg Rigele, *Die Großglockner Hochalpenstraße* (Vienna: WUV-Universitätsverlag, 1998); Barbara Schmucki, *Der Traum vom Verkehrsfluß: Städtische Verkehrsplanung seit 1945 im deutsch-deutschen Vergleich* (Frankfurt am Main: Campus, 2001); Carlos Arnaldo Schwantes, *Going Places: Transportation Redefines the Twentieth-Century West* (Bloomington: Indiana University Press, 2003); Thomas Zeller, *Strasse, Bahn, Panorama: Verkehrswege und Landschaftsveränderungen in Deutschland von 1930 bis 1990* (Frankfurt am Main: Campus, 2002); Thomas Zeller, "'The Landscape's Crown': Landscape, Perceptions, and Modernizing Effects of the German Autobahn System, 1934 to 1941," in *Technologies of Landscape: From Reaping to Recycling,* ed. David E. Nye (Amherst: University of Massachusetts Press, 1999); Thomas Zeller, "Landschaften des Verkehrs: Autobahnen im Nationalsozialismus und Hochgeschwindigkeitsstrecken für die Bahn in der Bundesrepublik," *Technikgeschichte* 64, no. 4 (1997): 323–40.

5. David Louter, "Glaciers and Gasoline: The Making of a Windshield Wilderness, 1900–1915," in *Seeing and Being Seen: Tourism in the American West,* ed. David M. Wrobel and Patrick T. Long (Lawrence: University Press of Kansas, 2001).

6. Quinta Scott and Susan Croce Kelly, *Route 66: The Highway and Its People* (Norman: University of Oklahoma Press, 1988); Quinta Scott, *Along Route 66* (Norman: University of Oklahoma Press, 2000).

7. Christoph Maria Merki, *Der holprige Siegeszug des Automobils, 1895–1930: Zur Motorisierung des Strassenverkehrs in Frankreich, Deutschland und der Schweiz* (Vienna: Böhlau, 2002), 21.

8. This premise appears to be the point of departure for a major new research initiative on European mobility history, the key hypothesis of which is that, "from a user perspective, the road system and the centrally controlled systems are different in several fundamental respects"; see Gijs Mom and Laurent Tissot, "Mobility History and the European Road Network: Planning, Building, Use and Spatial Organization (1920–2000)—A Proposal," *La Lettre du Gerpisa* 161 (July 2002): 10–11, esp. 10.

9. Daniel Miller, "Driven Societies," in *Car Cultures,* ed. Daniel Miller (Oxford: Berg, 2001), 1–33; see also R. J. Koshar, "On the History of the Automobile in Everyday Life," *Contemporary European History* 10, no. 1 (2001): 143–54.

Virginia Scharff's *Taking the Wheel: Women and the Coming of the Motor Age* (Albuquerque: University of New Mexico Press [1992]) remains an important exception.

10. David Gartman, *Auto Opium: A Social History of American Automobile Design* (London: Routledge, 1994).

11. Kris Lackey, *RoadFrames: The American Highway Narrative* (Lincoln: University of Nebraska Press, 1997); Ronald Primeau, *Romance of the Road: The Literature of the American Highway* (Bowling Green, OH: Bowling Green State University Popular Press, 1996).

12. John Urry, *Sociology Beyond Societies: Mobilities for the Twenty-First Century* (London: Routledge, 2000).

13. Schmucki notes that the automobile became the norm for East German traffic planning even when relatively few cars plied East German roads (*Der Traum vom Verkehrsfluss*, chap. 3).

14. My perspective is also influenced by recent scholarship on the social construction of technology, although I concentrate more on the users of technology than on how social groups shape design decisions; for a recent example of this literature, see Ronald R. Kline, *Consumers in the Country: Technology and Social Change in Rural America* (Baltimore: Johns Hopkins University Press, 2000).

15. William H. Sewell Jr., "The Concept(s) of Culture," in *Beyond the Cultural Turn: New Directions in the Study of Society and Culture*, ed. Victoria E. Bonnell and Lynn Hunt (Berkeley: University of California Press, 1999), 51.

16. See, for example, Roger Cooter and Bill Luckin, eds., *Accidents in History: Injuries, Fatalities, and Social Relations* (Amsterdam: Rodopi, 1997).

17. M. G. Lay, *Ways of the World: A History of the World's Roads and of the Vehicles that Used Them* (New Brunswick, NJ: Rutgers University Press, 1992), 117.

18. See McShane, *Down the Asphalt Path*.

19. Curt McConnell, *Coast to Coast by Automobile: The Pioneering Trips, 1899–1908* (Stanford, CA: Stanford University Press, 2000). On the literature on transcontinental trips in America, see Carey S. Bliss, *Autos across America: A Bibliography of Transcontinental Automobile Travel, 1903–1940* (Los Angeles: Dawson's Book Shop, 1972). For accounts of other pioneering trips not only in North America but in Europe, Africa, South America, China, and the Middle East, see T. R. Nicholson, *The Wild Roads: The Story of Transcontinental Motoring* (London: Jarrolds, 1969); for the record of an early-twentieth-century German adventurer's roadtrip, see Paul Graetz, *Im Auto quer durch Afrika* (Berlin: G. Braunbeck and Gutenberg-Druckerei, 1910). As the foregoing title suggests, such pioneering trips may also be seen in the context of imperialist expansion. Finally, early car magazines are a good source for empirical material on early auto trips, e.g., H. Heiland, "Motortouristik auf Java," *Allgemeine Automobil-Zeitung* 11 (October 7, 1910): 33–35.

20. Merki, *Der holprige Siegeszug,* 257–64; see also Roger Casey, "The Vanderbilt Cup, 1908," *Technology and Culture* 40, no. 2 (1999): 359–63.

21. James J. Flink, *The Automobile Age* (Cambridge, MA: MIT Press, 1988), 29–33.

22. McConnell, *Coast to Coast,* 9.

23. Ibid., 19.

24. Ibid., 11.

25. Cited in Paul S. Sutter, *Driven Wild: How the Fight Against Automobiles Launched the Modern Wilderness Movement* (Seattle: University of Washington Press, 2002), 79.

26. See Drake Hokanson, *The Lincoln Highway: Main Street across America* (Iowa City: University of Iowa Press, 1988).

27. Hokanson, *The Lincoln Highway,* 31.

28. Benedict Anderson, *Imagined Communities: Reflections on the Origin and Spread of Nationalism,* rev. ed. (London: Verso, 1991).

29. Martin Heidegger, *Being and Time* (1927), trans. John Macquarrie and Edward Robinson (New York: Harper, 1962), 99, 109.

30. I accept the argument that biological and mechanical deep structures shape the interaction between driver, car, and road, as suggested in Steven L. Thompson's "The Arts of the Motorcycle: Biology, Culture, and Aesthetics in Technological Choice," *Technology and Culture* 41, no. 1 (January 2000): 99–115; but the process of cultural mediation still remains central to my analysis.

31. Quoted in McConnell, *Coast to Coast,* 22–23.

32. Merki, *Der holprige Siegeszug,* 42.

33. McConnell, *Coast to Coast,* 266–302.

34. Horatio Nelson Jackson, *From Ocean to Ocean in a Winton* (Cleveland, OH: privately printed, 1903).

35. McConnell, *Coast to Coast,* 269.

36. Owen John, *The Autocar-Biography of Owen John* (London: Iliffe and Sons, 1927), 194.

37. See Catherine Bertho Lavenir, "How the Motor Car Conquered the Road," in *Cultures of Control,* ed. Miriam R. Levin (Amsterdam: Harwood Academic, 2000), 113–34.

38. Lavenir, 116–21; McShane, *Down the Asphalt Path,* 188–89.

39. John, *Auto-car Biography,* 194.

40. McShane, *Down the Asphalt Path,* 189.

41. Karl Dieterich, "Aus den Kinderjahren des Automobilismus," *Motor* 1 (July 1913): 57–61.

42. Scharff, *Taking the Wheel.*

43. Urry, *Sociology beyond Societies,* 191.

44. Jack Barth et al., *Roadside America* (New York: Simon and Schuster, 1986); Karal Ann Marling, *The Colossus of Roads: Myth and Symbol along the*

American Highway (Minneapolis: University of Minnesota Press, 1984); Warren James Belasco, *Americans on the Road: From Autocamp to Motel, 1910–1945* (Cambridge, MA: MIT Press, 1979); Lucinda Lewis, *Roadside America: The Automobile and the American Dream* (New York: H. N. Abrams, 2000).

45. See, e.g., McShane, *Down the Asphalt Path*, 22–23.

46. Reiner Flik, *Von Ford lernen? Automobilbau und Motorisierung in Deutschland bis 1933* (Cologne: Böhlau, 2001), 38–43; Michael L. Berger, *The Devil Wagon in God's Country: The Automobile and Social Change in Rural America, 1893–1929* (Hamden, CT: Archon, 1979); Kline, *Consumers in the Country*, 55–86.

47. For examples from England, see Sean O'Connell, *The Car in British Society: Class, Gender and Motoring, 1896–1939* (Manchester: Manchester University Press, 1998).

48. Uwe Fraunholz, *Motorphobia: Anti-automobiler Protest in Kaiserreich und Weimarer Republik* (Göttingen: Vandenhoeck and Ruprecht, 2002); Kline, *Consumers in the Country*, 57–62.

49. See Alexa Geisthövel, review in *sehepunkte* 3, no. 1 (2003), http://www.sehepunkte.de/2003/01/2898.html (accessed September 6, 2006).

50. Walter Henry Nelson, *Small Wonder: The Amazing Story of the Volkswagen* (Boston: Little, Brown, 1965), 49.

51. Hans Mommsen, *Das Volkswagenwerk und seine Arbeiter im Dritten Reich* (Düsseldorf: ECON, 1996).

52. See R. J. Koshar, "Germans at the Wheel: Cars and Leisure Travel in Interwar Germany," in *Histories of Leisure*, ed. R. J. Koshar (Oxford: Berg, 2002), 215–30, esp. 219–24.

53. Raymond Williams, *Marxism and Literature* (Oxford: Oxford University Press, 1977), 121–27.

54. Michael Ermarth, "*The German Talks Back:* Heinrich Hauser and German Attitudes toward Americanization after World War II," in *America and the Shaping of German Society, 1945–1955*, ed. Michael Ermarth (Providence: Berg, 1993).

55. C. Volkhardt, "Autobahnsünder," *Motor-Kritik* 18 (September 1938): 623–27, esp. 623.

56. Max Domarus, *Hitler: Speeches and Proclamations, 1932–1945*, vol. 3, *The Years 1939 to 1940*, trans. Mary Fran Gilbert (Wauconda, IL: Bolchazy-Carducci, 1990–97), 1478.

57. The reference is to preservationist geographer Vaughan Cornish, as cited by David Matless, *Landscape and Englishness* (London: Reaktion, 1998), 55.

58. Lewis Mumford, *The Highway and the City* (New York: Harcourt, Brace and World, 1963), 234–46.

59. See the numerous examples in Erhard Schütz, "'Jene blaugrauen Bänder': Die Reichsautobahn in Literatur und anderen Medien des 'Dritten

Reiches,'" *Internationales Archiv für Sozialgeschichte der deutschen Literatur* 18, no. 2 (1993): 76–120.

60. John Brinckerhoff Jackson, *Landscape in Sight: Looking at America* (New Haven: Yale University Press, 1997), 208.

61. Ibid., 205.

62. Michael Burleigh, *The Third Reich: A New History* (New York: Hill and Wang, 2000).

63. See Zeller, "'The Landscape's Crown'"; William H. Rollins, "Whose Landscape? Technology, Fascism, and Environmentalism on the National Socialist Autobahn," *Annals of the Association of American Geographers* 85, no. 3 (1995): 494–520; Eckhard Gruber and Erhard Schütz, "'A Land of Bridges': On the Conception and Presentation of Bridges for the *Reichsautobahn* in the Third Reich," *Daidalos: Architektur Kunst Kultur* 57 (September 1995): 20–33.

64. Viktor Klemperer, *I Will Bear Witness: A Diary of the Nazi Years, 1933–1941*, trans. Martin Chalmers (New York: Random House, 1998), 193, 165.

65. See O'Connell, *The Car in British Society*, 102–6; and, for a report on the rash of auto thefts and joyriding in Germany, see the anonymous "Here and There," *Autocar* 70 (January 6, 1933): 29. For a typical example of contemporary American tuning culture, see Mike Kojima, "All Motor Madness: The Inner Secrets of the 10–Second N/A Hondas," *Sport Compact Car* 13, no. 8 (2001): 164–81.

66. Michel de Certeau, *The Practice of Everyday Life* (Berkeley and Los Angeles: University of California Press, 1984), xxii.

67. H. F. Moorhouse, *Driving Ambitions: An Analysis of the American Hot Rod Enthusiasm* (Manchester and New York: Manchester University Press, 1991), 26.

68. Moorhouse, *Driving Ambitions*, 29. See also Ashleigh Brilliant, *The Great Car Craze: How Southern California Collided with the Automobile in the 1920s* (Santa Barbara: Woodbridge Press, 1989).

69. Moorhouse, *Driving Ambitions*, 33.

70. Ibid., 173. European variants suggest the many uses to which the juxtaposition of "American" and "European" driving practices could be put. In Sweden, for example, cruising or speeding in large, chrome-bedecked American cars of the late 1950s attracted unruly working-class teenagers known as *raggare*. Their adoption of ostentatious, often elaborately decorated American cars was an affront to the Swedish middle class, whose car ideal was the understated Volvo, the symbol of the Social Democratic project of the postwar age; see Tom O'Dell, "Raggare and the Panic of Mobility: Modernity and Hybridity in Sweden," in Miller, ed., *Car Cultures*, 105–32. In American culture, of course, it was the bulbous American car of the 1950s that earned hot-rodders' ridicule.

71. See Moorhouse, *Driving Ambitions*, 177–87; Moorhouse does note, however, that American hot-rodding's exclusion of women as active participants was never total.

72. Paul Graves-Brown, "From Highway to Superhighway: The Sustainability, Symbolism and Situated Practices of Car Cultures," *Social Analysis* 4, no. 1 (1997): 64–75.

73. For examples, see Michael Karl Witzel and Kent Bash, *Cruisin': Car Culture in America* (Osceola, WI: Motorbooks International Publishers and Wholesalers, 1997).

74. Reyner Banham, *Los Angeles: The Architecture of Four Ecologies* (London: Allen Lane, 1971), 215.

75. Marc Augé, *Non-Places: Introduction to an Anthropology of Supermodernity*, trans. John Howe (London: Verso, 1995), 78.

Chapter 2

1. A comprehensive history of American parkway development has yet to be published. Brief discussions of the topic appear in several studies of American landscape architecture, city planning, and highway engineering. These include Norman T. Newton, *Design on the Land: The Development of Landscape Architecture* (Cambridge, MA: Harvard University Press, 1971); Christopher Tunnard and Boris Pushkarev, *Man-Made America: Chaos or Control?* (New Haven: Yale University Press, 1963); and David Schuyler, *The New Urban Landscape: The Redefinition of City Form in Nineteenth-Century America* (Baltimore: Johns Hopkins University Press, 1986). Clay McShane offers numerous insights into parkway development in his *Down the Asphalt Path: The Automobile and the American City* (New York: Columbia University Press, 1994). Bruce Radde's *The Merritt Parkway* (New Haven: Yale University Press, 1993) and Sara Amy Leach's "Fifty Years of Parkway Construction in and around the Nation's Capital," in *Roadside America: The Automobile in Design and Culture*, ed. Jan Jennings (Ames: Iowa University Press, 1990), 185–97, also offer brief summaries of the genre. My own dissertation provides an overview of American parkway history and examines the development of Mount Vernon Memorial Highway in detail; see Timothy Davis, "Mount Vernon Memorial Highway and the Evolution of the American Parkway" (PhD diss., University of Texas at Austin, 1997). For an expanded version of the present essay, see Timothy Davis, "The American Motor Parkway," *Studies in the History of Gardens and Designed Landscapes* 25, no. 4 (2005): 219–49.

2. See Warren Susman, *Culture as History: The Transformation of American Society in the Twentieth Century* (New York: Pantheon,1973); Michael Kam-

men, *Mystic Chords of Memory: The Transformation of Tradition in American Culture* (New York: Pantheon, 1991); Lawrence Levine, *The Unpredictable Past: Essays in American Cultural History* (New York: Oxford University Press, 1993); Jeffrey Meikle, "Domesticating Modernity: Ambivalence and Appropriation, 1920–40," in *Designing Modernity: The Arts of Reform and Persuasion, 1885–1945: Selections from the Wolfsonian,* ed. Wendy Kaplan (London: Thames and Hudson, 1995), 143–67. The contemporary penchant for historic preservation, colonial revivalism, and Anglo-centric public history has been examined in James Lindgren, *Preserving New England: Preservation, Progressivism, and the Remaking of Memory* (New York; Oxford University Press, 1995; Michael Wallace, "Visiting the Past" and "Reflections on the History of Historic Preservation," in *Presenting the Past: Essays on History and the Public,* ed. Susan Porter Benson, Stephen Brier, and Roy Rosenzweig (Philadelphia: Temple University Press, 1986), 137–99; Karal Ann Marling, *George Washington Slept Here: Colonial Revivals and American Culture, 1876–1986* (Cambridge, MA: Harvard University Press, 1988); David Gebhard, "The Colonial Revival in the 1930s," *Winterthur Portfolio* 22 (1987): 109–48; and Bridget May, "Progressivism and the Colonial Revival: The Modern Colonial House, 1900–1920," *Winterthur Portfolio* 26 (1991): 107–22.

3. See Frederick Law Olmsted and Calvert Vaux, "Report of the Landscape Architects and Superintendents to the President of the Board of Commissioners of Prospect Park, Brooklyn," in Board of Commissioners of Prospect Park, *Eighth Annual Report of the Board of Commissioners of Prospect Park, Brooklyn, January 1868* (New York: I. Van Anden, 1868). For the best overview of late-nineteenth-century parkway development and its role in the evolution of American urban planning, see Schuyler, *The New American Landscape,* 126–46.

4. For a detailed analysis of the evolving social, political, technological, and aesthetic facets of one particular parkway over a hundred-year period, see Timothy Davis, "Rock Creek and Potomac Parkway, Washington, DC: The Evolution of a Contested Urban Landscape," *Studies in the History of Gardens and Designed Landscapes* 19 (April-June 1999): 123–237.

5. "Unfit for Modern Motor Traffic," *Fortune* 14 (August 1936): 85–99; *Life* magazine, quoted in Phil Patton, *Open Road: A Celebration of the American Highway* (New York: Simon and Schuster, 1986), 66–67; *Saturday Evening Post* editorial, quoted in "Why Not Make Travel as Stimulating to the Eye as It Is to the Speedometer?" *American City* 41 (October 1929): 121; Benton Mackaye and Lewis Mumford, "Townless Highways for the Motorist: A Proposal for the Automobile Age," *Harper's Monthly* 163 (August 1931): 347–56; and Benton Mackaye, "The Townless Highway," *New Republic* 62 (March 12, 1930): 93–95.

6. For a detailed summary of American parkway development during the 1920s and '30s, see Davis, "Mount Vernon Memorial Highway and the

Evolution of the American Parkway," 158–203. Contemporary accounts include E. W. James, "Parkway Features of Interest to the Highway Engineer," *Public Roads* 10 (April 1929): 21–28; Jay Downer, "How Westchester Treats its Roadsides,"*American Civic Annual, 1930* (Washington, DC: American Civic Association, 1930), 165–67; Jay Downer, "Principles of Westchester's Parkway System," *Civil Engineering* 4 (February 1934): 85–87; Stanley Abbot, "Ten Years of the Westchester County Park System," *Parks and Recreation* 16 (March 1933): 305–14; and Gilmore Clarke's extensive writings on the subject, especially "Modern Motor Arteries," in National Conference on City Planning, *Planning Problems of Town, City and Region: Papers and Discussion at the Twenty-second National Conference on City Planning, June 23–26, 1930* (Philadelphia: William Fell, 1930), 61–75; "Is There A Solution for the Through Traffic Problem?" *Parks and Recreation* 13 (July-August 1930): 367–75; and "Modern Motorways," *Architectural Record* (December 1933): 430–37.

7. Subsequent critics, such as Robert Caro (in *The Power Broker: Robert Moses and the Fall of New York* [New York: Random House, 1974]), have assailed parkway-builders for this practice on the grounds that it represented a reprehensible form of class discrimination. Such complaints may cater to current academic fads, but they reflect a poor command of history and geography. Park-makers had long excluded such vehicles for the reasons outlined above. Contrary to popular myth, moreover, Long Island's Jones Beach has long been accessible by public transportation (the Wantagh Parkway, which connected Jones Beach with the Long Island Railroad station at Wantagh, was equipped with higher overpasses that accommodated bus traffic). Contemporary accounts also noted that many people hitchhiked along the parkways, though the practice was technically forbidden. "Robert (Or-I'll-Resign) Moses," *Fortune* (June 1938): 70–78 and 124–41, esp. 124.

8. This vein of criticism appears in a series of published responses to a Gilmore Clarke presentation at the Twenty-Second National Conference on City Planning in June 1930; see National Conference on City Planning, *Planning Problems of Town, City and Region*, 67–75.

9. U.S. Department of Agriculture, *The Mount Vernon Memorial Highway: History, Design, and Progress in Construction* (Washington, DC: Government Printing Office, 1930); U.S. Department of Agriculture, *Roadside Improvements; U.S. Department of Agriculture Miscellaneous Publication No. 191* (Washington, DC: Government Printing Office, 1934), republished in Germany as Wilbur H. Simonson and R. E. Royall, *Landschaftsgestaltung an der Straße* (Berlin: Volk und Reich, 1935). Italian coverage of the memorial highway included I. Vandone, "La Strada Commemorativa da Washington a Mount Vernon," *Strade* 13 (January 1931): 2–8; and "Consiglio Nazionale Delle Ricerche Comitato per L'Ingegneria, La Strada Commemorativa da Washington a Mount Vernon," in *La Partecipazione Italiana al sesto Congresso internationale*

della Strada, Washington, Ottobre 1930 (Rome Stabilimento tipo-litografico del Genio civile, 1931), 229–33.

10. Gilmore Clarke, "Beauty: A Wanting Factor In the Turnpike Design," *Landscape Architecture* 32 (January 1942): 53–54. Clarke underscored the American parkway's seminal status in "Westchester Parkways: An American Development in Landscape Architecture," *Landscape Architecture* 28 (October 1937): 318–21. See also Stanley Abbott, "Parkways—Past, Present, and Future," *Parks and Recreation* 31 (December 1948): 681–91, esp. 683.

11. Historians William Rollins and Joachim Wolschke-Buhlman have disagreed on the relationships between Nazi racial ideology and ecologically derived notions of biological correctness, but the end result was a more rigid interpretation of the terms *native species* and *natural landscaping* than can be found in the American parkway design context. See Joachim Wolschke-Buhlman and William Rollins, "Whose Landscape? Technology, Fascism, and Environmentalism on the National Socialist *Autobahn*," *Annals of the Association of American Geographers* 85 (1995): 494–519; and Joachim Wolschke-Bulmahn, "Political Landscapes and Technology: Nazi Germany and the Landscape Design of the *Reichsautobahnen*," in Council of Educators in Landscape Architecture, ed., *Nature and Technology* (Washington, DC: CELA, 1996).

12. Frederick Law Olmsted [Jr.], "Roadside Plantings on Hitler's Highways: An Inquiry from Germany and an American Answer," *Landscape Architecture* 30 (July 1940): 179–82; "The Nazi Autobahnen," *Landscape Architecture* 35 (July 1945): 157.

13. Leo Marx, *The Machine in the Garden: Technology and the Pastoral Ideal in America* (New York: Oxford University Press, 1964).

14. Wilbur H. Simonson, "Mount Vernon Memorial Highway Is Correct Name," *Washington Evening Star*, July 13, 1932.

15. "Building the Mount Vernon Memorial Highway," 31 min., b&w, 35 mm (1933); U.S. Department of Agriculture Films, Record Group 33, Moving Pictures Branch, National Archives.

16. U.S. Congress, House Committee on Roads, *Roads: Hearings before the Committee on Roads . . . on H.R. 524* (68th Cong., 1st Sess., 25 April 1924), 16–21.

17. These models are described in Albert Rose, "Landscape Construction Notes. XLI. The Models of the Mount Vernon Memorial Highway," *Landscape Architecture* 23 (1932): 61–69.

18. H. S. Fairbank, "Modern Design Characterizes Highway Memorial to Mount Vernon," *American City* 43 (September 1930): 149–50; Wilbur H. Simonson, "The Mount Vernon Memorial Highway: Most Modern Motorway, Designed as Memorial to Country's First President, Now under Construction," *American City* 43 (October 1930): 85–88; "A Notable Highway," *Engineering News-Record* 107 (July 23, 1931): 122; "The Mount Vernon Memorial

Highway," *Engineering News-Record* 107 (July 23, 1931): 124–27; "The Mount Vernon Memorial Highway," *American Highways* 11 (October 1932): 11–13; R. E. Toms and J. W. Johnson, "The Design and Construction of The Mount Vernon Memorial Highway," *Journal of the American Concrete Institute* 4 (April 1932): 563–84; R. E. Royall, "The Mount Vernon Memorial Highway," *Military Engineer* 24 (May-June 1932): 238–42.

19. Gilmore Clarke, "Mount Vernon Memorial Highway," *Landscape Architecture* 22 (April 1932): 179–89; R. E. Toms, "Design and Construction of Mount Vernon Memorial Highway," *Parks and Recreation* 15 (May 1932): 537–44; Ralph Griswold, "Modernistic Work and Its Natural Limitations," *Landscape Architecture* 22 (July 1932): 296–99.

20. "Blow the Horns for Mount Vernon's Superhighway," *Literary Digest* 112 (9 January 1932): 42–43.

21. "The Mt. Vernon Memorial Highway," *American Motorist* 6 (April 1932): 21 and 28.

22. Abbott, "Parkways—Past, Present, and Future," 684.

23. For more on the contrived nature of parkway landscapes and the tensions between the goals of institutionally empowered designers and local or vernacular interests, see Barry M. Buxton, *Mabry Mill Historic Resource Study* (Washington, DC: U.S. Department of the Interior, National Park Service, 1987); Phil Noblitt, "The Blue Ridge Parkway and the Myths of the Pioneer," *Appalachian Journal* 21 (Summer 1994): 394–409; Timothy Davis, "'A Pleasant Illusion of Unspoiled Countryside': The American Parkway and the Problematics of Institutional Vernacular," in *Constructing Image, Identity, and Place: Perspectives in Vernacular Architecture IX,* ed. Alison K. Hoagland and Kenneth A. Breisch (Knoxville: University of Tennessee Press, 2003), 228–46; and Kathleen LaFrank, "Real and Ideal Landscapes along the Taconic State Parkway," in Hoagland and Breisch, eds., *Constructing Image, Identity, and Place,* 247–62.

24. For the classic articulation of the concept of invented traditions, see Eric Hobsbawm and Terence Ranger, eds., *The Invention of Tradition* (New York: Cambridge University Press, 1983). Wendy Kaplan discusses the concept of romantic nationalism and its material expressions in "Traditions Transformed: Romantic Nationalism in Design, 1890–1920," in Kaplan, ed., *Designing Modernity,* 19–47; while Jeffrey Meikle explicitly addresses the tension between modernity and anti-modernity in "Domesticating Modernity," in Kaplan, ed., *Designing Modernity,* 143–67. John Bodnar's *Remaking America: Public Memory, Commemoration, and Patriotism in the Twentieth Century* (Princeton, NJ: Princeton University Press, 1992) explores various manifestations of these phenomena in early-twentieth-century America.

25. Cleveland Rodgers, "Highways and Parkways," *Studio* 127 (June 1944): 204–8.

26. "Robert (Or-I'll-Resign) Moses," 70–78, 124–41.

27. "Along the Bronx River," postcard published by the Ruben Publishing Company, Newburgh, NY, ca. 1935 (author's collection).

28. Siegfried Giedion, *Space, Time and Architecture: The Growth of A New Tradition* (Cambridge, MA: Harvard University Press, 1941), 550–59.

29. For further analysis of the cultural resonance of streamlining in America during the 1920s and '30s, see Jeffrey Meikle, *Twentieth Century Limited: Industrial Design in America, 1925–1939* (Philadelphia: Temple University Press, 1979), 135–87. Terry Smith recapitulates Meikle's observations and adds some interpretations of his own in *Making the Modern: Industry, Art, and Design in America* (Chicago: University of Chicago Press, 1993), 353–84.

30. The "friction"-based traffic theories of Dr. Miller McClintock, head of Harvard's Bureau of Street Traffic Research, were summarized in "Unfit for Modern Motor Traffic," *Fortune* 14 (August 1936): 85–99.

31. Wilbur H. Simonson, ""The Mount Vernon Memorial Highway Unit VI: Final Report: The Landscape Architectural Problems in Its Development," unpublished project report for the Bureau of Public Roads (U.S. Department of Agriculture, 1932), 17–18, 197; caption to plates 70, 79. An illustrated copy of this report is in the U.S. Department of Transportation Library, Washington, DC.

32. Edward Bassett, "The Freeway—A New Kind of Thoroughfare," *American City* 42 (February 1930): 95.

33. Norman Bel Geddes's *Magic Motorways* (New York: Random House, 1940) provided a comprehensive, profusely illustrated overview of the Futurama along with an elucidation of its underlying principles. Futurama's significance is discussed in many sources, including Meikle, *Twentieth Century Limited;* and Smith, *Making the Modern.*

34. U.S. Public Roads Administration, *Toll Roads and Free Roads* (Washington, DC: Government Printing Office, 1939), 41–52, plates 30–33, 54–55.

35. In *Landscape Architecture* 32 (January 1942), see the following five articles: Ralph Stewart, "The Pennsylvania Turnpike and Its Landscape Treatment," 47–52; Malcolm Dill, "The Cross-Section: Its Effect on Safety and Economy," 52–53; Gilmore Clarke, "Beauty: A Wanting Factor in the Turnpike Design," 53–54; Ralph Griswold, "Precedent for Superhighway Landscape Yet to Be Found," 54–55; and Laurie Cox, "Appearance: Essential Element in Highway Design," 55–56. See also "Streamlined Mountain Thoroughfare," *Better Roads* 10 (July 1940): 13–14, 31–32;

36. See Timothy Davis, Todd A. Croteau, and Christopher H. Marston, *America's National Park Roads and Parkways: Drawings from the Historic American Engineering Record* (Baltimore: Johns Hopkins University Press, 2004).

Chapter 3

1. Harry Middleton, "The Good Road of the Blue Ridge," *Southern Living* (September 1985): 72–79.

2. All materials here are taken from the four-part series "Parkway at a Crossroads," published in the *Asheville (NC) Citizen-Times* during the autumn of 2002. Specific articles include Julie Ball, "Historic Scenic Roadway Plays Big Role in Region's Identity and Economy," *Asheville (NC) Citizen-Times,* October 10, 2002, available online at http://www.citizen-times.com/parkway (accessed August 30, 2006); and Julie Ball, "Views Draw Visitors to Scenic Parkway," *Asheville (NC) Citizen-Times,* October 17, 2002.

3. See, for example, Barry M. Buxton and Steven M. Beatty, eds., *Blue Ridge Parkway: Agent of Transition: Proceedings of the Blue Ridge Parkway Golden Anniversary Conference* (Boone, NC: Appalachian Consortium Press, 1986), i.

4. S. A. Miller, Obids, NC, to Franklin D. Roosevelt, January 7, 1937, RG 79, Entry 7, Box 2731, National Archives at College Park, MD (NACP).

5. Fred B. Bauer, "Cherokee Indian Explains Opposition to Scenic Road" *Charlotte (NC) Observer,* January 15, 1939.

6. The Cherokee situation is discussed in Anne V. Mitchell, "Culture, History, and Development on the Qualla Boundary: The Eastern Cherokees and the Blue Ridge Parkway, 1935–40," *Appalachian Journal* 24 (1997): 144–91; and Whisnant, *Super-Scenic Motorway: A Blue Ridge Parkway History* (Chapel Hill: University of North Carolina Press, 2006), 183–213.

7. Harley E. Jolley, *The Blue Ridge Parkway* (Knoxville: University of Tennessee Press, 1969), 44, 51–56, 90, 49, 93–10, 115–19, 135–36.

8. In fact the Parkway must be comprehended within the context of all modernizing development in the region (of which there was a great deal), but my scope here is narrower than that. Some relevant literature includes David E. Whisnant, *Modernizing the Mountaineer: People, Power, and Planning in Appalachia,* rev. ed. (Knoxville: University of Tennessee Press, 1994); Ronald D. Eller, *Miners, Millhands, and Mountaineers: Industrialization of the Appalachian South, 1880–1930* (Knoxville: University of Tennessee Press, 1982); Mary Beth Pudup, Dwight B. Billings, and Altina L. Waller, eds., *Appalachia in the Making: The Mountain South in the Nineteenth Century* (Chapel Hill: University of North Carolina Press, 1995); Ronald L. Lewis, *Transforming the Appalachian Countryside: Railroads, Deforestation, and Social Change in West Virginia, 1880–1902* (Chapel Hill: University of North Carolina Press, 1998).

9. Phoebe Cutler, *The Public Landscape of the New Deal* (New Haven: Yale University Press, 1985), 51; Gilmore D. Clarke, "The Parkway Idea," in *The Highway and the Landscape,* ed. W. Brewster Snow (New Brunswick, NJ: Rut-

gers University Press, 1959), 38–39; John Nolen and Henry V. Hubbard, *Parkways and Land Values* (Cambridge, MA: Harvard University Press, 1937), 83; Phil Patton, *Open Road: A Celebration of the American Highway* (New York: Simon and Schuster, 1986), 69.

10. Clarke, "The Parkway Idea," 40–41; Cutler, *The Public Landscape of the New Deal*, 52. Some of the so-called parkways built in New York under Moses's direction in the 1930s include Grand Central Parkway, connecting Manhattan with Long Island and LaGuardia Airport; the Henry Hudson Parkway; the Grand Central Parkway; the Cross Island and Gowanus parkways; and the Interborough Parkway. All of these, Cutler notes, "made a mockery of the original vision of a parkway as a strip of land containing a road" (52).

11. Milwaukee and Cleveland built riverside parkways (the Root River, Honey Creek, and Oak Creek parkways in Milwaukee and the Strongsville-Brecksville River Parkway in Cleveland). Other examples included Cooper River and Egg Harbor River parkways in New Jersey and Pennsylvania; the Rahway River Parkway in New Jersey; the extension of the Hutchinson River Parkway north of New York City; and two parkways that were planned but never built: one in New England along the Merrimack River, and—through the heart of the United States—a National Mississippi River Parkway. See Cutler, *The Public Landscape of the New Deal*, 53; Clarke, "The Parkway Idea," 42; John A. Jakle, *The Tourist: Travel in Twentieth-Century North America* (Lincoln: University of Nebraska Press, 1985), 139. Washington-area parkways included the Mount Vernon Memorial Highway (later extended and called the George Washington Memorial Parkway) along the Potomac River, connecting Arlington Memorial Bridge with George Washington's home.

12. Bruce Radde, *The Merritt Parkway* (New Haven: Yale University Press, 1993), 2–11, 23, 40, 44–47, 54, 61–75, 83–93, 115–16, 123. Radde describes the tensions caused by Merritt's dual role as both commuter route and pleasure road.

13. These parkways are discussed in correspondence and other records of the National Park Service (hereafter cited as NPS) throughout the 1930s, but see, for example, Jakle, *The Tourist*, 139.

14. Thomas H. MacDonald and A. E. Demaray, "Parkways of the Future: Radio Address," broadcast April 13, 1935, on the NBC radio network (transcript dated April 14, 1935), RG 7, Series 36, Box 51, Folder 1, Blue Ridge Parkway Archives, Asheville, NC (hereafter cited as BRPA). On the important role of Thomas H. MacDonald in the development of America's modern highway system, see Bruce E. Seely, *Building the American Highway System: Engineers as Policy Makers* (Philadelphia: Temple University Press, 1987), 3, 56.

15. MacDonald and Demaray, "Parkways of the Future: Radio Address."

16. Jakle, *The Tourist*, 129; and Patton, *Open Road*, 71–75.

17. DOI, NPS, "Regulations and Procedure to Govern the Acquisition of Rights-of-Way for National Parkways," February 8, 1935, State Highway Commission, Right of Way Department, Blue Ridge Parkway, General Correspondence, 1934–35 (hereafter cited as SHC-RWD), Box 1, North Carolina State Archives (hereafter NCSA).

18. This routing battle is detailed in Whisnant, *Super-Scenic Motorway*, 52–107.

19. For the full story, see Mitchell, "Culture, History and Development on the Qualla Boundary."

20. Jakle describes how in the 1920s many U.S. highways, unprotected by any zoning or land-use laws, became clogged with billboards and smaller signs tacked to trees (135–37). Patton discusses the dangers posed by the numerous eateries, billboards, driveway entrances, and other distractions (66). Partly as a result of these things, he notes, the 1920s were the "deadliest highway decade ever," measured by the number of deaths per mile driven (69). See also Cutler, *The Public Landscape of the New Deal*, 51; Clarke, "The Parkway Idea," 33–39; and Nolen and Hubbard, *Parkways and Land Values*, 83.

21. Rather than calling for a standard width, Park Service policy required a more flexible 100 acres per mile in fee simple and an additional 50 acres per mile in scenic easements. Use of the acres-per-mile standard permitted variation based on specific conditions (topographical and political) at particular places. See U.S. Department of the Interior, National Park Service (hereafter cited as DOI, NPS), "Regulations and Procedure to Govern the Acquisition of Rights-of-Way for National Parkways," February 8, 1935, SHC-RWD, Box 1, NCSA. This policy is also discussed in DOI, NPS, "Requirements and Procedure to Govern the Acquisition of Land for National Parkways," June 9, 1941, RG 7, Series 36, Box 51, Folder 1, BRPA; and Granville Liles, "History of the Blue Ridge Parkway," n.d., RG 5, Series 38, Box 48, Folder 2, BRPA. These documents note that a hundred acres per mile of fee-simple acquisition amounted to a right-of-way approximately 825 feet wide. See also C. K. Simmers to Director, NPS, April 1, 1935, RG 7, Series 4, Box 5, Folder 1, BRPA; Sam P. Weems to Stanley W. Abbott, August 1936, RG 79, Entry 7, Box, 2746, NACP; Stanley W. Abbott, "Annual Report of the Blue Ridge Parkway, Roanoke, VA, to the Director, NPS," June 30, 1940, RG 7, Series 4, Box 5, Folder 1, BRPA; Edward H. Abbuehl, "History of the Blue Ridge Parkway," February 8, 1948, RG 5, Series 38, Box 48, Folder 6, BRPA; Sam P. Weems to NPS Director, May 10, 1940, RG 79, Entry 7, Box 2733, NACP.

22. DOI, NPS, "Regulations and Procedure to Govern the Acquisition of Rights-of-Way for National Parkways," February 8, 1935, NACP; DOI, NPS, "Requirements and Procedure to Govern the Acquisition of Land for National Parkways," June 9, 1941; and the following correspondence, all from RG 79, Entry 7, NACP: Harold L. Ickes to Clyde R. Hoey, July 2, 1938 (Box

2732); H. J. Spelman to A. E. Demaray, April 19, 1939 (Box 2733); Stanley W. Abbott, "Annual Report of the Blue Ridge Parkway, Roanoke, Va. to the Director, NPS," June 30, 1938; Thomas H. MacDonald to A. E. Demaray, May 19, 1939 (Box 2733); Sam P. Weems to J. P. Dodge, January 21, 1939 (Box 2732); A. E. Demaray to R. F. Camalier, April 17, 1940 (Box 2715); and C. K. Simmers to Chief Counsel, September 1, 1939 (Box 2715).

23. S. A. Miller, Obids, NC, to Franklin D. Roosevelt, January 7, 1937, RG 79, Entry 7, Box 2731, NACP.

24. See the following correspondence, all from RG 79, Entry 7, NACP: C. K. Simmers to Moskey, February 15, 1938 (Box 2719); Sam P. Weems to Director, NPS, September 22, 1939 (Box 2721); Stanley W. Abbott, "Superintendent's Monthly Narrative Report, February 1942," March 10, 1942 (Box 2718); Stanley W. Abbott, "Superintendent's Monthly Narrative Report, May 1942," June 11, 1942 (Box 2718); Stanley W. Abbott, "Superintendent's Monthly Narrative Report, September 1942," October 10, 1942 (Box 2718); Stanley W. Abbott, "Superintendent's Monthly Narrative Report, November 1942," December 9, 1942 (Box 2718); and Sam P. Weems, "Superintendent's Monthly Narrative Report, November 1945, December 11, 1945 (Box 2719).

25. See the following correspondence, all from RG 79, Entry 7, NACP: Josephus Daniels to Harold L. Ickes, December 26, 1934 (Box 2730); Bertha L. Cone, Baltimore, MD, to Harold L. Ickes, March 12, 1939 (Box 2733); Bertha L. Cone, Blowing Rock, NC, to Franklin D. Roosevelt, July 14, 1939 (Box 2733).

26. Harry Slattery to Mrs. Moses H. Cone, Baltimore, MD, April 23, 1935, SHC-RWD, Box 8, Section 2–F, 1934–39 Folder, NCSA; A. E. Demaray to Harold L. Ickes, January 10, 1935, RG 79, Entry 7, Box 2730, NACP; Frank L. Dunlap to Josephus Daniels, July 13, 1938, Josephus Daniels Papers, Box 677, Great Smoky Mountains Files, LC; and Frank L. Dunlap to J. Gordon Hackett, December 20, 1938, SHC-RWD, Box 3, December 1938 Folder, NCSA; Frank L. Dunlap to R. L. Doughton, January 24, 1939, SHC-RWD, Box 3, January 1939 Folder, NCSA; A. E. Demaray to The Files, May 25, 1939, RG 79, Entry 7, Box 2733, NACP; Stanley W. Abbott, "Annual Report of the Blue Ridge Parkway, Roanoke, VA, to the Director, NPS," June 30, 1939, RG 79, Entry 7, Box 2717, NACP; Frank L. Dunlap to Benjamin Cone, July 20, 1939, SHC-RWD, Box 3, July 1939 Folder, NCSA; Bertha L. Cone, Blowing Rock, NC, to A. E. Demaray, July 28, 1939, SHC-RWD, Box 3, August 1939 Folder, NCSA; Frank L. Dunlap to A. E. Demaray, July 29, 1939, SHC-RWD, Box 3, July 1939 Folder, NCSA; Frank L. Dunlap to J. R. White, August 7, 1939, SHC-RWD, Box 3, August 1939 Folder, NCSA; Bertha L. Cone, Blowing Rock, NC, to Frank L. Dunlap, September 10, 1939, SHC-RWD, Box 3, September 1939 Folder, NCSA; Arno B. Cammerer to Mrs. Moses H. Cone, Baltimore, MD, April 5, 1939, SHC-RWD, Box 3, April 1939 Folder, NCSA.

27. For more on the Cone Estate, see Philip T. Noblitt, *A Mansion in the Mountains: The Story of Moses and Bertha Cone and Their Blowing Rock Manor* (Boone, NC: Parkway, 1996).

28. Sam P. Weems to Eli Richardson, Laurel Springs, NC, October 17, 1939, RG 7, Series 13, Box 13, Folder 21, BRPA.

29. Blackwell P. Robinson, ed., *The North Carolina Guide* (Chapel Hill: University of North Carolina Press, 1955), 528–36, 551; Edward H. Abbuehl, "Memorandum for Files," n.d. [in November 1937 file], RG 7, Series 4, Box 6, Folder 47, BRPA.

30. The full story of the Switzerland Company's fight against the Parkway is told in Anne Mitchell Whisnant, "Public and Private Tourism Development in 1930s Appalachia: The Blue Ridge Parkway Meets Little Switzerland," in *Southern Journeys: Tourism, History, and Culture in the Modern South,* ed. Richard Starnes (Tuscaloosa: University of Alabama Press, 2003).

31. A. E. Demaray to L. F. Caudill, Sparta, NC, January 23, 1936, RG 79, Entry 7, Box 2731, NACP; Sam P. Weems to Stanley W. Abbott, August 1936, RG 79, Entry 7, Box 2746, NACP.

32. Stanley W. Abbott, "Appalachian National Parkway . . . Report on Recreation and Service Areas," December 15, 1934; Martha Armstrong, Norris, TN, to A. E. Demaray, December 12, 1937, RG 79, Entry 7, Box 2746, NACP; Hillory A. Tolson to Martha Armstrong, Norris, TN, January 19, 1938, RG 79, Entry 7, Box 2746, NACP.

33. *Blue Ridge Parkway News* 5, no. 3 (April 1942); A. E. Demaray to Secretary of the Interior, December 26, 1941, RG 79, Entry 7, Box 2747, NACP; A. E. Demaray to Secretary of the Interior, December 26, 1941, RG 79, Entry 7, Box 2747, NACP; Stanley W. Abbott, "Annual Report of the Blue Ridge Parkway, Roanoke, Va. to the Director, NPS," June 30, 1943, RG 79, Entry 7, Box 2718, NACP.

34. In fact, the initial decisions made in 1942 set the specific course for much of the future development of concessions along the Parkway up until the present day. A Park Service document produced in 1988 indicated that the Park Service had leased concessions at twelve sites along the Parkway. Six different concessionaires ran operations at those sites, but the services were dominated by two firms: National Park Concessions and the Virginia Peaks of Otter Company. While Virginia's Peaks of Otter Company ran three of four Virginia sites, National Park Concessions held contracts for concessions at four sites—the one remaining Virginia site and three North Carolina installations (Doughton Park, Julian Price Park, and Crabtree Meadows). See Division of Resource Planning and Professional Services, Blue Ridge Parkway, "Blue Ridge Parkway Statement for Management," June 1988, RG 5, Series 2, Box 1, Folder 3, BRPA.

35. Granville Liles, "History of the Blue Ridge Parkway," n.d., RG 5, Series 38, Box 48, Folder 2, BRPA.

36. David E. Whisnant discusses the interrelationship between the social and cultural workers in the mountains after 1890 and the economic changes that came during the same period in *All That Is Native and Fine: The Politics of Culture in an American Region* (Chapel Hill: University of North Carolina Press, 1983), 5–16, 43, 110–18, 161–63. See also David E. Whisnant, *Modernizing the Mountaineer*, xv–xii, 8, 272. The economic dislocations themselves—caused by coal, timber, and textiles—are described in Eller, *Miners, Millhands, and Mountaineers*. Henry D. Shapiro discusses the creation of the popular (mis)understanding of Appalachia as a region distinct from—and lagging behind—the rest of mainstream America and offers a comprehensive bibliography of the many articles and books on Appalachian people that spilled forth from publishers after the 1850s in *Appalachia on Our Mind: The Southern Mountains and Mountaineers in the American Consciousness, 1870–1920* (Chapel Hill: University of North Carolina Press, 1978), ix–xix, 18, 30–31, 188–89. The notion that such a "backward" society fostered an uncivilized citizenry especially prone to feuding is detailed in Altina L. Waller, *Feud: Hatfields, McCoys, and Social Change in Appalachia, 1860–1900* (Chapel Hill: University of North Carolina Press, 1988). On early films with Appalachian subjects, see J. W. Williamson, *Southern Mountaineers in Silent Films: Plot Synopses of Movies about Moonshining, Feuding and Other Mountain Topics, 1904–1929* (Jefferson, NC: McFarland and Co., 1994).

37. Leo A. Borah, "A Patriotic Pilgrimage to Eastern National Parks," *National Geographic* 65 (June 1934): 663–97; Cabell Phillips, "New Scenic Ridge Road," *New York Times*, February 11, 1934, XX8.

38. David E. Whisnant, *All That Is Native and Fine*, 5–16, 68, 78, 110–18, 161–63. For more on these economic dislocations, see Eller, *Miners, Millhands, and Mountaineers*; Shapiro, *Apppalachia on Our Mind*, ix–xix, 18, 30–31 188–89; and David E. Whisnant, *Modernizing the Mountaineer*, 3–17. The journal *Mountain Life and Work* (1925–88) detailed the labors of these missionaries and schools. On the Southern Highland Handicraft Guild, see Jane S. Becker, *Selling Tradition: Appalachia and the Construction of an American Folk, 1930–1940* (Chapel Hill: University of North Carolina Press, 1998), 73–92.

39. Roy Edgar Appleman, "Report on Preservation of Mountain Culture, Marking of Historic Sites, and Promotion of Handicraft, Blue Ridge Parkway," October 9, 1940, RG 5, Series 46, Box 61, Folder 4, BRPA.

40. NPS, "Planning the Complete Landscape Development: The Problem and the Program," 1939, RG 7, Series 36, Box 51, Folder 3, BRPA; Ronald F. Lee to Regional Director, Region I, August 19, 1940, RG 79, Entry 7, Box 2733, NACP; Roy E. Appleman to J. P. Dodge, September 5, 1940, RG 79, Entry 7, Box 2733, NACP.

41. Stanley W. Abbott, "Annual Report of the Blue Ridge Parkway, Roanoke, Va. to the Director, NPS," June 30, 1941, RG 79, Entry 7, Box 2718, NACP;

and Stanley W. Abbott, "Superintendent's Monthly Narrative Report, May 1942," June 11, 1942, RG 79, Entry 7, Box 2718, NACP; Stanley W. Abbott to Director, NPS, November 10, 1942, RG 5, Series 50, Box 70, Folder 4, BRPA; Stanley W. Abbott, "Draft of the Interpretive Statement of the Blue Ridge Parkway," December 1942, RG 5, Series 10, Box 13, Folder 1, BRPA; Stanley W. Abbott, "Annual Report of the Blue Ridge Parkway, Roanoke, Va. to the Director, NPS," June 30, 1943, RG 79, Entry 7, Box 2718, NACP.

42. Stanley W. Abbott, "Draft of the Interpretive Statement of the Blue Ridge Parkway," December 1942, RG 5, Series 10, Box 13, Folder 1, BRPA.

43. Roy Edgar Appleman, "Report on Preservation of Mountain Culture, Marking of Historic Sites, and Promotion of Handicraft, Blue Ridge Parkway," October 9, 1940, RG 5, Series 46, Box 61, Folder 4, BRPA.

44. Roy Edgar Appleman, "Recommendations (for Blue Ridge Parkway)," October 9, 1940, RG 5, Series 46, Box 61, Folder 4, BRPA.

45. Thor Borreson, "Report on Mountain Culture and Handicraft, Blue Ridge Parkway," October 7, 1940, RG 5, Series 46, Box 61, Folder 4, BRPA.

46. Phil Noblitt, "The Blue Ridge Parkway and the Myths of the Pioneer," *Appalachian Journal* 21 (June 1994): 394–409, esp. 394–98.

47. Thor Borreson, "Report on Mountain Culture and Handicraft, Blue Ridge Parkway," October 7, 1940, RG 5, Series 46, Box 61, Folder 4, BRPA.

48. Noblitt, "The Blue Ridge Parkway and the Myths of the Pioneer," 394–98. In his study of the Cades Cove community, which was taken into the Great Smoky Mountains National Park, Durwood Dunn argues that indeed mountain people had never been "isolated." Rather, he finds, throughout their history they were not in a substantial way different than people of mainstream America; they were in touch and involved with local, state, national politics, they participated actively in the market economy, and they used the court system and abided by state laws. See Durwood Dunn, *Cades Cove: The Life and Death of a Southern Appalachian Community, 1818–1937* (Knoxville: University of Tennessee Press, 1988).

49. Blue Ridge Parkway Headquarters, "Research and Interpretation," Section of Blue Ridge Parkway Master Plan, October 1950, RG 5, Series 10, Box 13, Folder 1, BRPA.

50. O. B. Taylor to Regional Director, June 9, 1945, RG 5, Series 25, Box 33, Folder 4, BRPA; Granville Liles, "History of the Blue Ridge Parkway," n.d., RG 5, Series 38, Box 48, Folder 2, BRPA.

51. Noblitt, "The Blue Ridge Parkway and the Myths of the Pioneer," 400–404. For a fuller discussion of the history of the Cone estate, see Noblitt, *A Mansion in the Mountains*, 143–59.

52. Stanley W. Abbott, "Annual Report of the Blue Ridge Parkway, Roanoke, Va. to the Director, NPS," June 30, 1943, RG 79, Entry 7, Box 2718, NACP; Noblitt argues effectively that this portrayal of Appalachian life has been

difficult to challenge because it has both mirrored and perpetuated the widespread public misunderstanding of the Appalachian region (*A Mansion in the Mountains,* 148–59).

53. This body of scholarship began to emerge in the late 1960s and was well developed by the 1980s. Some major works included Shapiro, *Appalachia on Our Mind;* David E. Whisnant, *Modernizing the Mountaineer;* Eller, *Miners, Millhands, and Mountaineers;* David E. Whisnant, *All That Is Native and Fine;* Stephen Foster, *The Past Is Another Country: Representation, Historical Consciousness, and Resistance in the Blue Ridge* (Berkeley: University of California Press, 1988); Dunn, *Cades Cove;* and Waller, *Feud.*

54. Jean Haskell Speer, Frances H. Russell, and Gibson Worsham, *The Johnson Farm at Peaks of Otter, Blue Ridge Parkway, Milepost 86,* Historic Resources Study and Historic Structures Report (DOI, NPS, Blue Ridge Parkway, 1990), 63–80.

55. Ibid.

56. Ibid.

57. Ibid., 86–96.

58. Scholarship on Appalachia has continued to mushroom in the 1990s and 2000s. A few important books published in this period include Margaret Lynn Brown, *The Wild East: A Biography of the Great Smoky Mountains* (Gainesville: University Press of Florida, 2000); Stephen Wallace Taylor, *The New South's New Frontier: A Social History of Economic Development in Southwestern North Carolina* (Gainesville: University Press of Florida, 2001); Pudup, Billings, and Waller, eds., *Appalachia in the Making;* J. W. Williamson, *Hillbillyland: What the Movies Did to the Mountains and What the Mountains Did to the Movies* (Chapel Hill: University of North Carolina Press, 1995); and Becker, *Selling Tradition.*

Chapter 4

1. P. D. Peterson, *Through the Black Hills and Bad Lands of South Dakota* (Pierre, SD: J. Fred Olander, 1929), 103.

2. A good study of recreational automobile travel through World War II is Warren James Belasco's *Americans on the Road: From Autocamp to Motel, 1910–1945* (Baltimore: Johns Hopkins University Press, 1979).

3. For a discussion of society preceding and during the Progressive Era, see Steven J. Diner, *A Very Different Age: Americans of the Progressive Era* (New York: Hill and Wang, 1998). John Buell provides a concise discussion of the development of industrialization and corporations and resulting effects on workers in *Democracy by Other Means: The Politics of Work, Leisure, and Environment* (Chicago: University of Illinois Press, 1995), 17–23.

4. For a contemporary view of leisure and recreation, especially as it relates to workers, see *Recent Social Trends in the United States: Report of the President's Research Committee on Social Trends*, 2 vols. (New York: McGraw-Hill, 1933), 2:801–56, 912–14, 921–25.

5. Harold K. Steen, *The U.S. Forest Service: A History* (Seattle: University of Washington Press, 1976), 113–17; Ronald A. Foresta, *America's National Parks and Their Keepers* (Washington, DC: Resources for the Future, 1984), 17, 20–21; Hal K. Rothman, *Preserving Different Pasts: The American National Monuments* (Chicago: University of Illinois Press, 1989), xiv–xv, 43–49, 86–90.

6. John Ise, *Our National Park Policy: A Critical History* (Baltimore: Johns Hopkins Press for Resources for the Future, 1961), 191–92.

7. Ibid., 193–99, 202–5.

8. Ibid., 197; Marguerite S. Shaffer, *See America First: Tourism and National Identity, 1880–1940* (Washington, DC: Smithsonian Institution Press, 2001), 26–27, 100–108; John A. Jakle, *The Tourist: Travel in Twentieth-Century North America* (Lincoln: University of Nebraska Press, 1985), 102–3, 236.

9. For discussions of state park developments in other areas of the country, particularly the West and Midwest, see Thomas R. Cox, *The Park Builders: A History of State Parks in the Pacific Northwest* (Seattle: University of Washington Press, 1988); Freeman Tilden, *The State Parks: Their Meaning in American Life* (New York: Alfred A. Knopf, 1962); Ise, *Our National Park Policy*, 294–96; and Rebecca Conard, "Hot Kitchens in Places of Quiet Beauty: Iowa State Parks and the Transformation of Conservation Goals," *Annals of Iowa* 51 (Summer 1992): 441–79, esp. 444–45.

10. Gilbert Courtland Fite, *Peter Norbeck, Prairie Statesman* (Columbia: University of Missouri Press, 1948), 25–53, 78; For an overview of Norbeck's aesthetic philosophy, see Norbeck to Harry Gandy, October 17, 1935, File Sylvan Lake Hotel, Rebuilding of, Box 70, Peter Norbeck Papers, University of South Dakota Special Collections, Richardson Archives, Vermillion, South Dakota (hereafter cited as Peter Norbeck Papers). For a full discussion of Norbeck's work in Custer State Park, see Suzanne Barta Julin, "Public Enterprise: Politics, Policy, and Tourism Development in the Black Hills Through 1941" (PhD diss., Washington State University, 2001).

11. Peter Norbeck, "South Dakota State Park: The Black Hills Are Not Hills but High Mountains," *Outlook* 14 (June 1, 1927): 153. For a concise overview of Progressivism and conservation, see Char Miller, *Gifford Pinchot and the Making of Modern Environmentalism* (Washington, DC: Island Press, 2001), 4–12. See also Samuel Hays, *Conservation and the Gospel of Efficiency: The Progressive Conservation Movement, 1890–1920* (Cambridge, MA: Harvard University Press, 1959, repr., Pittsburgh: University of Pittsburgh Press, 1999).

12. Norbeck to John A. Stanley, May 4, 1921, File Custer State Park, Stanley, Hon. J. A. (1921–22), Box 70, Peter Norbeck Papers.

13. Peter Norbeck to J. A. Stanley, January 2, 1923, Historical Correspondence Materials, Custer State Park Archives, Custer State Park, Custer, South Dakota (hereafter cited as CSPA); Peter Norbeck to Bureau of Roads, October 3, 1932, File State Highways 1932, Box 35, Peter Norbeck Papers; Peter Norbeck to Paul Bellamy, December 26, 1928, File Bellamy, Hon. Paul E. (1923–32), Box 66, Peter Norbeck Papers.

14. For examples of Norbeck's attitude toward professionals, see Norbeck to J. C. Dennison, May 8, 1927, File "Custer State Park Board, Correspondence-C, 16.1 (Highways, 1924–1927)," CSPA; Norbeck to C. W. Robertson, March 24, 1931 (telegram), File Robertson, Hon. C. W., Jan-Apr 1931, Box 129, Peter Norbeck Papers; Norbeck to C. C. Gideon, October 23, 1931, File "Gideon, C. C., 1931–32," Box 67, Peter Norbeck Papers; Paul E. Bellamy to Norbeck, January 21, 1932 (one of two letters), File "Bellamy, Paul E., 1932–1934," Box 49, Peter Norbeck Papers; Norbeck to Chauncey L. Bates, March 21, 1932, File "State Highways, 1932," Box 35, Peter Norbeck Papers.

15. Norbeck to J. Harper Hamilton, January 22, 1932, File State Highways-1932, Box 35, Peter Norbeck Papers.

16. Peter Norbeck to J. C. Dennison, May 8, 1927, Custer State Park Board, C-C, 16.1 (Highways) 1924–1927, CSPA.

17. Gail Bederman, *Manliness and Civilization: A Cultural History of Gender and Race in the United States, 1880–1917* (Chicago: University of Chicago Press, 1995; paperback edition, 1996), 85–88, 192–96 (citations are to the paperpack edition); Warren James Belasco, *Americans on the Road: From Autocamp to Motel, 1910–1945* (Cambridge, MA: MIT Press, 1979), 30–35.

18. Belasco, *Americans on the Road,* 26–39, 61.

19. See Paul Sutter, *Driven Wild: How the Fight Against Automobiles Launched the Modern Wilderness Movement* (Seattle: University of Washington Press, 2002), 30–41 for a concise treatment of recreational driving, automobile tourism, and autocamping during the interwar period.

20. Peter Norbeck to Doane Robinson, September 19, 1924, File 161 Box 10, Doane Robinson Papers, South Dakota State Historical Society Archives, Pierre, South Dakota (hereafter cited as Doane Robinson Papers).

21. Norbeck to Kenneth Scurr, April 18, 1932, File State Highways 1932, Box 35, Peter Norbeck Papers.

22. Peter Norbeck to Owen Mann, April 12, 1934, File Custer State Park—Mann, Owen, Box 69, Peter Norbeck Papers.

23. Norbeck to Scovel Johnson, November 14, 1919, File "1920 Corres. #4," Box 95, Peter Norbeck Papers; Norbeck to Stephen T. Mather, February 6, 1920, File "1920 Corres. #3," Box 95, Peter Norbeck Papers; Scovel Johnson to Peter Norbeck, September 21, 1920, File 1920 Corres. #4, Box 95, Peter Norbeck Papers; Fite, *Peter Norbeck: Prairie Statesman,* 76; Scovel Johnson to Norbeck, August 27, 1920, File "Highways by Name, H-J," Box 6,

Governor Peter Norbeck Papers, South Dakota State Historical Society Archives, Pierre, South Dakota (hereafter cited Governor Norbeck Papers); Norbeck to M. L. Shade, October 7, 1921, File "Shade, M. L., 1916, 1921–1925, Box 80, Peter Norbeck Papers; Scovel Johnson to Norbeck, September 17, 1921, Norbeck to Scovel Johnson, October 26, 1921, Scovel Johnson to Norbeck, October 28, 1921, File "Custer State Park, Johnson, Scovel (1921–22)," Box 68, Peter Norbeck Papers.

24. A. A. Schwartz, "Reconnoissence [*sic*] Estimate of the Cost of a Portion of the Proposed Scenic Highway, 2, 4, File "Custer State Park, 1921–1931," Box 97, Peter Norbeck Papers; Scovel Johnson to State Highway Commission, April 1, 1921; Scovel Johnson to Norbeck, October 28, 1921, File "Custer State Park, Johnson, Scovel (1921–1922)," Box 68, Peter Norbeck Papers.

25. Scovel Johnson to Norbeck, September 17, 1921, File "Custer State Park, Johnson, Scovel (1921–1922)," Box 68, Peter Norbeck Papers.

26. Scovel Johnson to Norbeck, December 10, 1921, File "Custer State Park, Johnson, Scovel (1921–1922)," Box 70, Peter Norbeck Papers; Scovel Johnson to Norbeck, File "Custer State Park, Johnson, Scovel (1921–1922)," Box 68, Peter Norbeck Papers; Scovel Johnson to Norbeck, File "Highways by Name, H-J," Box 6, Governor Norbeck Papers; John A. Stanley to Norbeck, November 9, 1921, File "Stanley, Hon. J. A., (1921–1922)," Box 70, Peter Norbeck Papers.

27. "Road to Sylvan Lake Is Proposed," *Rapid City Daily Journal,* August 26, 1920.

28. M. L. Shade to Peter Norbeck, April 11, 1921, File Shade, L. N. [*sic*], 1916, 1921–1925, Box 80, Peter Norbeck Papers.

29. John A. Stanley to Peter Norbeck, November 9, 1921, File Custer State Park, Stanley, Hon. J. A. (1921–22), Box 70, Peter Norbeck Papers.

30. Ibid.

31. *National Geographic* 52 (September 1927): 311. The South Dakota State Historical Society Archives, in Pierre, South Dakota, hold a significant number of early photographs of the Needles Highway.

32. See *South Dakota Historical Collections Cumulative Index,* comp. Suzanne Julin (Pierre: South Dakota State Historical Society, 1989), 1–3; Gilbert Fite, *Mount Rushmore,* 2nd ed. (Norman: University of Oklahoma Press, 1964), 5–6; "South Dakota State Meeting of the Black and Yellow Trail Association Held in Huron on Tuesday, January 22nd, at the Call of vice-president Phelps: Official Bulletin," n.d. [1924], File 9, Tourism and Highway Travel Collection, South Dakota State Historical Society Archives, Pierre, South Dakota.

33. Robinson to J. B. Green [*sic*], March 7, 1924, File 149, Box 9, Doane Robinson Papers.

34. Fite, *Mount Rushmore*, 5–9; Norbeck to Robinson, December 13, 1924, File 161, Box 10, Doane Robinson Papers; Robinson to Gutzon Borglum, July 1, 1925, File Doane Robinson, 1925, July 1, 1925, Box 130, Peter Norbeck Papers; Norbeck to Robinson, January 20, 1925, Box 10 File 162, Doane Robinson Papers.

35. Fite, *Mount Rushmore*, 6, 12, 25–27, 50–52; Borglum to Robinson, June 29, 1925, File 149, Box 9, Doane Robinson Papers.

36. "Our Needles—and Borglum," *Sunshine State and Progress Magazine* 6 (April 1925), n.p.

37. Cora B. Johnson to Robinson, December 6, 1924, File 149, Box 9, Doane Robinson Papers. This file contains additional correspondence between Robinson and people who objected to the proposed carving. See also Fite, *Mount Rushmore*, 27–28, 54–55.

38. *Deadwood Daily Pioneer Times,* April 26, 1925.

39. Robinson to F. W. Meyers, December 4, 1924, File 149, Box 9, Doane Robinson Papers.

40. For a description of the struggle to launch and fund the project, see Fite, *Mount Rushmore*, 3–95.

41. Ibid., 108, 122.

42. Norbeck to Julian Blount, May 6, 1930, File "Custer State Park 1930," Box 96, Peter Norbeck Papers.

43. Peter Norbeck to John A. Stanley, December 4, 1930, File Stanley 30–31, Box 70, Peter Norbeck Papers; Scovel Johnson to Norbeck, September 12, 1928, File "Custer State Park, Johnson, Scovel (1927–1932)," Box 68, Peter Norbeck Papers.

44. Jessie Y. Sundstrom, *Pioneers and Custer State Park: A History of Custer State Park and Northcentral Custer County* (privately printed, 1994), 124.

45. Peter Norbeck to C. B. Howell, December 21, 1931, File State Highways-1932, Box 35, Peter Norbeck Papers.

46. Charles E. Smith to Peter Norbeck, February 14, 1932, File State Highways-1932, Box 35, Peter Norbeck Papers; Norbeck to Charles W. Robertson, October 30, 1931, File Robertson Hon. C. F. [*sic*], Nov.-Dec. 1931, Box 129, Peter Norbeck Papers; Norbeck to Charles W. Robertson, March 24, 1931, File Robertson, C. W., Jan.-Apr. [1931], Box 129, Peter Norbeck Papers; Francis Case, "Remarks for Ceremonies at Unveiling of Plaque to Peter Norbeck and Dedication of Norbeck Wildlife Preserve, September 13, 1952," File Norbeck Memorial, Box 12, Paul E. Bellamy Papers, University of South Dakota Special Collections, Richardson Archives, Vermillion, South Dakota (hereafter cited as Paul E. Bellamy Papers.). When the National Park Service director requested a photo of what Norbeck's wife called the "Aisle of Pines," Norbeck rather acidly pointed out the site to the park superintendent as "that part of the Sylvan Lake highway which was not built by the Engineers, where all the trees remain along the

roadside." Peter Norbeck to Charles W. Robertson, March 24, 1931, File Robertson, Hon. C. W., Jan.-Apr. [1931], Box 129, Peter Norbeck Papers.

47. Norbeck to Cecil C. Gideon, October 23, 1931, File Gideon, C. C., 1931–1932, Box 67, Peter Norbeck Papers; Paul E. Bellamy to Norbeck, January 21, 1932, (two letters); Norbeck to Paul E. Bellamy, January 26, 1932, File Bellamy, Paul E., 1932–1934, Box 49, Peter Norbeck Papers; C. C. Gideon to Norbeck, January 10, 1932, C. C. Gideon to Norbeck, February 20, 1932, File Gideon, C. C., 1931–1932, Box 67, Peter Norbeck Papers; C. E. Smith to Norbeck, February 14, 1932, File State Highways-1932, Box 35, Peter Norbeck Papers; Frederic L. Quivik and Lon Johnson for Renewable Technologies, Inc., *Historic Bridges of South Dakota* ([Pierre, South Dakota]: South Dakota Department of Transportation, 1990), 3–4. For information on park rustic style, see Albert A. Good, *Park and Recreation Structures, Part 1: Administration and Basic Services Facilities* (Washington, DC: National Park Service, Department of the Interior, 1938), 38, and Laura Soulliere Harrison, *Architecture in the Parks: National Historic Landmark Theme Study* ([Washington, DC]: National Park Service, Department of the Interior, 1986), 4–9.

48. Norbeck to Scovel Johnson, May 6, 1927, and Scovel Johnson to Norbeck, May 8, 1927, File Custer State Park, Box 68, Johnson, Scovel (1927–1932), Peter Norbeck Papers; Norbeck to Charles W. Robertson, October 3, 1931, File Robertson Hon. C. F. [*sic*] Nov-Dec 1931, Box 129, Peter Norbeck Papers; Norbeck to C. C. Gideon, October 23, 1931, File Gideon, C. C., 1931–1932, Box 67, Peter Norbeck Papers; Norbeck to J. A. Stanley, July 7, 1931, File Stanley, John A., 1930–31, Box 70, Peter Norbeck Papers.

49. Charles W. Robertson to Peter Norbeck, March 20, 1931, File Robertson Hon. C. W. Jan-Apr 1931, Box 129, Peter Norbeck Papers.

50. Paul Bellamy to Peter Norbeck, March 30, 1932, File Bellamy, Paul E.-1932–1934, Box 49, Peter Norbeck Papers.

51. Norbeck to J. A. Stanley, July 7, 1931, File Stanley, John A., 1930–31, Box 70, Peter Norbeck Papers.

52. *Rapid City Daily Journal*, June 24, 1932.

53. Paul E. Bellamy to Norbeck, March 30, 1932, File Bellamy, Paul E., 1932–1934, Box 49, Peter Norbeck Papers.

54. "The Black Hills of South Dakota," *South Dakota Hiway Magazine* 7 (June 1932): 9.

55. Roderick Frazier Nash offers a discussion of sublimity and romanticism in *Wilderness and the American Mind* (1962), 4th ed. (New Haven: Yale University Press, 2001), 44–66.

56. Peterson, *Through the Black Hills*, 103.

57. Manuscript, File Custer State Park, Outlook Article, Box 96, Peter Norbeck Papers. The Cathedral Spires are a particular group of the Needles formations.

58. "Address of Calvin Coolidge, President of the United States, Delivered at the Beginning of the Carving of the National Memorial on Rushmore Mountain, August 10, 1927." Program, MORU 675, Box 3, National Park Service, Mount Rushmore National Memorial, Keystone, South Dakota.

59. Francis Case, "Remarks for Ceremonies at Unveiling of Plaque to Peter Norbeck and Dedication of Norbeck Wildlife Preserve, September 13, 1952," File Norbeck Memorial, Box 12, Paul E. Bellamy Papers.

60. John A. Stanley, *From Then until Now* (privately printed [1948]), 62–63.

Chapter 5

1. This essay concentrates on the attention paid to advertising and scrap along the highways. Yet the industries associated with those highway phenomena comprise a fraction of the commercial activity visible to drivers in the United States. John A. Jakle and Keith A. Sculle, in a series of books about roadside businesses, demonstrate that American roads have developed a sophisticated network of chains and small businesses designed to attract drivers. Their work indicates a long-standing vision of the American road as a place of commerce, and commercial developments after World War II grew in size and sophistication. John A. Jakle and Keith A. Sculle, *The Gas Station in America* (Baltimore: Johns Hopkins University Press, 1994); John A. Jakle, Keith A. Sculle, and Jefferson S. Rogers, *The Motel in America* (Baltimore: Johns Hopkins University Press, 1996); John A. Jakle and Keith A. Sculle, *Fast Food: Roadside Restaurants in the Automobile Age* (Baltimore: Johns Hopkins University Press, 1999).

2. Lady Bird Johnson, quoted in Chester H. Liebs, *Main Street to Miracle Mile: American Roadside Architecture* (Boston: Little, Brown, 1985): 65.

3. Joseph A. Califano, *The Triumph and Tragedy of Lyndon Johnson: The White House Years* (New York: Simon and Schuster, 1991); Louis L. Gould, *Lady Bird Johnson: Our Environmental First Lady* (Lawrence: University Press of Kansas, 1999).

4. Important overviews of the evolution of environmental regulations from a local to a federal jurisdiction in the United States include Joel A. Tarr, *The Search for the Ultimate Sink: Urban Pollution in Historical Perspective* (Akron, OH: University of Akron Press, 1996); and Martin V. Melosi, *The Sanitary City: Urban Infrastructure in America from Colonial Times to the Present* (Baltimore: Johns Hopkins University Press, 2000).

5. William H. Wilson, "The Billboard: Bane of the City Beautiful," *Journal of Urban History* 13, no. 4 (August 1987): 394–425, esp. 396.

6. Ibid., 415–17.

7. John Margolies and Emily Gwathmey, *Signs of Our Time* (New York: Abbeville Press, 1993), 13.

8. Laura Steward Heon, Peggy Diggs, and Joseph Thompson, *Billboard Art on the Road: A Retrospective Exhibition of Artists' Billboards of the Last 30 Years* (Cambridge, MA: MIT Press, 1999), 16.

9. Margolies and Gwathmey, *Signs of Our Time*, 15–16.

10. *Wall Street Journal*, April 14, 1960, quoted in Peter Blake, *God's Own Junkyard: The Planned Deterioration of America's Landscape* (New York: Holt, Rinehart and Winston, 1964), 12.

11. *Reader's Digest*, March 1960, quoted here from Blake, *God's Own Junkyard*, 12.

12. On the growing importance of steel, see Thomas J. Misa, *A Nation of Steel: The Making of Modern America, 1865–1925* (Baltimore: Johns Hopkins University Press, 1995). The number of junk, rag, and scrap businesses listed in New York City city directories rose from 356 in 1890 to 455 in 1910 and to 543 in 1917. *Trow's New York, New York City Directory for 1890* (New York: Trow Directory, 1891); *Trow's General Directory of the Boroughs of Manhattan and Bronx City of New York, New York for 1910* (New York: Trow Directory, 1909); *R. L. Polk and Co.'s Trow General and Business Directory of the Boroughs of Manhattan and Bronx City of New York, New York for 1917* (New York: Trow Directory, 1917).

13. "America's Richest War Bride," *Scientific American* (November 24, 1917), cited here from the American Iron and Steel Archive, Record Group 1631, Box 116, Folder 9, "Scrap 1917–1918," Hagley Museum and Library, Wilmington, DE.

14. "Aims of a Scrap-Iron Organization," *Iron Age* (July 16, 1914): 141.

15. "American Iron and Steel Institute Asked to Condemn Direct Dealing and to Make Scrap Marketing Survey," *Institute Bulletin of the Institute of Scrap Iron and Steel, Inc.* 3 (May-June 1930): 1–2.

16. John A. Kouwenhoven, *The Beer Can by the Highway: Essays on What's American about America* (Garden City, NY: Doubleday, 1961).

17. Melosi, *The Sanitary City*, 271–73.

18. Adam Ward Rome, *The Bulldozer in the Countryside: Suburban Sprawl and the Rise of American Environmentalism* (Cambridge: Cambridge University Press, 2001).

19. Samuel P. Hays, *A History of Environmental Politics since 1945* (Pittsburgh: University of Pittsburgh Press, 2000), 17–18.

20. "U.S. to Step Up Auto-Graveyard Scrap Flow; Also Studying Far East Salvage Program," *New York Times*, November 4, 1951, 143.

21. American Automobile Manufacturers Association, *Motor Vehicles Facts and Figures*, quoted here from John B. Rae, *The American Automobile Industry* (Boston: Twayne, 1984), 180–82; *Automobile Manufacturers Association*,

Motor Vehicles Facts and Figures 1998 (Detroit: Motor Vehicle Manufacturers Association, 1999), 21.

22. Charles H. Lipsett, *Industrial Wastes and Salvage* (New York: Atlas, 1963), 159.

23. Blake, *God's Own Junkyard*, 12.

24. Senator Robert S. Kerr of Oklahoma, quoted here from Blake, *God's Own Junkyard*, 10.

25. Blake, *God's Own Junkyard*, 16.

26. Ibid., 69.

27. Ibid., 109.

28. Ibid.

29. Ibid., 142.

30. Gould, *Lady Bird Johnson*, 93.

31. Ibid., 96.

32. Ibid., 94.

33. Lady Bird Johnson, *A White House Diary* (New York: Holt, Rinehart and Winston, 1970), 234.

34. Lady Bird Johnson, quoted here from *Lady Bird: The Biography of First Lady Lady Bird Johnson*, a PBS documentary first aired on December 12, 2001, and available online at http://www.pbs.org/ladybird/shattereddreams/shattereddreams_report.html.

35. President Lyndon B. Johnson, "Special Message to the Congress on Conservation and Restoration of Natural Beauty," delivered on February 8, 1965, archived at the Lyndon B. Johnson Library and Museum (National Archives and Records Administration) and available online at http://www.lbjlib.utexas.edu/johnson/archives.hom/speeches.hom/650208.asp.

36. "Text of the President's Letter on Highway Beauty," *New York Times*, May 27, 1965, 23.

37. "The Problems of Beautification," *Scrap Age* 22, no. 7 (1965): 5.

38. "Senate Hearing on 'Beautification' Bill," *Scrap Age* 22, no. 9 (1965): 1–4.

39. "It's Time to Wake Up . . . Scrap Is Not Junk!" *Scrap Age* 22, no. 6 (1965): 1–3.

40. Schwartz was speaking on behalf of the larger scrap firms, many of whom risked losing customers amid municipal regulations designed to reduce nuisances associated with smaller firms operating in residential neighborhoods. His dichotomy between "scrap" and "junk" firms attempted to improve the reputation of the larger firms by distancing them from traditional notions of the junk trade as a nuisance. "American Iron and Steel Institute Asked to Condemn Direct Dealing and to Make Scrap Marketing Survey," *Institute Bulletin of the Institute of Scrap Iron and Steel, Inc.* 3 (May-June 1930): 1–2.

41. "It's Time to Wake Up . . . Scrap Is Not Junk!"

42. "Beautification—Good or Bad?" *Scrap Age* 22, no. 6 (1965): 5.

43. "Highway Beautification Act. It's [*sic*] Effect on Scrap Industry," *Scrap Age* 22, no. 11 (1965): 16–17.

44. "Connor Challenged in House on Road Beauty Plans," *New York Times*, July 21, 1965, 21.

45. *Congressional Record* 111 (1965): 26139–322. Opposition was not uniformly Republican; Representative Jim Wright (D-TX) was one of several Democrats who voiced concern about the bill's effects on commerce.

46. "Advertising: Case for Highway Billboards," *New York Times*, June 2, 1965, 71.

47. "Advertising: Billboard Proposal Welcomed," *New York Times*, May 27, 1965, 59.

48. President Lyndon B. Johnson, "Remarks at the Signing of the Highway Beautification Act of 1965, October 22, 1965," archived at the Lyndon B. Johnson Library and Museum, Austin, TX (National Archives and Records Administration) and available online at http://www.lbjlib.utexas.edu/johnson/archives.hom/speeches.hom/651022.asp.

49. Califano, *The Triumph and Tragedy of Lyndon Johnson*, 81. See also Charles F. Floyd and Peter J. Shedd, *Highway Beautification: The Environmental Movement's Greatest Failure* (Boulder, CO: Westview Press, 1979).

50. U.S. Senate, *Federal Highway Beautification Assistance Act of 1979: Hearings Before the Committee on Transportation of the Committee on Environment and Public Works of the United States Senate*, 96th Cong., 1st sess., 1979, 42; Gould, *Lady Bird Johnson*, 103–7.

51. Gould, *Lady Bird Johnson*, 90–108.

52. Martin T. Katzman, "From Horse Carts to Minimills," *Public Interest* 92 (1988): 121–35, esp. 131–32.

53. Jakle and Sculle, *Fast Food*, 10–12; John B. Jackson, *Discovering the Vernacular Landscape* (New Haven: Yale University Press, 1984), 5; D. W. Meinig, ed., *The Interpretation of Ordinary Landscapes* (New York: Oxford University Press, 1979). See also Robert Venturi, Denise Scott Brown, and Steven Izenour, *Learning from Las Vegas* (Cambridge, MA: MIT Press, 1972); and Catherine Gudis, *Buyways: Automobility, Billboards, and the American Cultural Landscape* (New York: Routledge, 2004).

54. Jakle and Sculle, *The Gas Station in America*, 18–47.

55. Mary Douglas, *Purity and Danger: An Analysis of Concepts of Pollution and Taboo* (London: Routledge and Kegan Paul, 1966), 36.

Chapter 6

1. Renato Bonelli, "Le autostrade in Italia," *Comunità* 86 (January 1961): 3–9. Translations from Italian to English throughout this essay are my own.

I would like to thank Erin O'Loughlin for her help in editing the original English text of this essay.

2. The themes of Bonelli's article were taken up by the architect Bruno Zevi in a famous article in the weekly *L'Espresso;* see Bruno Zevi, "Auto-strade italiane: I dittatori dell'asfalto," *L'Espresso,* 19 February 1961. See also Pier Luigi Beretta, "Le autostrade d'Italia," *Universo* 3 (1968): 523–66, esp. 555–61.

3. Until a few decades ago, national literature—including scientific works—continued to perpetuate the legend created during the Fascist period that Italy had been the first country in the world to build highways. The self-congratulatory "Autostrada" entry by Piero Puricelli (the first constructor of highways in Italy) in the *Enciclopedia Italiana* (Rome: Istituto Enciclopedia Italiana, 1930) makes this claim, and it appears again in a volume published more than fifty years later: S.p.A. per l'Autostrada Serravalle-Milano-Ponte Chiasso, ed., *Le autostrade della prima generazione* (Milan: S.p.A. per l'Au-tostrada Serravalle-Milano-Ponte Chiasso, 1984), 35. It is interesting to note how historians' attention to the subject of highways has been inconsistent, despite widespread acknowledgment of highways' social and economic importance.

4. The idea of the Italians being "behind" was a topic of much discussion after World War II: see Paul Ginsborg, *Storia d'Italia dal dopoguerra a oggi* (Turin: Einaudi, 1989); on the transport field, see Aldo Farinelli, "Pro-duzione e diffusione dell'autoveicolo," in *I trasporti automobilistici,* ed. Camera di commercio industria e artigianato di Torino (Turin: Camera di commercio industria e artigianato di Torino, 1949), 10–12.

5. On preunification road networks in Italy, see F. Borlandi, *Il problema delle comunicazioni nel secolo XVIII nei suoi rapporti con il Risorgimento italiano* (Pavia: Soc. an. Treves Treccani Tumminelli, 1932); G. Guderzo, *Vie e mezzi di comunicazione in Piemonte dal 1831 al 1861: I servizi di posta* (Turin: Museo Nazionale del Risorgimento, 1961); M. Di Gianfrancesco, *La rivoluzione dei trasporti in Italia nell'età risorgimentale. L'unificazione del mercato e la crisi del Mezzogiorno* (L'Aquila: Japadre, 1979). See also L. Orusa, *L'evoluzione della legislazione sulla classificazione delle strade,* in *I lavori pubblici: Atti del Congresso Celebrativo del Centenario delle leggi amministrative di unificazione,* ed. Istituto per la scienza dell'amministrazione pubblica (Vicenza: Neri Pozza, 1969). A generous bibliography on the subject of the Italian road system can be found in S. Maggi, *Politica ed economia dei trasporti italiani (secoli XIX–XX): Una storia della modernizzazione italiana* (Bologna: Il Mulino, 2001).

6. See A. Mioni, *Metamorfosi d'Europa. Popolamento, campagne, infrastrut-ture e città. 1750–1950* (Bologna: Compositori, 1999). On infrastructures in Italy, see C. Mochi, *Opere pubbliche,* in the various volumes of the *Annali dell'economia*

italiana, ed. Ipsoa (Milan: Ipsoa, 1982–84). For details on the expenses incurred for public works, see the tables given in S. Potenza, *Ruolo del settore delle costruzioni non residenziali e delle opere pubbliche nello sviluppo economico italiano,* in *Opere pubbliche, lavori pubblici, capitale fisso sociale,* ed. Marino Folin (Milan: Franco Angeli, 1978).

7. See Lando Bortolotti, "Viabilità e sistemi infrastrutturali," in *Annali della storia d'Italia: Insediamenti e territorio,* ed. Cesare De Seta (Turin: Einaudi, 1989).

8. See Anfia, ed., *Automobile in cifre* (Turin: Anfia, 1962).

9. It should be noted that the increase was only relative, since in 1923 the number of vehicles on Italian roads was about 40,000, a figure by no means comparable to the ten million automobiles that year in the United States.

10. On the activities of the *Azienda autonoma statale della strada,* see Aass, ed., *Aass. Relazione sul primo biennio di gestione* (Rome: Grafia, 1930); Aass, ed., *Aass. Il primo quadriennio di gestione* (Rome: Grafia, 1932); Aass, ed., *L'opera dell'Aass al 30 giugno 1934* (Rome: Ricci, 1934); Aass, ed., *L'Azienda autonoma statale della strada nel decennio 1° luglio 1928 VI–30 giugno 1938 XVI* (Rome: Ricci, 1938); and Anas, ed., *La strada in Italia dall'unità ad oggi, 1861–1987* (Rome: Anas, 1987).

11. In 1938 the number of vehicles on Italian roads was about 372,000; in Germany, about 1,670,000; in France, about 2,270,000; in the United Kingdom, about 2,600,000; and in the United States, about 29,400,000. See Anfia, ed., *Automobile in cifre,* 71.

12. For the case of Turin, see Pietro Abate Daga, *Alle porte di Torino. Studio storico-critico dello sviluppo della vita e dei bisogni nelle regioni periferiche della città* (Turin: Italia industriale artistica editrice, 1926).

13. Information on Piero Puricelli can be found in Lando Bortolotti, "Origini e primordi della rete autostradale in Italia, 1922–1933," *Storia urbana* 59 (1992): 35–70.

14. The Touring Club Italiano was a private tourism club founded in Milan in 1894. Its members were mainly cyclists and motorists, and it was to play an important role in the transport sector. See Giuseppe Vota, *I sessant'anni di Touring Club Italiano, 1894–1954* (Milan: Tci, 1954). The club's periodical, *Le strade: rivista mensile tecnico-amministrativa della viabilità ordinaria* is also very interesting. Published from 1898, this journal provided an excellent overview of the road-network sector.

15. Information about the highway between Milan and Venice is contained in *Atti del III Convegno nazionale stradale promosso e organizzato dal Touring Club Italiano: Napoli 30 Marzo—4 Aprile 1922* [Proceedings of the Third National Road Conference . . .] (Milan: Tci, 1922). It is worth recalling that the first proposal for an "autovia" was put forward in 1906 by the engineer Spera for the Rome-Naples stretch; see Lando Bortolotti and Giuseppe De Luca,

Fascismo e autostrade. Un caso di sintesi: La Firenze-mare (Milan: Franco Angeli, 1994).

16. One of the main characteristics of Italian highways built during the Fascist period (1922–1943) was that they provided transportation links between the main cities and holiday resorts. The Milan-Lakes, the Rome-Ostia, and Florence-Sea are the clearest examples, designed to provide a luxury service for wealthy automobile owners going on vacation. The extremely low level of motorization in Italy made these sections the only ones with a sufficient number of users to ensure some chance of commercial success. For information about the highway from Milan to the lakes, see Società Anonima Autostrade, ed., *Le autostrade da Milano ai Laghi* (Milan: Società Anonima Autostrade, 1923); Società Anonima Autostrade, ed., *Le autostrade e la Milano-Laghi* (Milan: Bestetti e Tumminelli, 1925); Giovanni Da Rios, Savino Rivelli, "Autostrada Milano-Laghi," in S.p.A. per l'Autostrada Serravalle-Milano-Ponte Chiasso, ed., *Le autostrade della prima generazione;* Sergio Mattia, "La costruzione dell'autostrada Milano-laghi," in *Costruire in Lombardia. Rete e infrastrutture territoriali,* ed. Ornella Selvafolta and Aldo Castellano (Milan: Electa, 1984).

17. See Società Anonima Autostrade, ed., *Le autostrade da Milano ai Laghi.*

18. For data on the quality of Italian roads, see Sileno Fabbri, *Il problema delle strade in Italia* (Milan: Cooperativa Grafica Operai, 1927).

19. Right from the beginning, access to Italian highways was limited to motor vehicles only. To modern eyes, the highway to the lakes may appear rudimentary, like all prewar highways, with a single, three-lane carriageway about ten meters across, with two-way traffic. For technical details on Italian highways, see S.p.A. per l'Autostrada Serravalle-Milano-Ponte Chiasso, ed., *Le autostrade della prima generazione;* and S.p.A. per l'Autostrada Serravalle-Milano-Ponte Chiasso, ed., *Le autostrade della seconda generazione* (Milan: S.p.A. per l'Autostrada Serravalle-Milano-Ponte Chiasso, 1990).

20. There was also the *strada camionabile,* a road suitable for trucks, between Genoa and Serravalle Scrivia in the Po Valley, which was completed in 1935. The camionabile had some particular characteristics: even though a toll was charged, it was built directly by the state, partly because no private company was willing to undertake the work immediately after the great crash of 1929 and partly because there was considerable military interest in linking Genoa, Italy's largest port, with the industrial centers in the plains. See Ministero dei lavori pubblici, ed., *L'autocamionabile Genova-Valle Po* (Rome: Ministero dei lavori pubblici, 1938).

21. The cheerful optimism of the financial estimates—which projected unrealistic revenues, underestimated the running costs, and overestimated potential traffic—and the economic crisis of 1929 combined to deal a mortal blow to Italy's small network of highways. Almost none of the licensee

companies were able to bear the liabilities accumulated, and in the 1930s the state, through the national road authority, took over management of the highways while leaving the tolls in place. For more details of these events, see S.p.A. per l'Autostrada Serravalle-Milano-Ponte Chiasso, ed., *Le autostrade della prima generazione.*

22. On the company policies of Fiat, see Valerio Castronovo, *Giovanni Agnelli* (Turin: Einaudi, 1977). On the entry of Fiat into the highway sector in the late 1920s, see Massimo Moraglio, "L'autostrada Torino-Milano, 1923–1933: I progetti e la costruzione," *Storia urbana* 86 (1999): 103–22.

23. On the administrative and political aspects of Italian highways after the Second World War, see the memoir by Fedele Cova, *Autostrade e altri episodi di vita vissuta* (Milan: Editoriale Domus, 1983). Cova, an engineer, was for many years the managing director of the highway company and was personally responsible for overseeing the construction of the Autostrada del Sole.

24. See Mauro Tebaldi, *La politica dei trasporti* (Bologna: Il Mulino, 1999).

25. On the development of the Italian highway network, cf. *The Development of the Italian Highway Network, 1924–1993: A Computerized Atlas,* ed. Albert Carreras and Elena Cefis (Badia Fiesolana: European University Institute, 1996). On highway projects in the 1920s and 30s, see Lando Bortolotti and Giuseppe De Luca, *Fascismo e autostrade.*

26. On Italian highways after World War II, see Lando Bortolotti, *Viabilità e sistemi infrastrutturali,* 358–66; S.p.A. per l'Autostrada Serravalle-Milano-Ponte Chiasso, ed., *Le autostrade della seconda generazione;* Maggi, *Politica ed economia dei trasporti italiani;* see also Enrico Menduni, *L'autostrada del Sole* (Bologna: Il Mulino, 1999).

27. On Puricelli's initiatives in Europe, from Germany to Poland to France, cf. Lando Bortolotti, "Fra politica, propaganda e affari: l'autostrada Roma-Berlino, 1927–1942," *Storia urbana* 81 (1997): 47–80; and Lando Bortolotti, "Italia, Europa e oltre: proposte e utopie autostradali al tramonto degli imperialismi e del colonialismo," *Storia urbana* 72 (1995): 133–62, esp. 134–40. Specifically on Finland, cf. Kimmo Antila, "Foreign Models, Private Initiatives and Relief Works: Roots of Highway Building in Finland," lecture delivered at the Mobility History and the European Road Network: Planning, Building, Use and Spatial Organization conference, held in Neuchâtel, France, 13–15 February 2003.

28. In addition to the rich German literature on autobahns, see also Thomas Zeller, "'The Landscape's Crown': Landscape, Perceptions, and Modernizing Effects of the German Autobahn System, 1934–1941," in *Technologies of Landscape: From Reaping to Recycling,* ed. David E. Nye (Amherst: University of Massachusetts Press, 1999); Thomas Zeller, "Building and Rebuilding the Landscape of the Autobahn, 1930–70," chapter 7 in this volume; and Joachim Wolschke-Bulmahn, "Landscape Planning and *Reichsautobahnen*

during the Nazi Period," lecture delivered at the Landscapes and Roads in North America and Europe: Cultural History in Transatlantic Perspective conference, held at the German Historical Institute in Washington, DC, October 11–13, 2002; see also Volker Ziegler, "Il progetto autostradale tedesco tra fra città e territorio 1925–1955," *Storia urbana* 100 (2002): 85–120.

29. Cf. Gianfranco Pala and Maurizio Pala, *Lo sviluppo dei trasporti*, in *Lo sviluppo economico in Italia. Storia dell'economia italiana negli ultimi cento anni*, ed. Giorgio Fua (Milan: Franco Angeli, 1969).

30. See Maggi, *Politica ed economia dei trasporti italiani*, 113–37.

31. Partial but interesting information about the role of the IRI can be found in Fedele Cova, *La rete autostradale Iri* (Rome: Firema, 1963); and Fedele Cova, *Autostrade e altri episodi di vita vissuta*. On state investments and Italian legislation, see Aiscat, ed., *Legislazione autostradale* (Rome: Aiscat, 1994). The 1955 highway plan provided for an initial ten-year public investment of 100 billion lire: see Vito Rocco, "La legislazione autostradale italiana dal '55 al '75," in S.p.A. per l'Autostrada Serravalle-Milano-Ponte Chiasso, ed., *Le Autostrade della seconda generazione*, 28–35.

32. See Carreras and Cefis, *The Development of the Italian Highway Network*.

33. On Italian cultures after World War II, see Silvio Lanaro, *Storia dell'Italia repubblicana* (Venice: Marsilio, 1992), 223–79.

34. See Menduni, *L'autostrada del Sole*, 7–35.

35. Paolo Capuzzo, "La conquista della mobilità. Contributo ad una storia sociale dei trasporti urbani in Europa (1870–1940)," *Ricerche storiche* 3 (2000): 621–40.

36. The historical photographic archive of Fiat, kept by Satiz in Turin, is a perfect example of this tendency. See also the images in the previously cited S.p.A. per l'Autostrada Serravalle-Milano-Ponte Chiasso, ed., *Le autostrade della prima generazione* and *Le autostrade della seconda generazione*. A similar approach can be seen in the case of the ordinary road network: see *La strada in Italia dall'unità ad oggi, 1861–1987*.

37. Of interest here is Tci, ed., *Le autostrade in Italia e all'estero* (Milan: Tci, 1963). It is worth noting that the volumes on the first- and second-generation highways, referred to above and published in the 1980s, contain no critical comments whatever or even any considerations of the environmental impact of highways in Italy.

38. A clothoid, or Cornu spiral, has a variable radius. The advantage of the clothoid is that, from a dynamic point of view, it is the best possible type of connection between a straightaway and a curve. This is because when a car follows a straight line, the centrifugal acceleration (and thus also the centripetal acceleration produced by the grip of the tires to counterbalance it) is equal to zero, while it has a certain value in a curve. The clothoid proceeds from a curve of infinite radius to one of a circle, bringing about the

centrifugal acceleration only gradually and thus maintaining the stability of the vehicle.

39. Eugenio Gra, "Strada" in *Enciclopedia Italiana, Aggiornamento 1938–1948*, vol. 2 (Rome: Istituto dell'Enciclopedia Italiana, 1949), 2:2, emphasis added.

40. Bortolotti and De Luca, *Fascismo e autostrade*, 11.

41. See, for example, Società Autostrade, ed., *Autostrada del Sole: Ponte sul Po* (Milan: Tip. Scotti, 1959).

42. Menduni, *L'autostrada del Sole*, 44, 55. See also Società Autostrade, ed., *Autostrada del Sole, 1956–1964* (Rome: Firema, 1964); Società Autostrade, ed., *L'autostrada del Sole attraverso gli Appennini* (Rome: Società Autostrade, 1960); and Società Autostrade, ed., *Autostrade, un'esperienza italiana* (Rome: Società Autostrade, 1983).

43. On the design philosophy of the Ministry of Public Works (Ministero dei lavori pubblici) and of the state road authority (Azienda statale della strada), see Bonelli, "Le autostrade in Italia."

Chapter 7

1. Mark Rask, in *American Autobahn: The Road to an Interstate Freeway with No Speed Limit* (Minneapolis, MN: Vanguard, 1999), praises the autobahn as a paragon of automotive freedom.

2. In the original: "Wir fahr'n fahr'n fahr'n auf der Autobahn / Vor uns liegt ein weites Tal / Die Sonne scheint mit Glitzerstrahl / Die Fahrbahn ist ein graues Band / Weiße Streifen, grüner Rand / Jetzt schalten wir das Radio an / Aus dem Lautsprecher klingt es dann: / Wir fahr'n auf der Autobahn."

3. Kurt Möser, *Geschichte des Autos* (Frankfurt: Campus, 2002), 313–16.

4. Dirk van Laak, "Infra-Strukturgeschichte," *Geschichte und Gesellschaft* 27 (2001): 367–93. Van Laak draws on a large body of literature in the history of technology, which cannot be dealt with here.

5. David E. Nye, ed., *Technologies of Landscape: From Reaping to Recycling* (Amherst: University of Massachusetts Press, 1999); Thomas Lekan and Thomas Zeller, "Introduction: The Landscape of German Environmental History," in *Germany's Nature: Cultural Landscapes and Environmental History*, ed. Thomas Lekan and Thomas Zeller (New Brunswick, NJ: Rutgers University Press, 2005), 1–14.

6. Pascal Bussy, *Kraftwerk: Man, Machine and Music,* 2nd ed. (London: SAF, 2001), 53–59. According to this account, "Autobahn" was the first record with German lyrics to enter the American charts (59). See also Michael Bracewell, "Fade to Grey: Motorways and Monotony," in *Autopia: Cars and Culture*, ed. Peter Wollen and Joe Kerr (London: Reaktion, 2003), 288–92. Kraftwerk's status in U.S. popular culture is further evidenced by the fact that it has become

the subject of multiple parodies, as in *Sprockets*, a fictional West German TV show featured on *Saturday Night Live* during the 1990s, and the German techno-pop band Autobahn in Joel Coen's 1998 film *The Big Lebowski*.

7. Wolfgang Sachs, *For Love of the Automobile: Looking Back into the History of Our Desires* (Berkeley: University of California Press, 1992). For a criticism of historians' eagerness to rely on these accounts, see Christoph Maria Merki, *Der holprige Siegeszug des Automobils 1895–1930: Zur Motorisierung des Strassenverkehrs in Frankreich, Deutschland und der Schweiz* (Vienna: Böhlau, 2002).

8. See Massimo Moraglio's essay in chapter 6 of this volume.

9. In the case of the autobahn, these strictly enforced regulations include service stations located within the right of way of the roads run by state-licensed managers, a new body of laws, and a separate police force. For general reflections, see Gijs Mom, "Roads without Rails: European Highway-Network Building and the Desire for Long-Range Motorized Mobility," *Technology and Culture* 46, no. 4 (2005): 745–72.

10. Joachim Radkau, *Technik in Deutschland. Vom 18. Jahrhundert bis zur Gegenwart* (Frankfurt am Main: Suhrkamp, 1989), 308.

11. Michael Stolz, "Am Beginn des modernen Straßenbaus — Sächsische Straßenbaupolitik und -technik zur Zeit der Weimarer Republik," *Bautechnik* 75 (1998): 391–402, 394; Alfred P. Sloan Jr., *My Years with General Motors* (Garden City: Doubleday, 1972), 380.

12. Merki, *Siegeszug*, 40, 429; Kurt Möser, "World War I and the Creation of Desire for Automobiles in Germany," in *Getting and Spending: European and American Consumer Societies in the Twentieth Century*, ed. Susan Strasser, Charles McGovern, and Matthias Judt (Cambridge: Cambridge University Press, 1998), 195–222.

13. Martin Kornrumpf, *HAFRABA e.V. Deutsche Autobahn-Planung 1926–1934* (Bonn: Kirschbaum, 1990).

14. Richard J. Overy, "Cars, Roads, and Economic Recovery in Germany, 1932–1938," in *War and Economy in the Third Reich* (Oxford: Clarendon Press; New York: Oxford University Press, 1994), 68–89; Christopher Kopper, "Modernität oder Scheinmodernität nationalsozialistischer Herrschaft: Das Beispiel der Verkehrspolitik," in *Von der Aufgabe der Freiheit. Politische Verantwortung und bürgerliche Gesellschaft im 19. und 20. Jahrhundert. Festschrift für Hans Mommsen*, ed. Christian Jansen, Lutz Niethammer, and Bernd Weisbrod (Berlin: Akademie, 1995), 399–411; Dan P. Silverman, *Hitler's Economy: Nazi Work Creation Programs, 1933–1936* (Cambridge, MA: Harvard University Press, 1998).

15. Todt to Seifert, 23 November 1933, Deutsches Museum, Munich, Archives (hereafter DMA), NL 133/56.

16. Wilbur H. Simonson and R. E. Royall, *Landschaftsgestaltung an der Straße* (Berlin: Volk und Reich, 1935); Wolfgang Singer, "Parkstraßen in den Vereinigten Staaten," *Die Straße* 2 (1935): 175–77; Bruno Wehner, "Die

landschaftliche Ausgestaltung der nordamerikanischen Park- und Verkehrsstraßen," *Die Straße* 3 (1936): 599–601. Cf. Timothy Davis's essay in chapter 2 of this volume.

17. In the original: "Die Straße muß Ausdruck ihrer Landschaft und Ausdruck deutschen Wesens sein." Fritz Todt, "Geleitworte," in *Reichsautobahnen: Vom ersten Spatenstich—zur fertigen Fahrbahn*, ed. Otto Reismann (Berlin: Naturkunde und Technik-Verlag Fritz Knapp, 1935), n.p.

18. For the massive multimedia propaganda campaign, see Erhard Schütz and Eckhard Gruber, *Mythos Reichsautobahn. Bau und Inszenierung der "Straßen des Führers" 1933–1941* (Berlin: Links, 1996); and Rainer Stommer, ed., *Reichsautobahn: Pyramiden des Dritten Reiches. Analysen zur Ästhetik eines unbewältigten Mythos* (Marburg: Jonas, 1982).

19. Alfred C. Mierzejewski, *The Most Valuable Asset of the Reich: A History of the German Railway Company*, vol. 2, *1933–1945* (Chapel Hill: University of North Carolina Press, 2000), 40–42; Schütz and Gruber, *Mythos*, 12; Alfred Gottwaldt, *Julius Dorpmüller, die Reichsbahn und die Autobahn: Verkehrspolitik und das Leben des Verkehrsministers bis 1945* (Berlin: Argon, 1995).

20. Mierzejewski, *Most Valuable Asset*, 42; Gottwaldt, *Julius Dorpmüller*, 41.

21. For an extended discussion, see Thomas Zeller, *Driving Germany: The Landscape of the German Autobahn, 1930–1970* (New York and Oxford: Berghahn, 2007), 79–179; Thomas Zeller, *Straße, Bahn, Panorama: Verkehrswege und Landschaftsveränderung in Deutschland 1930 bis 1990* (Frankfurt am Main: Campus, 2002), 128–287; and Thomas Zeller, "'The Landscape's Crown': Landscape, Perceptions, and Modernizing Effects of the German *Autobahn* System, 1934–1941," in Nye, ed., *Technologies of Landscape*, 218–38.

22. Seifert to Todt, 19 June 1937, DMA NL 133/57.

23. Alwin Seifert, "Reichsautobahnen und deutsche Landschaft," *Reichsautobahnen*, n.p. For a different interpretation of this topic based solely on published sources, see Gert Gröning and Joachim Wolschke-Bulmahn, "Some Notes on the Mania for Native Plants in Germany," *Landscape Journal* 11 (1992): 116–26.

24. Weber to Todt, 25 January 1940, Federal Archives Berlin [hereafter FAB] 46.01/140; Seifert to Todt, February 17, 1940, FAB 46.01/140.

25. "Vorläufige Richtlinien über die Bepflanzung der Kraftfahrbahnen auf Grund der Besprechung beim Generalinspektor," November 11, 1936, Alwin Seifert Papers, Technical University Munich-Weihenstephan (hereafter cited as ASP), 116.

26. Seifert to Gauleiter of Lower Silesia, 24 February 1943, ASP 148.

27. Both the East and the West German departments of transportation relied on the expertise of "Generalinspektor" engineers; see Axel Dossmann, *Begrenzte Mobilität: Eine Kulturgeschichte der Autobahnen in der DDR* (Essen: Klartext, 2003), 71–83.

28. "Rede des Bundesverkehrsministers Dr. Ing. Seebohm auf der Mitgliederversammlung der Forschungsgesellschaft für das Straßenwesen in Hamburg am 22. Juli 1950," *Straße und Autobahn* 1, no. 7 (1960): 1–6, esp. 4.

29. Hans-Christoph Seebohm, "Straßenplanung und Forschung. Vortrag vor der Straßenbautagung und Mitgliederversammlung der Forschungsgesellschaft für das Straßenwesen am 24. Oktober 1952 in Düsseldorf," *Straße und Autobahn* 3 (1952): 361–80, 371.

30. Seebohm encouraged a scientification of civil engineering, likening it to chemistry and physics, which utilize quantitative anlaysis and comparative observation in research ("Straßenplanung," 362). For West German transportation policy, see Dietmar Klenke, *Bundesdeutsche Verkehrspolitik und Motorisierung. Konfliktträchtige Weichenstellungen in den Jahren des Wiederaufstiegs* (Stuttgart: Steiner, 1993); and Klenke, *"Freier Stau für freie Bürger": Die Geschichte der bundesdeutschen Verkehrspolitik* (Darmstadt: Wissenschaftliche Buchgesellschaft, 1995).

31. Hermann Kunde, "Rationeller Straßenbau," *Straße und Autobahn* 5 (1954): 336–41, esp. 338.

32. Hans Lorenz, "Moderne Trassierung," *Straße und Autobahn* 5 (1954): 370–73.

33. Kurt Becker,"Straßenbautechnik und Straßenbaukunst," *Brücke und Straße* 3 (1951): 174.

34. Klenke, *"Freier Stau"*, 46, 50. In the larger Germany of 2005, with a traffic volume about twenty times higher than it was in 1950, some 5,400 traffic deaths occurred. http://www.destatis.de/basis/d/verk/verktab6.php (accessed July 27, 2006).

35. *Die Verkehrspolitik in der Bundesrepublik Deutschland 1949–1965: Ein Bericht des Bundesministers für Verkehr* (Hof: Hoermann, 1965), 23.

36. Leopold Örley, *Übergangsbogen bei Straßenkrümmungen* (Berlin: Volk und Reich, 1937); Walther Schürba, *Klothoiden-Abstecktafeln. Anleitung zu Entwurf, Berechnung und Absteckung* (Berlin: Volk und Reich, 1942); Hans Lorenz, "Sinn und Anwendung von Übergangsbögen," in *Trassierungsgrundlagen der Reichsautobahn*, ed. Hans Lorenz (Berlin: Volk und Reich, 1943), 43–51.

37. Theodore M. Porter, *Trust in Numbers: The Pursuit of Objectivity in Science and Public Life* (Princeton, NJ: Princeton University Press, 1995); Louis Ward Kemp, "Aesthetes and Engineers: The Occupational Ideology of Highway Design," *Technology and Culture* 27 (1986): 759–97, esp. 774–75.

38. T. Spielmann, "Zweckgebundene Straßengrünflächen," *Straße und Autobahn* 3 (1952): 43–46.

39. Wilhelm Hirsch, "Sicherheitspflanzungen an den Autobahnen," *Straße und Autobahn* 5 (1954): 304–8.

40. Immanuel Kant, preface to *A Critique of Pure Reason*, quoted here from Bruno Latour, "Visualization and Cognition: Thinking with Eyes and Hands," *Knowledge and Society* 6 (1986): 1–40, esp. 15.

41. For newer interpretations that have been useful for this paper, see Monika Renneberg and Mark Walker, eds., *Science, Technology and National Socialism* (Cambridge: Cambridge University Press, 1994); Mitchell G. Ash, "Verordnete Umbrüche, konstruierte Kontinuitäten: Zur Entnazifizierung von Wissenschaftlern und Wissenschaften nach 1945," *Zeitschrift für Geschichtswissenschaft* 43 (1995), 903–23; Kees Gispen, *Poems in Steel: National Socialism and the Politics of Inventing from Weimar to Bonn* (New York: Berghahn, 2002); Mark Walker, ed., *Science and Ideology: A Comparative History* (London: Routledge, 2003).

42. Kranzberg, one of the founding figures of the history of technology in the United States, stated in the first of his six stipulations that technology is neither good nor bad, nor is it neutral. Melvin Kranzberg, "Technology and History: 'Kranzberg's Laws,'" *Technology and Culture* 27 (1986): 544–60.

43. See Axel Dossmann's essay in chapter 8 of this volume.

Chapter 8

1. Karl Schawelka, "*Ut hortus poesis:* The Garden Art of Ian Hamilton Finlay," *Daidalos: Architektur, Kunst, Kultur* 38 (December 1990): 81–89, esp. 88.

2. VEB Autobahnbaukombinat, *Straßenbau—Road building—La construction de routes—Construção de estradas* (Berlin: VEB Autobahnbaukombinat, 1984), 9.

3. See Thomas Zeller, *Straße, Bahn, Panorama: Verkehrswege und Landschaftsveränderung in Deutschland von 1930 bis 1990* (Frankfurt am Main: Campus, 2002).

4. For an extended discussion, see Axel Dossmann, *Begrenzte Mobilität. Eine Kulturgeschichte der Autobahnen in der DDR* (Essen: Klartext, 2003).

5. Langdon A. Winner, "Do Artifacts Have Politics?" *Daedalus* 109 (1980): 121–36; Raymond Stokes, "In Search of the Socialist Artefact: Technology and Ideology in East Germany, 1945–1962," *German History* 15 (1997): 221–39; Bernward Joerges, "Do Politics Have Artefacts?" *Social Studies of Science* 29 (1999): 411–31.

6. See Werner Durth, *Deutsche Architekten. Biographische Verflechtungen 1900–1970* (Munich: Deutscher Taschenbuch Verlag, 1992); and Werner Durth, Jörn Düwel, and Niels Gutschow, *Architektur und Städtebau der DDR, Band 1: Ostkreuz: Personen, Pläne, Perspektive* and *Band 2: Aufbau: Städte, Themen, Dokumente* (Frankfurt am Main: Campus, 1998), hereafter cited as Durth, Ostkreuz or Durth, *Aufbau.*

7. Christopher Kopper, "Die Deutsche Reichsbahn 1949–1989," in *Die Eisenbahn in Deutschland: Von den Anfängen bis zur Gegenwart,* ed. Lothar Gall and Manfred Pohl (Munich: Beck, 1999), 281–316.

8. Michael Geyer, "Industriepolitik in der DDR: Von der großindustriellen Nostalgie zum Zusammenbruch," in *Die DDR als Geschichte: Fragen—Hypothesen—Perspektiven,* ed. Jürgen Kocka and Martin Sabrow (Berlin: Akademie Verlag, 1994), 122–34.

9. Walter Ulbricht, *Der Siebenjahrplan des Friedens, des Wohlstands und des Glück des Volkes* (Berlin: Dietz, 1959), 8–155, esp. 30.

10. Ibid., 30.

11. See Erhard Schütz and Eckhard Gruber, *Mythos Reichsautobahn: Bau und Inszenierung der "Straßen des Führers" 1933–1945* (Berlin: Ch. Links, 1996).

12. Karl Böhm, "Sprung über sieben Jahre," *Magazin* 2 (1960): 46–48.

13. Ibid., 47.

14. James C. Scott, *Seeing Like a State: How Certain Schemes to Improve the Human Condition Have Failed* (New Haven: Yale University Press, 1998).

15. Böhm, "Sprung über sieben Jahre," 47.

16. See Johannes Roskothen, *Verkehr. Zu einer poetischen Theorie der Moderne* (Munich: Fink, 2003), 31–40; Alf Lüdtke, "Ikonen des Fortschritts. Eine Skizze zu Bild-Symbolen und politischen Orientierungen in den 1920er und 1930er Jahren in Deutschland," in *Amerikanisierung: Traum und Alptraum im Deutschland des 20. Jh.,* ed. Alf Lüdtke, Inge Marßolek, and Adelheid von Saldern (Stuttgart: Steiner, 1996), 199–210. On the transformation of this pictorial world of the 1920s and 1930s in the Federal Republic during the 1950s, see Westfälisches Landesmuseum für Kunst und Kulturgeschichte, ed., *Die nützliche Moderne: Graphik- und Produktdesign in Deutschland 1935–1955* (Münster: Westfälisches Landesmuseum für Kunst und Kulturgeschichte, 2000).

17. "Socialist progress is powered by an automobile motor and one which has been made into a tank," as two literary critics put it in the analysis of automobile metaphors in the works of East German authors. Gerd Katthage and Karl-Wilhelm Schmidt, *Langsame Autofahrten. Studien zu Texten ostdeutscher Schriftsteller* (Weimar: Böhlau, 1997), 180.

18. On the historical origins of the GDR insignia, see Harry D. Schurdel, "Die Hoheitssymbole der Deutschen Demokratischen Republik," in *Parteiauftrag: Ein neues Deutschland: Bilder, Rituale und Symbole der frühen DDR,* ed. Dieter Vorsteher (Munich: Koehler and Amelang, 1997), 44–62, esp. 48–56.

19. See Uwe Johnson, *Begleitumstände. Frankfurter Vorlesungen* (Frankfurt am Main: Suhrkamp Verlag, 1992), 289.

20. Ina Merkel, *Utopie und Bedürfnis: Die Geschichte der Konsumkultur in der DDR* (Cologne: Böhlau, 1999).

21. See Burghard Ciesla and Helmuth Trischler, "Die andere 'Verkehrsnot': Verkehrspolitik und Leistungsentwicklung des ostdeutschen Verkehrssystems," in *Deutsch-deutsche Wirtschaft 1945 bis 1990. Strukturveränderungen, Innovationen*

und regionaler Wandel. Ein Vergleich, Lothar Baar and Dietmar Petzina, eds. (St. Katharinen: Scripta Mercaturae Verlag, 2000), 152–91.

22. Axel Dossmann, "Auto-Suggestionen. Zur Autobahnplanung in der DDR bis 1961," *WerkstattGeschichte* 7, no. 21 (1998): 65–85.

23. This was meant to be better and faster than West Germany, but not on the same level; not by assimilating the Western countries but by searching for new, different, "socialist" methods of production and consumption.

24. The rail lines of the Deutsche Reichsbahn, which was the main long-distance transporter of goods in the GDR until 1989, were in no way forgotten but were severely neglected in the 1950s, just like the roads. The construction of the network of connections, which had been severely cut back, was put off many times because other projects had to be advanced for reasons primarily of political security. See Kopper, "Deutsche Reichsbahn," 302–12.

25. See Peter Hübner, "Menschen—Macht—Maschinen: Technokratie in der DDR," in *Eliten im Sozialismus: Beiträge zur Sozialgeschichte der DDR,* ed. Peter Hübner (Cologne: Böhlau, 1999), 327–60; Agnes Charlotte Tandler, *Geplante Zukunft: Wissenschaftler und Wissenschaftspolitik in der DDR 1955–1971* (Freiberg: Universitätsverlag Freiberg, 2000).

26. Vorschläge zur Streichung von bisher bekannten Vorhaben zugunsten des Autobahnneubaus, 18.9.1967, in Landeshauptarchiv Sachsen-Anhalt, Magdeburg (hereafter cited as LAM), Rep. J 85/749; Werner Pardemann, Probleme des Autobahnbaues, Vortrag, 15.12.1967, ibid.

27. Stefan Wolle, *Die heile Welt der Diktatur. Alltag und Herrschaft in der DDR 1971–1989* (Munich: Econ and List, 1999), 359.

28. Wolfgang Kaschuba, Ina Merkel, Leonore Scholze-Irrlitz, and Thomas Schulze, "Freizeitverhalten in der DDR und in den neuen Ländern: Geselligkeit, Fest- und Konsumkultur," in *Alltagsleben in der DDR und in den neuen Ländern,* vol. 5 of *Materialien der Enquete-Kommission "Überwindung der Folgen der SED-Diktatur im Prozeß der deutschen Einheit,"* ed. Deutscher Bundestag (Baden-Baden: Nomos-Verlagsgesellschaft, 1999), 655–744. See also Hasso Spode, ed., *Goldstrand und Teutonengrill: Kultur- und Sozialgeschichte des Tourismus in Deutschland 1945 bis 1989* (Berlin: Moser, 1996).

29. Jonathan R. Zatlin, "The Vehicle of Desire: The Trabant, the Wartburg, and the End of the GDR," *German History* 15, no. 3 (1997): 358–80, esp. 358. See also Gerd Katthage and Karl-Wilhelm Schmidt, *Langsame Autofahrten,* 63.

30. Most pieces of the concrete Berlin Wall were not sold as souvenirs; they were smashed, and the fragments were used to build new roads around the reunified Berlin.

31. Dorothee Wierling, "A German Generation of Reconstruction: The Children of the Weimar Republic in the GDR," in *Memory and Totalitarism,* ed. Luisa Passerini, International Yearbook of Oral History and Life Stories 1 (Oxford: Oxford University Press, 1992), 71–88, esp. 71 and 86.

32. See Durth, *Aufbau*, 49–61, 462.

33. Durth, *Ostkreuz*, 282–84.

34. See examples in Durth, *Aufbau*, 211–12.

35. Ibid., 101.

36. Ibid., 116.

37. Ibid., 109.

38. *Unsere Straßen: Ein Überblick über die Entwicklung des Straßenwesens in der Deutschen Demokratischen Republik,* ed. Ministry of Communication and Traffic (Berlin: Transpress, 1963), 132–37.

39. Ibid., 182–86, esp. 182.

40. See Alf Lüdtke, "'Ehre der Arbeit': Industriearbeiter und Macht der Symbole: Zur Reichweite symbolischer Orientierungen im Nationalsozialismus," in his *Eigen-Sinn: Fabrikalltag, Arbeitserfahrungen und Politik vom Kaiserreich bis in den Faschismus* (Hamburg: Ergebnisse Verlag, 1993), 283–350.

41. See Norbert Frei, *Vergangenheitspolitik: Die Anfänge der Bundesrepublik und die NS-Vergangenheit* (München: dtv, 1999), 297, translated by Joel Golb as *Adenauer's Germany and the Nazi Past: The Politics of Amnesty and Integration* (New York: Columbia University Press, 2002).

42. See my interview with Rolf Näser, June 5, 1998 and Waldemar Gromzig, "Gestaltung und Technologie der Autobahn Berlin-Rostock," *Wissenschaftliche Zeitschrift der Hochschule für Verkehrswesen* 8, no. 3 (1960/61): 768–70.

43. *Bau der Autobahn Leipzig-Dresden, Präsentationsmappe zum 22: Jahrestag der Gründung der DDR,* ed. Ministerium für Verkehr (Berlin: n.p., 1971), 14–16.

44. Ulrich Krüger, "Sachzeugen der Produktivkraftentwicklung," in *Denkmale zur DDR-Geschichte im Bezirk Leipzig,* ed. Kulturbund der DDR (Leipzig: Gesellschaft für Denkmalpflege, 1984), 11–15, esp. 14–15.

45. Ernst Ullmann, "Gedanken zu Denkmalen aus der Geschichte der DDR," in *Denkmale zur DDR-Geschichte im Bezirk Leipzig,* e. Kulturbund der DDR, 3–5, esp. 4.

46. Schütz/Gruber, *Mythos,* 97.

47. Tape-recorded interview with Hermann Gärlich, conducted by the author on September 1, 2000.

48. *Bau der Autobahn Leipzig-Dresden, Präsentationsmappe zum 22. Jahrestag der Gründung der DDR,* 1 and 22.

49. See also Paul Josephson and Thomas Zeller, "The Transformation of Nature under Hitler and Stalin," in *Science and Ideology: A Comparative History,* ed. Mark Walker (London: Routledge, 2003), 124–55.

50. *Unsere Straßen,* 4, 151.

51. "Diese Ingenieure, die früher tätig waren im Autobahnbau, die haben ein Wissen gespeichert, kein Buchwissen . . . und ham das meistens sehr

geschickt, manchmal auch nicht so geschickt, an uns weitergegeben. Ein Beispiel: Ich sagte Ihnen, wir sind mit Herrn Roesmer und der ganzen Truppe das [Gelände für die Trasse Berlin-Rostock] abgelaufen oder mit den Jeeps abgefahren. Im Norden gibt es viele Seen. . . . Und da hat der Herr Roesmer uns aber eingebleut: Legt die Trasse um! . . . Legt die nicht etwa so, daß die direkt am Wasser lang führt. Wenn wir einen Wald haben, dann paßt immer auf, das zwischen dem See und der Autobahn noch fünfzig oder hundert Meter Wald [liegen]. Es ist viel schöner, wenn man durch die Bäume das Wasser sieht. Nicht etwa als Schutz oder was, . . . Der Mann hat Recht gehabt. Es gibt so tausend kleine Dinge, wo Roesmer uns getrimmt hat." Rolf Näser, quoted here from my June 5, 1998, interview with Näser, cited above.

52. Näser, "Bericht zur Trasse für die Bestimmung der Linienführung, Variante D," November 28, 1959, in Bundesarchiv Berlin-Licherfelde (hereafter cited as BArchB), DM 1/3706.

53. Ibid.

54. "Bei der Trassenführung wurde soweit wie möglich versucht, einen ständigen Wechsel des Landschaftsbildes zu erreichen. An einigen Stellen ist die Trasse so geführt, daß Blickpunkte auf Seen und andere reizvolle Punkte entstehen." "Stellungnahme der Hauptverwaltung Straßenwesen an die Staatliche Plankommission zur Studie Berlin-Rostock," June 3, 1960, BArchB, DE 1/20 841.

55. There were plans to travel to England, France, the Federal Republic of Germany, Austria, Italy, Switzerland, and Sweden; see "Protokoll über Beratung für den Autobahnbau Berlin-Rostock," January 9, 1960, BArchB, DM 1/3706.

56. "Bericht über die Reise einer Delegation des Ministeriums für Verkehrswesen zum Studium der Autobahn und des Straßenbaus in England vom 6.9. bis 16.9.1960 und in Frankreich vom 17.9. bis 24.9.1960," *Das Straßenwesen*, 5. Sonderheft (1961): 22f.

57. Johannes Kastl, *Der Straßenbau*, vol. 2 (Leipzig: Teubner, 1960), 4–7, 170–82. See also Kastl, *Entwicklung der Straßenbautechnik vom Saumpfad bis zur Autobahn* (Berlin: Verlag der Technik, 1953); and *Studienmaterial der Fachschule des Bauwesens*, ed. Zentralabteilung Fachmethodik der Fachschule des Bauwesens (Leipzig: Deutsche Baukadademie, 1956); Ortleb/Christfreund, *Lehrbriefe für das Fernstudium*, ed. TH Dresden (Berlin: n.p., 1955).

58. "Das breite Band der Autobahn muß sich als neues Gestaltungselement harmonisch der Landschaft einfügen, andernfalls kann das Landschaftsbild erheblich beeinträchtigt werden. Da es keine mathematisch begründeten Gesetzmäßigkeiten für die Linienführung im Landschaftsraum gibt, ist es notwendig, die bisherigen Erfahrungen und Erkenntnisse, die bei den bestehenden Autobahnen gesammelt wurden, systematisch auszuwerten." Johannes Kastl, *Der Straßenbau*, rev. ed., 2 vols. (Leipzig: Teubner, 1968), 2:181.

59. Scheibe, "Richtlinien für die Anlage von Autobahnen—Linienführung und Querschnittsgestaltung," *Das Straßenwesen*, 8. Sonderheft (1960): 37–50, esp. 40 and 44. For the Federal Republic, see Thomas Zeller, "Landschaft als Gefühl und Autobahn als Formel: Der Autobahnbau in der frühen Bundesrepublik als Abgrenzungsversuch gegen die 'Straßen Adolf Hitlers,'" *WerkstattGeschichte* 7, no. 21 (1998): 29–41; Zeller, *Straße, Bahn, Panorama*, 228–50. See also Benjamin Steininger, *Raum-Maschine Reichsautobahn. Zur Dynamik eines bekannt/unbekannten Bauwerks* (Berlin: Kadmos, 2005), 85–133.

60. Sergej Anatoljevic Treskinskij, *Estetika avtomobilnych dorog* (Moscow: Transport, 1967).

61. "Die Frage, wie wird der Mittelstreifen? Was glauben Sie, wie wir diskutiert haben! Es gibt in Amerika Autobahnstrecken, da ist der Autobahnstreifen wesentlich breiter und hat eine Mulde. Und dieser Mittelstreifen ist natürlich sehr üppig bepflanzt, aber nur mit Büschen, keine Bäume, und das hat den großen Vorteil, sie brauchen keine Leitplanken. . . . Solche Gedanken ham wir unerhört diskutiert. Geht nicht! Unser Grund und Boden ist zu kostbar hier in der DDR—oder damals in der DDR." Rolf Näser, quoted here from my June 5, 1998, interview with Näser.

62. Sitzung des Präsidiums des Ministerrates vom June 8, 1988, BArchB, C 20/I/4–6263, 1–39, p. 6. See also Heinz Stehling, *Die Entwicklung des Straßenwesens in der sowjetischen Besatzungszone Deutschlands und der Deutschen Demokratischen Republik 1945–1989* (Bonn: Kirschbaum Verlag, 1992), 71.

63. Interview with Hermann Gärlich.

64. See, among others, the Bericht der Staatlichen Plankommission zur Vorlage in der Beratung im ZK am October 13, 1960, erstellt im Auftrag des ZK durch die Mitglieder der Unterkommission "Autobahnbau Berlin-Rostock," September 20, 1960, 21–28, BArchB, DM 1/2632.

65. Petitions from 1987/88, without signature, in Verwaltungsarchiv des Brandenburgischen Autobahnamtes Stolpe (hereafter cited as VBAS).

66. Petitions to the Autobahnmeisterei Freienhufen (Dresden), September 25, 1987, and January 15, 1988, in VBAS.

67. Petition to the Autobahndirektion Dresden, January 30, 1988, in VBAS.

68. Letter to the Autobahndirektion Berlin, October 13, 1987, in VBAS.

69. Ibid.

70. Letter to the Ministerium für Verkehrswesen, January 19, 1988; petition to the Autobahnbaukombinat, Betrieb Weimar, April 8, 1987; petition to Mitropa, February 15, 1987, in VBAS.

71. Letter to the Autobahndirektion Berlin, October 13, 1987, in VBAS.

72. Letter to the Dresden Council, Bereich Straßenwesen, March 17, 1987, in VBAS.

73. Letter to the Autobahnbaukombinat, Betrieb Weimar, April 8, 1987, in VBAS.

74. Replies to petition, January 30, 1988, and February 11, 1988, in VBAS.

75. Axel Dossmann, "Transit: Die Autobahn im Blick von Polizei und Staatssicherheit," in *Die DDR im Bild. Zum Gebrauch der Fotografie im anderen deutschen Staat,* ed. Karin Hartewig and Alf Lüdtke (Göttingen: Wallstein, 2004), 107–24.

76. Friedrich Christian Delius, "Angenehme Weiterreise!" in *Transit Westberlin. Erlebnisse im Zwischenraum,* ed. Friedrich Christian Delius and Peter Joachim Lapp (Berlin: Ch. Links, 1999), 9–38, esp. 38.

77. Peter Schneider, *Der Mauerspringer* (Darmstadt: Luchterhand, 1987), 64.

78. Delius, "Angenehme Weiterreise!" 30.

79. Steininger, *Raum-Maschine Reichsautobahn,* 132.

80. Axel Dossmann, "'Wer ist wer?' Feindaufklärung an den Transitautobahnen in der DDR," *Traverse* 3 (2004): 85–99; and the documentary *Autobahn Ost,* directed by Gerd Kroske, written by Axel Dossmann and Gerd Kroske (Leykauf Film, Germany, 2004).

Chapter 9

1. The quoted phrase in my title is drawn from Brenda Colvin, "Roadside Planting in Country Districts," *Landscape and Garden* 6, no. 2 (1939): 86–88, esp. 86. Colvin herself is, of course, quoting from *Hamlet* 2.2.

2. In the case of the German autobahns, landscape advocates were frequently consulted *after* a road had been planned, while economic constraints limited the extent of landscaping and planting. See Thomas Zeller, "'The Landscape Crown': Landscape, Perceptions, and Modernizing Effects of the German *Autobahn* System, 1934 to 1941," in *Technologies of Landscape: From Reaping to Recycling,* ed. David E. Nye (Amherst: University of Massachusetts Press, 1999), 218–38. On the landscaping of the autobahns, see also W. H. Rollins, "Whose Landscape? Technology, Fascism, and Environmentalism on the National Socialist *Autobahn,*" *Annals of the Association of American Geographers* 85 (1995): 494–520; E. Dimendberg, "The Will to Motorization: Cinema, Highways, and Modernity," *October* 73 (1995): 91–137; G. Gröning, "The Feeling of Landscape—a German example," *Landscape Research* 17 (1992): 108–15; James D. Shand, "The *Reichsautobahn*: Symbol for the Third Reich," *Journal of Contemporary History* 19 (1984): 189–200.

3. On debates surrounding the design, construction, and use of Britain's roads and motorways in early- and mid-twentieth-century Britain, see Peter Merriman, *Driving Spaces: A Cultural-Historical Geography of England's M1 Motorway* (Oxford: Blackwell, 2007).

4. J. Sheail, *Rural Conservation in Inter-war Britain* (Oxford: Clarendon Press, 1981).

5. On the formation of the Roads Beautifying Association, see E. Ford, "Byways Revisited," *Landscape Design* 234 (1994): 34–38; M. Spitta, "A Quarter of a Century of Highway Planting," *Journal of the Royal Horticultural Society* 77 (1952): 4–12; and Merriman, *Driving Spaces*. Fox was a consulting physician for diseases of the skin at St. George's Hospital before running his father's firm of general merchants, Duncan, Fox and Co. He also established an arboretum at his home in Winkworth, Surrey, which he gifted to the National Trust in 1952. See "Dr Wilfrid Fox" (obituary), *Times* (London), May 24, 1962, 25.

6. "Arterial Roads to Be Avenues," *Daily Express*, July 25, 1928. This news story, like several others cited below, is collected in a scrapbook of press cuttings preserved in the Roads Beautifying Association Archive at the Civic Trust Library, London, hereafter cited as RBA Archive Scrapbook.

7. See "Roadside Tree Protests," *Star*, October 31, 1928, in the RBA Archive Scrapbook.

8. Edwin Campbell, "Roadside Tree Planting: Art *versus* Utility," *The Queen: The Lady's Newspaper*, December 19, 1928, in the RBA Archive Scrapbook.

9. "Mrs. Ashley and the Trees," *Daily News*, December 29, 1928, in the RBA Archive Scrapbook.

10. Wilfrid Fox, "Roadside Planting (Including Post-war Suggestions)," *Journal of the Royal Horticultural Society* 69 (1944): 231–39, esp. 239. These discussions are clearly complicated by references to both Britain and England, and by the very different cultures of landscape which are invoked in discussions of Britain and its nations. What's more, the organizations examined in this paper operate in different regions and nations within Britain: the CPRE focuses on England, ILA members work throughout Britain, while the RBA worked on schemes in England and Wales (though the majority of these were in the South-East and Midlands of England). This tension is evident throughout the debates in this chapter.

11. "The Road Beautiful," *Country Life*, November 17, 1928, 708–10, esp. 708.

12. Roads Beautifying Association, *Eighth Report of the Roads Beautifying Association 1935–1936* (London: Roads Beautifying Association, 1936), 7. A similar assertion is made in a 1937 publication titled *The Highway Beautiful*, jointly authored and published by the Automobile Association and the Roads Beautifying Association; the copy of this booklet that I consulted is in the RBA Archive at the Civic Trust Library, London.

13. Fox, "Roadside Planting," 233, 235.

14. Roads Beautifying Association, *Seventh Report of the Roads Beautifying Association October, 1933–March, 1935* (London: Roads Beautifying Association,

1935), 15. See also Fox, "Roadside Planting"; and AA and RBA, *The Highway Beautiful.*

15. AA and RBA, *The Highway Beautiful,* 4, 18–20.

16. Wilfrid Fox, "The Roads Beautifying Association," *Roads and Road Construction* 6 (December 1928): 411.

17. Edward W. S. Cavendish, F. R. S. Balfour, and Wilfrid Fox, "Roadside Planting," *Times* (London), January 14, 1944, 8.

18. David Matless, *Landscape and Englishness* (London: Reaktion, 1998), 34.

19. See, e.g., ibid., 54–61; Matless, "Ordering the Land: The 'Preservation' of the English Countryside, 1918–1939" (PhD diss., University of Nottingham, 1990); Matless, "Ages of English Design: Preservation, Modernism, and Tales of Their History, 1926–1939," *Journal of Design History* 3 (1990): 203–12; C. Williams-Ellis, *England and the Octopus* (London: Geoffrey Bles, 1928). The CPRE is now officially known as the Campaign to Protect Rural England.

20. H.H.P. and N.L.C., eds., *The Face of the Land: The Yearbook of the Design and Industries Association, 1929–1930* (London: George Allen and Unwin, 1930); Design and Industries Association, *The Village Pump: A Guide to Better Garages* (London: Sidgwick and Jackson, 1930); "Roads," *Architectural Review* 81 (1937): 155–78.

21. German Roads Delegation, *Report upon the Visit of Inspection and Its Conclusions* (London: German Roads Delegation, 1938); Merriman, *Driving Spaces.*

22. Editorial preface to A. H. Brodrick, "The New German Motor-Roads," *Geographical Magazine* 6 (January 1938): 193–210, esp. 193.

23. See Leslie Burgin, "The German Motor Roads," undated note ca. January 1938, National Archives of the United Kingdom, Kew (hereafter cited as TNA), shelfmark MT 39/96.

24. Letter from H. G. Griffin to the Earl of Crawford and Balcarres, November 25, 1936, Council for the Preservation of Rural England Archives (hereafter cited as CPRE Archives), Museum of English Rural Life, University of Reading, shelfmark 241/16/I. See also Trunk Roads Joint Committee of the Council for the Preservation of Rural England and the Roads Beautifying Association, *Report of the Trunk Roads Joint Committee* (London: CPRE, 1937).

25. Letter from W. Fox to H. G. Griffin, December 8, 1936, CPRE Archives, shelfmark 241/16/I. From 1938 the CPRE and RBA decided to "cooperate in road planting by mutually sending representatives to all discussions." *Eleventh Report of the Roads Beautifying Association 1938–1939* (London: Roads Beautifying Association, 1939), 13. Between 1938 and 1947, the RBA was paid an annual fee of £200 to act as advisers to the Ministry of Transport. Letter from P. Faulkner to W. Fox, May 12, 1947, TNA, shelfmark MT 121/73.

26. "History of The Roads Beautifying Association from formation in 1928 to dismissal by the Minister of Transport in 1947," Roads Beautifying Association to the Ministry of Transport, December 4, 1951, TNA, shelfmark MT 121/575, esp. p. 3.

27. Letter from P. A. Barnes to H. G. Griffin, September 10, 1947, CPRE Archives, shelfmark 241/9; and C. Williams-Ellis, "Our New Roads," *Manchester Guardian*, September 26, 1947, in the RBA Archive Scrapbook.

28. During World War II, Lord Reith (Minister of Town and Country Planning), Thomas Sharp (President, Town Planning Institute), Clough Williams-Ellis, and geographer Dudley Stamp were all elected members of the Institute of Landscape Architects. By 1947, membership stood at 170, of which 65 were categorized as horticulturists and 81 as town planners or architects. See L. J. Fricker, "Forty Years a Growing," *Journal of the Institute of Landscape Architects* 86 (1969): 8–15; and G. A. Jellicoe, "War and Peace," *Landscape Design* 125 (1979): 10–13.

29. G. A. Jellicoe, "The Wartime Journal of the Institute of Landscape Architects," in *Fifty Years of Landscape Design, 1934–84*, ed. Sheila Harvey and Stephen Rettig (London: Landscape Press, 1985), 9–25, esp. 9.

30. Brenda Colvin, "Presidential Address," *Journal of the Institute of Landscape Architects* 22 (1951): 3–7, esp. 4. It is important to note that both Brenda Colvin and Sylvia Crowe studied horticulture and garden design rather than architecture, reflecting the gendering of these professions in early-twentieth-century Britain. See Sylvia Crowe, "Dame Sylvia Crowe," in *Reflections on Landscape: The Lives and Work of Six British Landscape Architects*, ed. Sheila Harvey (Aldershot, Hants, UK: Gower Technical Press, 1987), 31–51; and Sheila Harvey, "Brenda Colvin (1897–1981)," in Harvey, ed., *Reflections on Landscape*, 139–50.

31. Brenda Colvin, *Land and Landscape* (London: John Murray, 1948), 244.

32. Ibid., 245. For an early attempt to apply the concept of the fitted highway to British roads, see Memorandum, H. E. Aldington to All Divisional Road Engineers, "Trunk Roads: Fitting the Road to the Landscape," 12 June 1946, TNA, shelfmark MT 95/499. For a discussion of the same topic in relation to American practices, see F. W. Cron, "The Art of Fitting the Highway to the Landscape," in *The Highway and the Landscape*, ed. W. Brewster Snow (New Brunswick, NJ: Rutgers University Press, 1959), 78–109.

33. Sylvia Crowe, "From Coast to Coast," *Journal of the Institute of Landscape Architects* 44 (1958): 4–6 and 22, esp. 6.

34. G. A. Jellicoe, "Motorways—Their Landscaping, Design and Appearance," *Journal of the Town Planning Institute* 44 (1958): 274–83, esp. 274.

35. "Marginalia: Motorways," *Architectural Review* 95 (1944): liv.

36. "Exhibitions: British Road Federation," *Wartime Journal of the Institute of Landscape Architects* 5 (1944): 18–19, esp. 18.

37. See G. A. Jellicoe, "Sir Geoffrey Jellicoe," in Harvey, ed., *Reflections on Landscape*, 1–29; and Jellicoe, "The Aesthetic Aspect of Civil Engineering Design (Fifth Lecture)," in *The Aesthetic Aspect of Civil Engineering Design*, ed. Institution of Civil Engineers (London: Institution of Civil Engineers, 1945), 83–95, esp. 90. Jellicoe's major private/industrial commission at this time was his landscape plan for G. F. Earle's cement works in Hope Valley, Derbyshire; see G. A. Jellicoe, *Blue Circle Cement Hope Works Derbyshire: A Progress Report on a Landscape Plan, 1943–93* (Blue Circle Industries, 1980).

38. British Road Federation, *The Case for Motorways* (London: British Road Federation, 1948).

39. Jellicoe, "The Aesthetic Aspect," 91.

40. British Road Federation, *The Case for Motorways*, 6.

41. See Special Roads Bill, second reading, *Parliamentary Debates*, Commons, 5th ser., vol. 457 (November 11, 1948), cols. 1737–1848, esp. col. 1748.

42. Jellicoe, "Motorways." Painted between 1808 and 1810, *The Shadowed Road* is said to be one of Crome's best watercolors; see Norman L. Goldberg, *John Crome the Elder*, vol. 1, *Text and a Critical Catalogue* (Oxford: Phaidon Press, 1978), and Andrew Hemingway, *The Norwich School of Painters, 1803–1833* (Oxford: Phaidon Press, 1979).

43. Jellicoe, "Motorways," 276.

44. Sylvia Crowe, *The Landscape of Roads* (London: Architectural Press, 1960), 114.

45. Colvin, *Land and Landscape*, 246, 247.

46. Ibid., 246.

47. Ibid., 248.

48. Crowe, *The Landscape of Roads*, 25, 48–55, 85–87. Crowe also gave her verdict on the design of the newly opened M1 motorway. See below.

49. Ibid., 85. The Mickleham Bypass is a two- to three-mile section of the A24 north of Dorking (Surrey). Box Hill, a famous chalk escarpment and tourist attraction in Surrey, is now owned and managed by the National Trust.

50. Ibid., 87 and 114.

51. Ibid., 20.

52. Ian Nairn, "Outrage," special issue, *Architectural Review* 117 (1955): 363–460.

53. Ibid., 363, 371.

54. Ibid., 448.

55. See David Matless, "Visual Education and Geographical Citizenship: England in the 1940s," *Journal of Historical Geography* 22 (1996): 424–39.

56. R. Banham, "On the Road and on the Scene," *New Statesman* 67 (May 15, 1964): 769–70, esp. 770; Nairn, "Outrage," 371, 383, 389, 451.

57. Nairn, "Outrage," 451.

58. See Williams-Ellis, *England and the Octopus,* 136, 161–68; and Matless, *Landscape and Englishness,* 54–61.

59. Nairn, "Outrage," 389. For an earlier use of the term *municipal rustic,* see Donald Campbell, "Municipal Rustic," *Architectural Review* 112 (1952): 235–40.

60. Ibid., 389.

61. I borrow the phrase "ordering modernism" from Matless, *Landscape and Englishness,* 223, although he uses it to refer specifically to the work of landscape architects. While James Scott has described how the modernist designs of planners and architects have been, and could be, criticized for inferring *"functional* order from . . . purely visual order," I would argue that many of the diverse design philosophies that envisage such an ordering modernism place issues of practicality and performative encounters at the heart of their conception of functional order. See James C. Scott, *Seeing Like a State: How Certain Schemes to Improve the Human Condition Have Failed* (New Haven: Yale University Press, 1998), 133.

62. E.g., Sylvia Crowe wrote regular articles and columns on landscape for the *Architectural Review* in the mid 1950s, while three of her books were published by the Architectural Press. See Sylvia Crowe, *Tomorrow's Landscape* (London: Architectural Press, 1956); Sylvia Crowe, *The Landscape of Power* (London: Architectural Press, 1958); and Crowe, *The Landscape of Roads.*

63. See S. Crowe, I. Nairn, J. K. Boynton, and J. Adams, "Symposium on Subtopia," *Journal of the Institute of Landscape Architects* 35 (1956): 2–9; and Ian Nairn, "Counter-attack," special issue, *Architectural Review* 120 (1956): 353–440.

64. E. de Maré, review of *To-morrow's Landscape,* by Sylvia Crowe, *Journal of the Royal Society of Arts* 105 (1956): 121–22, esp. 121.

65. Ian Nairn, "Outrage Twenty Years After," *Architectural Review* 158 (1975): 328–37, esp. 329.

66. Ibid., 329.

67. On the work of the Advisory Committee on the Landscape Treatment of Trunk Roads (Landscape Advisory Committee), see C. Williams-Ellis (Ministry of Transport), *Roads in the landscape* (London: HMSO, 1967); Bruno de Hamel (Department of the Environment), *Roads and the Environment* (London: HMSO, 1976); Peter Merriman, "'A New Look at the English Landscape': Landscape Architecture, Movement, and the Aesthetics of Motorways in Early Post-war Britain," *Cultural Geographies* 13 (2006): 78–105; and Merriman, *Driving Spaces.*

68. The Roads Beautifying Association was conducting very little work on roadside planting at this time. After the Ministry of Transport terminated their funding in 1947, the Association diversified and took on increasing levels of private work, providing planting advice on housing estates, industrial estates, the ESSO oil refinery at Fawley, the ICI plant near Stockton, and over

twenty power stations and numerous other buildings for the British Electricity Authority. See Philippa Bassett, *A List of the Historical Records of the Roads Beautifying Association* (Birmingham: Centre for Urban and Regional Studies, University of Birmingham, and Reading: Institute of Agricultural History, University of Reading, 1980).

69. "Advisory Committee on the Landscape Treatment of Trunk Roads. Minutes of First Meeting, held in Room 6042, Berkeley Square House, at 2.30 p.m. on 30 April 1956," dated May 17, 1956, TNA, shelfmark MT 121/74.

70. See Zeller, "'The Landscape Crown'"; Rollins, "Whose Landscape?"; Dimendberg, "The Will to Motorization"; Shand, "The *Reichsautobahn*"; and G. Gröning and J. Wolschke-Bulmahn, "The Native Plant Enthusiasm: Ecological Panacea or Xenophobia?" *Landscape Research* 28 (2003): 75–88.

71. Letter from Wilfrid Fox to Mr. Watkinson, September 6, 1956, TNA, shelfmark MT 121/81.

72. Minute 15, by Mr. Haynes, December 23, 1954, TNA, shelfmark MT 121/576. For a more detailed discussion of the design, construction, and use of the M1 motorway in 1950s and 1960s Britain, see Peter Merriman, "'A Power for Good or Evil': Geographies of the M1 in Late-Fifties Britain," in *Geographies of British Modernity: Space and Society in the Twentieth Century*, ed. David Gilbert, David Matless and Brian Short (Oxford: Blackwell, 2003); Peter Merriman, "'Operation Motorway': Landscapes of Construction on England's M1 Motorway," *Journal of Historical Geography* 31 (2005): 113–33; Merriman, "Driving Places: Marc Augé, Non-places, and the Geographies of England's M1 Motorway," *Theory, Culture, and Society* 21, nos. 4–5 (2004): 145–67; Merriman, "A New Look at the English Landscape"; Merriman, "Materiality, Subjectification, and Government: The Geographies of Britain's Motorway Code," *Environment and Planning D: society and space* 23, no. 2 (2005): 235–50; Merriman, "'Mirror, Signal, Manoeuvre': Assembling and Governing the Motorway Driver in Late-1950s Britain," in *Against Automobility: Representation, Subjectivity, Politics*, ed. Steffen Böhm, Campbell Jones, Chris Land, and Mat Paterson (Oxford: Blackwell, 2006), 75–92; and Merriman, *Driving Spaces*.

73. Letter from Godfrey Samuel to the Minister of Transport, April 20, 1956, TNA, shelfmark MT 121/577.

74. "Note of meeting held on the 31st July to discuss the appointment of a landscape architect for the London-Yorkshire Motorway," August 10, 1956, TNA, shelfmark MT 121/77; letter from A. E. Dale, Secretary of the ILA, to A.H.M. Irwin, Ministry of Transport and Civil Aviation, August 14, 1956, TNA, shelfmark MT 121/77.

75. Letter from E. O. Williams to Mr. Jeffery, Ministry of Transport and Civil Aviation, February 13, 1957, TNA, shelfmark MT 95/503. A. P. Long was President of the Society of Foresters of Great Britain, a retired Director of

Forestry for Wales, and former Assistant Commissioner for Forestry for England and Wales. See also the unattributed article "Motorways," *Journal of the Institute of Landscape Architects* 47 (1959): 13, 16; Sylvia Crowe, "Roads through the Landscape," *Times* (London), May 20, 1959, 11; Royal Fine Art Commission [RFAC], *Sixteenth Report of the Royal Fine Art Commission, January 1958–August 1959,* Cmnd. 909 (London: HMSO, 1959); and TNA, shelfmark MT 121/77.

76. See Crowe, "Roads through the Landscape," 11; Crowe, *The Landscape of Roads,* 42–43, 93–95; and Merriman, "A New Look at the English Landscape," 87–89.

77. See Brenda Colvin, "The London-Birmingham Motorway: A New Look at the English Landscape," *Geographical Magazine* 32 (1959): 239–46; Ian Nairn, "Look Out," *Architectural Review* 133 (1963): 425–26; G. A. Jellicoe, "Corridors of Communication," *Architectural Review* 148 (1970): 381–84; Nikolaus Pevsner, *Buckinghamshire* (Harmondsworth: Penguin, 1960); Nikolaus Pevsner, *Northamptonshire* (Harmondsworth: Penguin, 1961); J. Betjeman, "Men and Buildings: Style on Road and Rail," *Daily Telegraph and Morning Post,* June 27, 1960, 15.

78. Crowe, *The Landscape of Roads,* 94.

79. Ibid.; see also Colvin, "The London-Birmingham Motorway," 239, 243.

80. Sylvia Crowe, "The London/York Motorway: A Landscape Architect's View," *Architects' Journal* 130 (September 10, 1959): 156–61, esp. 160.

81. Colvin, "The London-Birmingham Motorway," 246.

82. Sir Owen Williams and Partners (A. P. Long), "London-Yorkshire Motorway (South of Luton-Watford Gap-Dunchurch Special Road): Landscape Report and Model," Report to Ministry of Transport and Civil Aviation, 1957. The copy of this report that I consulted is held in the Institution of Civil Engineers Archive, London.

83. Minute by L. E. Morgan, "London-Yorkshire Motorway: Landscaping Proposals: Meeting between Representatives of Sir Owen Williams and Partners and Ministry of Transport and Civil Aviation. 27 Feb 58," March 7, 1958, TNA, shelfmark MT 121/78.

84. Ibid.

85. "Advisory Committee on the Landscape Treatment of Trunk Roads: Minutes of 15th meeting, held in Room 6042 Berkeley Square House at 3 P.M. on Wednesday 17th July, 1957," TNA, shelfmark MT 123/59.

86. Ibid.

87. Ibid.

88. "Advisory Committee on the Landscape Treatment of Trunk Roads: London-Birmingham Motorway: Mr. Williams-Ellis' Observations Arising from the Committee's Inspection of the Motorway on 21st May, 1959," TNA, shelfmark MT 123/59.

89. Letter from Eric Savill to Mr. Lodge, Ministry of Transport and Civil Aviation, February 6, 1958, TNA, shelfmark MT 121/78.

90. Matless, *Landscape and Englishness,* 223.

Chapter 10

1. Carl Abbott, *Political Terrain: Washington, D.C. From Tidewater Town to Global Metropolis* (Chapel Hill: University of North Carolina Press, 1999), 128, 214–15; Douglas B. Feaver, "Washington's Main Drag," *Washington Post,* August 30, 1999, A1.

2. See Payne-Maxie Consultants and Blayney-Dyett, Urban and Regional Planners, *The Land Use and Urban Development Impacts of Beltways: Executive Summary,* Final Report No. DOT-OS-90079, U.S. Department of Transportation and Department of Housing and Urban Development (Washington, DC: U.S. Government Printing Office, 1980). On the history of American beltways, see Christopher John Sutton, "The Socioeconomic, Land-Use, and Land-Value Impacts of Beltways in the Denver Metropolitan Area" (PhD diss., University of Denver, 1995), 42–50; and Jeremy Louis Korr, "Washington's Main Street: Consensus and Conflict on the Capital Beltway, 1952–2001" (PhD diss., University of Maryland, College Park, 2002), 68–75, 440–47.

3. Payne-Maxie Consultants and Blayney-Dyett, Urban and Regional Planners, *Land Use and Urban Development Impacts,* 5–6.

4. Lester Wilkinson, tape-recorded telephone interview conducted by author on October 27, 1998.

5. F. L. Burroughs, "The Capital Beltway," *Virginia Highway Bulletin* (January 1961): 36.

6. "Public Notice," *Fairfax (Virginia) Herald,* April 19, 1957.

7. *Fairfax (Virginia) Newsletter,* April 6, 1957, Virginia Room, Fairfax County Public Library.

8. "Chamber Asks Three Links with New Road," *Fairfax County (Virginia) Journal-Standard,* April 26, 1957.

9. *Transcript of Proceedings of Public Hearings by the Maryland State Roads Commission on the Proposed Interstate Route 495 and the Cabin John Connection to the George Washington Memorial Parkway, Dec. 17, 1959, Glen Echo Town Hall* (Washington, DC: Hart and Haskins, Shorthand and Stenotype Reporting, 1959), 75.

10. Ibid.

11. Grady Clay, "The Tiger Is Through the Gate," *Landscape Architecture* 49 (Winter 1958–59): 79–82, esp. 80–81.

12. "Road Work to Demolish Shop Center, 53 Homes," *(Bethesda, MD) Suburban Record,* October 22, 1959.

13. Joan L. Donegan, letter to the editor, *Washington Evening Star*, August 30, 1964, B1.

14. Tape-recorded interview with Isidore Elrich and Lisa Loflin, conducted by author on January 23, 2001, in Silver Spring, Maryland.

15. Tape-recorded telephone interview with Paul Foer, conducted by author on October 11, 2000.

16. Interview with Isidore Elrich and Lisa Loflin.

17. Edward M. Bassett, "The Freeway—A New Kind of Thoroughfare," *American City* 42 (February 1930): 95. See also Timothy J. Davis, "Rock Creek and Potomac Parkway, Washington, DC: The Evolution of a Contested Urban Landscape," *Studies in the History of Gardens and Designed Landscapes* 19 (April-June 1999): 123–237, esp. 229n160.

18. Cliff Ellis, "Professional Conflict over Urban Form: The Case of Urban Freeways, 1930 to 1970," in *Planning the Twentieth-Century American City*, ed. Mary Corbin Sies and Christopher Silver (Baltimore: Johns Hopkins University Press, 1996), 262–79, esp. 273.

19. See Korr, "Washington's Main Street," 186–204.

20. Edward Weiner, *Urban Transportation Planning in the United States: An Historical Overview*, rev. ed. (Westport, CT: Praeger, 1999), 61–62.

21. See U.S. Department of Transportation, Federal Highway Administration, "TEA-21 Planning and Environmental Provisions: Options for Discussion," http://www.fhwa.dot.gov/environment/tea21opt.htm#iiia; and "Statewide Transportation Planning; Metropolitan Transportation Planning; Proposed Rule[s]," *Federal Register* 65, no. 102 (May 25, 2000): 33926–33938, http://www.fhwa.dot.gov/environment/plng_fr.pdf .

22. On Maryland's current planning process and residents' response to it, see Korr, "Washington's Main Street," 216–38.

23. "Public Involvement," http://project1.parsons.com/capitalbeltway/New_Public_Home.htm.

24. "Overview," http://project1.parsons.com/capitalbeltway/New_Overview_MIS_Public.htm; "Capital Beltway Study," http://project1.parsons.com/capitalbeltway/Newhome.htm.

25. Bahram Jamei, tape-recorded interview conducted by author on January 22, 2001, in Chantilly, Virginia.

26. Virginia Department of Transportation, *Capital Beltway Study: Summary Report, Citizen Workshops, June 8, 9, 10, 1999*, 3 vols., 2:15–17.

27. Ibid., vol. 2, comment #63.

28. Ibid., vol. 2, comment #73.

29. Ibid, vol. 3, comment #256.

30. Ibid., vol. 2, comment #60.

31. In a tape-recorded oral-history interview conducted on February 1, 1999, in Beltsville, Maryland, William Shook, the assistant district engineer

for the Maryland State Roads Commission at the time of the Beltway's design and construction, confirmed that similar deceptive practices occurred regularly during the 1950s.

32. Virginia Department of Transportation, vol. 2 of 3, comment #250.

33. Tape-recording of Virginia Department of Transportation, Capital Beltway Study Location Public Hearing, McLean, VA, May 29, 2002, speaker #25, in possession of the author.

34. Tape-recording of Fairfax County Beltway Improvement Task Force, McLean Area Community Meeting, McLean, VA, February 9, 1999, in the author's possession.

35. This summary of remarks at the Virginia Department of Transportation's Capital Beltway Location Study Public Hearing, held in McLean, Virginia, on May 29, 2002, is drawn from notes I took at this hearing.

36. Gary M. Bowman, *Highway Politics in Virginia* (Fairfax, VA: George Mason University Press, 1993), 16.

37. [Name withheld by request], tape-recorded telephone interview conducted by the author on December 20, 2000.

38. ICF Kaiser Consulting Group, *Assessment of Public Involvement in Transportation Planning for the Washington Metropolitan Region* (Washington, DC: Metropolitan Washington Council of Governments, 1998), IV-2.

39. Gordon Fellman, "Neighborhood Protest of an Urban Highway," in *Transport Sociology: Social Aspects of Transport Planning*, ed. Enne de Boer (Oxford: Pergamon Press, 1986), 29–38, esp. 37.

40. Fellman, "Neighborhood Protest of an Urban Highway," 37.

41. On social construction, see Peter L. Berger and Thomas Luckmann, *The Social Construction of Reality: A Treatise in the Sociology of Knowledge* (Garden City, NY: Doubleday, 1967).

42. J. Edward Hood, "Social Relations and the Cultural Landscape," in *Landscape Archaeology: Reading and Interpreting the American Historical Landscape*, ed. Rebecca Yamin and Karen Bescherer Metheny (Knoxville: University of Tennessee Press, 1996), 122–23.

43. Beltway Survey #577. Citations with this designation refer to 620 responses to a World Wide Web survey I conducted between June 7, 2000, and August 17, 2001, using nonprobability snowball sampling. The "Capital Beltway Questionnaire," comprising thirty-five questions, was posted on the Web server of the University of Maryland at College Park and was publicized by personal e-mail, by announcements on Usenet newsgroups, and by coverage on local television and radio stations and in local newspapers. Among the 620 submissions, 607 answered between two and thirty-five questions, 6 were resubmissions with additional information, and 7 included single narrative anecdotes rather than answers to the specific questions. Of the 604 respondents who provided demographic data, 58 percent lived in Maryland; 29

percent in Virginia; 3 percent in Washington, DC; and the remainder elsewhere. For further discussion of the survey's methodology and sample, see
Korr, "Washington's Main Street," 50–64, 350–63.

44. Beltway Survey #595.

45. Beltway Survey #216.

46. Beltway Survey #187.

47. Beltway Survey #583.

48. Beltway Survey #51.

49. Beltway Survey #117.

50. Beltway Survey #441 and #410.

51. Beltway Survey #385 and #347.

52. Beltway Survey #112.

53. Beltway Survey #284.

54. Sandra Fleishman, "Traffic May Cause Some to Leave Area," *Washington Post,* June 23, 2001, H9; and online under the title "Bad Traffic Leads Many Residents to Consider Leaving the Washington Area," http://www
.aaamidatlantic.com/livenew/aboutus/pga/pga_dc/021901leaving_area.asp.

55. Beltway Survey #553.

56. Beltway Survey #453.

57. Beltway Survey #340.

58. Beltway Survey #337.

59. Beltway Survey #212.

60. Beltway Survey #194.

61. Beltway Survey #290.

62. Alan K. Henrickson, "'A Small, Cozy Town, Global in Scope': Washington, DC," *Ekistics* 299 (March/April 1983): 123–45, esp. 126.

63. Larry Van Dyne, "Getting There," *Washingtonian Magazine* (May 1990): 122–29 and 201–11, esp. 203.

64. Beltway Surveys #220, 490, 485, 203.

65. Beltway Survey #607.

66. Beltway Survey #203.

67. Beltway Surveys #239, 307, 322, 368, 436, 477, 604.

68. See Korr, "Washington's Main Street," 414–21.

69. This figure is cited in Hugh Sidey, "Life in the Capital Cocoon," *Time,* March 4, 1985, 20.

70. See Rudy J. Koshar, "Driving Cultures and the Meaning of Roads: Some Comparative Examples," in this volume, 30–31.

71. Beltway Survey #259.

72. Beltway Survey #257.

73. Beltway Survey #253, ellipses in original.

74. Beltway Survey #605.

75. Beltway Surveys #546, 357.

76. Beltway Survey #596.

77. Beltway Survey #436.

78. Beltway Survey #597. A similar account appears in Beltway Survey #600.

79. Beltway Survey #491.

80. Beltway Survey #78.

81. [Name withheld by request], tape-recorded telephone interview conducted by the author on October 11, 2000.

82. Angus K. Gillespie and Michael Aaron Rockland, *Looking for America on the New Jersey Turnpike* (New Brunswick, NJ: Rutgers University Press, 1989), 147.

83. Beltway Survey #238.

84. Beltway Survey #603; see also Beltway Surveys #83, 546, 614, 615.

85. "Housing Group Enters Second Day of Beltway Hike," *(Washington, DC) Evening Star,* June 9, 1966, B4.

86. Beltway Survey #596.

87. David Nakamura, "A 'Track' for Race Fans' Tears," *Washington Post,* February 26, 2001, B1.

Contributors

TIMOTHY DAVIS is the lead historian for the Park Historic Structures and Cultural Landscapes Program of the U.S. National Park Service. His writings on the American landscape have appeared in such publications as *Landscape Journal, Perspectives in Vernacular Architecture,* and *Studies in the History of Gardens and Designed Landscapes;* he is also a coeditor of *America's National Park Roads and Parkways: Drawings from the Historic American Engineering Record* (Johns Hopkins University Press, 2004).

AXEL DOSSMANN, lecturer in the Historical Institute at the University of Jena, is the author of *Begrenzte Mobilität. Eine Kulturgeschichte der Autobahnen in der DDR* (Klartext, 2003) and coauthor, with Jan Wenzel and Kai Wenzel, of *Architektur auf Zeit. Baracken, Pavillons, Container* (metroZones/b_books, 2006). Dossmann participated in the 2004 international exhibition *Shrinking Cities* at the KW Institute for Contemporary Art in Berlin. Since 2000 he has also been producing radio documentaries, and in 2004 he coauthored the film documentary *Autobahn Ost,* directed by Gerd Kroske.

SUZANNE JULIN received her doctorate in U.S. and public history from Washington State University. She is a consultant specializing in cultural-resource assessment and oral histories. Her published articles and professional presentations focus on the link between public policy and the development of tourism-related buildings, landscapes, and regions. She received the Western History Association's 2003 Michael P. Malone Award for her article "Art Meets Politics: Peter Norbeck, Frank Lloyd Wright, and the Sylvan Lake Hotel Commission," which appeared in the summer 2002 issue of *South Dakota History.*

JEREMY L. KORR is assistant professor of social science at Chapman University in Ontario, California. He holds a PhD in American studies from the University of Maryland, College Park. Korr's research and teaching specialties include transportation history and American foodways.

RUDY J. KOSHAR is the George L. Mosse Professor of History at the University of Wisconsin–Madison and the author of *From Monuments to Traces: Artifacts of German Memory, 1870–1990* (University of California Press, 2000), *German Travel Cultures* (Berg, 2000), *Germany's Transient Pasts: Preservation and National Memory in the Twentieth Century* (University of North Carolina Press, 1998), and *Social Life, Local Politics, and Nazism: Marburg, 1880–1935* (University of North Carolina Press, 1986), among others. *Sociologist*

CHRISTOF MAUCH holds the Chair in American History and Transatlantic Relations at the University of Munich. From 1999 to 2007 he was the director of the German Historical Institute, Washington, DC. He has authored and edited many books in the fields of German history and literature, U.S. history, and environmental history.

PETER MERRIMAN is a lecturer in the Institute of Geography and Earth Sciences at the University of Wales, Aberystwyth, UK. His research focuses on mobility, space and social theory, and cultures of landscape in twentieth-century Britain. He is the author of *Driving Spaces* (Blackwell, 2007), and his articles have appeared in several geography and social sciences journals and edited collections.

MASSIMO MORAGLIO, assistant professor of contemporary history in the political science faculty at the Università degli Studi di Torino, Italy, is also the author of *Strade e Politica: Storia della viabilita nella provincia di Torino* (Edizioni dell'Orso, 2003) and coauthor, with Michele Bonino, of the bilingual exhibition catalogue *Inventare gli spostamenti: Storia e immagini dell'autostrada Torino-Savona/Inventing Movement. History and Images of A6 Motorway* (Allemandi, 2006).

DAVID E. NYE, professor of history and American studies at the University of Southern Denmark, is the author of ten books, including *Electrifying America: Social Meanings of a New Technology* (MIT Press, 1990), *American Technological Sublime* (MIT Press, 1994), and *Technology Matters: Questions to Live With* (MIT Press, 2006). In 2005 the Society for the History of Technology awarded him the Leonardo da Vinci Medal. He is currently writing a cultural history of electrical blackouts.

ANNE MITCHELL WHISNANT received her doctorate in history from the University of North Carolina at Chapel Hill, where she is now Director of Research, Communications, and Programs for the Office of Faculty Governance. The author of *Super-Scenic Motorway: A Blue Ridge Parkway History* (University of North Carolina Press, 2006) as well as articles in several scholarly and popular publications, she is also a member of the Board of Directors of the Blue Ridge Parkway Foundation.

THOMAS ZELLER, associate professor of history at the University of Maryland, College Park, was also a research fellow and a visiting research fellow at the German Historical Institute, Washington, DC. He is the author of *Driving Germany: The Landscape of the German Autobahn, 1930–1970* (Berghahn, 2007), which is a revised translation of *Strasse, Bahn, Panorama: Verkehrswege und Landschaftsveränderung in Deutschland von 1930 bis 1990*. Zeller is also the coeditor of *How Green Were the Nazis? Nature, Environment, and Nation in the Third Reich* (Ohio University Press, 2005), *Germany's Nature: Cultural Landscapes and Environmental History* (Rutgers University Press, 2005), and *Rivers in History: Perspectives on Waterways in Europe and North America* (University of Pittsburgh Press, 2008).

CARL A. ZIMRING is an affiliate scholar at Oberlin College, where he has taught courses on environmental history, urban history, consumer culture, and the history of technology and the environment in the United States. He holds a doctorate in history from Carnegie Mellon University and is the author of *Cash for Your Trash: Scrap Recycling in America* (Rutgers University Press, 2005).

Index